Effective Leadership

Effective Leadership

Strategies for Maximizing Executive Productivity and Health

LEN SPERRY

Routledge
Taylor & Francis Group
LONDON AND NEW YORK

First published 2002 by Brunner-Routledge
Published 2014 by Routledge
2 Park Square, Milton Park, Abingdon, Oxfordshire OX14 4RN
711 Third Avenue, New York, NY 10017
First issued in paperback 2014

Routledge is an imprint of the Taylor & Francis Group, an informa business

Library of Congress Cataloging-in-Publication Data
Sperry, Len.
Effective leadership : strategies for maximizing executive productivity and health / by Len Sperry.
p. cm.
Includes bibliographical references and index.
ISBN 978-1-58391-083-2 (hbk)
ISBN 978-0-41576-340-0 (pbk)
1. Leadership. 2. Management—Psychological aspects. 3. Executive ability. I. Title.

HD57.7 .S6947 2002
658.4'092—dc21

2002018289

Contents

Foreword

When I had just begun my clinical training, too many years ago to try to remember without the refreshing help of old scrapbook pictures, my 19 fellow students and I were caught up in the zealous wish to become the top-notch psychologists we assumed our mentors to be. If only we could infer from test responses and patients' verbalizations those profound conclusions our mentors seemed to pull out of the psychological air! And if only we could watch them at work and learn to do what they did, we, too, could acquire the magic wand of sophisticated technique that would convert us from bumbling students who were not yet allowed to administer Rorschach tests to full-fledged, card-carrying (in the American Psychological Association, of course) psychologists.

Fortunately, we could watch in small groups, through the one-way glass as the chief magician, Dr. David Rapaport—our revered Hungarian genius mentor—demonstrated his skill. But there were two problems. The first problem was that it was hard to stay awake in that hot, stuffy, makeshift observation room in a not-yet air-conditioned building that the Menninger Clinic had pieced together from a hot-dog stand and a barn. Yet somehow we must, for certainly, later, he would pointedly ask us what we had seen and how we understood it. He, who in his lectures on psychological testing could draw on illustrations from Dick Tracy to Schopenhauer—not to mention on his inexhaustible knowledge of Freud—would not be satisfied with banalities. No, he expected us to be scientists, to observe, record, infer, interpret, and arrive at logical conclusions. Even so, our heads nodded. From time to time, one or another of us suddenly would snap our head back in a desperate effort not to miss even the patient's subtle twitches. To make matters more difficult, no matter how hard we concentrated, Dr. Rapaport's heavy accent masked our understanding of what he was saying. Yet somehow, the patient understood. That was a lesson in itself.

The second problem was that no matter how much one observes, no matter how much one tries to imitate the master, imitation is not the same as understanding. Even a parrot can imitate. But understanding evolves out of experience that generates insights. If transmitted experience is to generate insight, ideally it must be organized in steps that the learner can follow, with illustrations that make the point. In real estate the identifying slogan is "Location, location, location." In teaching, the parallel might well be "Organize, synthesize, exemplify, repeat." That parallel is followed in this book. Thus, learners establish a frame of reference to systematize their learning and a method to apply what they learn. Without a system, there is just a jumble of facts, theories, or analogies. (The literature on leadership behavior ranges from applying psychology derived from research with rats to urging the reader to emulate examples that range from ancient military heroes to contemporary football coaches.) Without a method for application, one cannot test what one practices, nor can practice lead to insight and, ultimately, wisdom. It is wisdom, after all, that characterizes effective practice and earns the respect of patients, learners, and colleagues alike.

This book is a life history. It is not an autobiography in the usual sense. Nor is it an evolutionary document that starts from a birth and continues to a death. It does not explain what great predecessors have done. It does not lend itself to banner headlines or glib psychological answers to complex questions, nor does it delve into complex theory. It is a thoughtful digestion, reorganization, reintegration, and recounting of the author's lifetime professional experience, which takes advantage of what he has learned from a surprising number of other people. The book draws on more than 30 years of the author's labor and learning and is intended to guide those who help executives professionally or who wish to do so.

In addition to integrating the literature on leadership to include not only behavior, but also issues of selection, coaching, counseling, and the fit of the individual to the organization, the author develops two themes that are not usually integrated into books of this genre. The first is an emphasis on the *concurrent* roles of emotions and productivity in leadership effectiveness. The second is an emphasis on health. Although much has been written about the health of leaders, rarely has it been the specific and integrated focus, as in this book, on leadership effectiveness. Furthermore, rather than merely citing the usual generalities about the relationship of exercise, diet, and tension relief to leaders' health, the author takes the reader into specific energy patterns, body shapes, personality patterns, and stress responses that then become the basis for custom-tailored nutritional strategy, exercise strategy, and stress-reduction strategy. The combination of more than three decades of extensive consultation practice with leaders, based on training in psychology and psychiatry, as well as on an understanding of management, makes for a unique and uniquely helpful book.

Harry Levinson, PhD
—Author of *Executive*, chairman of the Levinson Institute, and Emeritus Clinical Professor of Psychology in Psychiatry, Harvard Medical School

Acknowledgments

For over 30 years I have enjoyed consulting with senior executives. This opportunity has been intellectually challenging, growth-producing, and immensely gratifying. I wish to express my sincerest appreciation to all the male and female executives who have permitted me to be a part of their lives and their work.

It is paramount that I acknowledge those individuals who have served as mentors along the way. My heartfelt appreciation to Harry Levinson, PhD, for pioneering the practice of executive consultation and helping me forge my identity and skills in this field. His book *The Exceptional Executive* and its revision, *Executive*, formed an entire generation of my fellow executive consultants. In addition to his extraordinary grasp of the mind and heart of the executive, Dr. Levinson has been a wonderfully caring and generous mentor and colleague.

Recently, two other mentors, William "Bill" Humber, PhD, and Alan McLean, MD, have passed away. I mourn their loss, while cherishing the memory of the times we worked and played together. My intellectual debt to Eliot Jaques, MD, PhD, and Manfred Kets de Vries, PhD, must be noted.

I would also mention many others. From the Division of Consulting Psychology of the American Psychological Association I would like to especially recognize Rodney Lowman, PhD; H. Skipton Leonard, PhD; Paul Lloyd, PhD; Arthur Freedman, PhD; Ann O'Roark, PhD; and John Deleray, PhD. From the Academy of Organizational and Occupational Psychiatry I would like to recognize Don Williams, MD; Steve Heidel, MD; Barry Greiff, MD; Duane Hagen, MD; Robert Larsen, MD; and Peter Brill, MD. From the American Psychiatric Association I want to recognize members of the Committee on Psychiatry/Business Relationship Initiatives; I would recognize Drew Clemens, MD; Daniel Bornstein, MD; Marcia Goin, MD; Jeff Kahn, MD; Al Herzog, MD; Sandra DeJong, MD; Bob Gordon, MD; Marcia Scott, MD; and Larry Kraus. Furthermore, I would note Harry Prosen, MD; Jon Gudeman, MD; Carl Chan, MD; John Kasen Frei, O.P., PhD; Alan Whiteman, PhD; Lenore S. Blum, PhD; and Lee R. Hess, PhD.

Finally, I want to thank Linda Hollick, George Zimmar, Emily Epstein, and Hope Breeman at Brunner-Routledge for their expertise and support in bringing this work to fruition, Julie Thompson for her administrative support, and to Tim Julet, now of Lippincott, who helped launch this project.

I would also like to thank Paul Lloyd, C. Donald Williams, and Maureen White for their thoughtful and helpful comments on this manuscript.

Introduction

A recent Gallup poll indicates that nearly 55% of workers across all corporations, large and small, have such low motivation for their jobs that corporate productivity and profits have been notably compromised. Successful corporations employ management practices that motivate employees at all levels. Such corporations require their executives to meet a performance standard and expect these individuals to mobilize employee commitment and motivation. On a day-to-day basis, this means ensuring that competent and motivated employees are hired, developed, and retained. For instance, Jack Welch, the recently retired CEO of General Electric, initiated the policy of eliminating 10% of GE's least effective employees every year since the 1980s, when he became CEO. The goal of this policy was to replaced unproductive, unmotivated employees with more motivated ones. Although undoubtedly there may be less dramatic ways of dealing with this critical issue, the point is that major differences exist between effective and less effective corporations, just as differences exist between effective leaders and less effective leaders.

This book is based on three premises. The first is that leadership effectiveness is a function of both leader productivity and health. The second is that leadership effectiveness significantly leverages and impacts corporate effectiveness—that is, corporate productivity and health. The third is that corporations are continually searching for strategies to increase leadership effectiveness in order to maximize corporate productivity and health.

In other words, effective executives can significantly impact the productivity and health of an entire organization. Such executives wield considerable power and influence and make decisions that affect the lives of many individuals every day. When executives function optimally, people who report to them are likely to be highly productive and to enhance the success of their corporations. When executives function suboptimally, the opposite occurs. It is no wonder, then, that corporate boards of directors and top management place a high priority on finding and retaining effective executives and on supporting leadership-development initiatives that maximize the productivity and health of these leaders.

Before proceeding further, I should say what effective leadership is not. Effective is not synonymous with being "successful," if success only means being highly productive or profitable. Rather, effectiveness means balancing personal development—of self and employees—with productivity. Furthermore, the effective leader is ethical, generative, and self-transcending—meaning that leaders can look and act beyond their own needs and concerns to the needs of the organization and of the community. By these criteria, many leaders are ineffective. Nevertheless, awareness is growing on the part of corporate boards and CEOs that effective leaders are essential to the development and maintenance of vital and effective corporations. Accordingly, they are responding in two decisive ways: first, by aligning this leadership-development initiative with corporate strategy and, second, by allocating the necessary resources to achieve this initiative.

This book is a response to that important initiative. It is based on my experience as an executive and as a consultant to executives. It covers the determinants of effective leadership. It also describes and illustrates strategies that executives, and those who consult to them, can use to maximize productivity and health. Seven such strategies are given: organizational consultation, leadership development, executive policy advisement, executive coaching, executive consultation, executive counseling, and executive health promotion.

Executive coaching, executive counseling, executive consultation, and executive health promotion are four powerful strategies for maximizing an executive's effectiveness. Executive coaching increases executive effectiveness by increasing both strategic management and interpersonal or "emotional intelligence" skills. Executive counseling increases executive effectiveness by removing emotional blocks to high performance, whereas executive consultation increases executive effectiveness by assisting the executive in critically reviewing personal and corporate concerns, circumstances, and alternatives. Executive health promotion will maximize executive energy, stamina, and well-being, as well as reduce and possibly eliminate chronic disease processes.

Nonpsychologically trained management consultants may have much to offer corporations by increasing organizational effectiveness, usually through improving operational and management systems, as well as work group performance. Although increasing numbers of these consultants provide coaching to executives, it is the contention of this book that psychologically trained professionals can be even more effective in coaching, counseling, and consulting with executives. In other words, professionals with training and experience in individual, couples, and group therapy have much to offer executives who need to increase their leadership effectiveness. This book introduces such professionals to the knowledge and skill base they need to work with executives. It will be of particular interest to clinicians who want to learn more about the psychological and organizational dynamics that drive executive behavior, as well as how to increase leader effectiveness.

This book reviews and integrates the latest information and research data on the determinants of executive productivity and health in a reader-friendly fashion. It provides capsule descriptions of theories and research findings, along with tables and figures that summarize key points. Several examples and detailed case studies explain and illustrate how this information and the seven leadership development strategies can be practically and usefully applied.

Effective Leadership: Strategies for Maximizing Executive Productivity and Health breaks new ground in emphasizing the link and interaction between productivity and health. A unique feature is the discussion of the determinants of executive health and well-being and their relationship to leadership and corporate effectiveness. Case material illustrates specific strategies for maximizing executive health. Another unique feature is a discussion and illustration of the importance of recognizing and assessing the impact of an executive's character on productivity and health.

This book will be of interest to three groups. The first group is clinicians—psychologists, social workers, psychiatrists, marital and family therapists, and other professional counselors who want to expand their professional horizons and practice patterns—and management consultants. The second group is students and trainees in course work and seminars on leadership, coaching, consultation, and corporate counseling. The third group is executives who want and need to increase their own productivity and health. Increasingly, executives are becoming more aware of how their energy level and stamina, as well as the stress of extensive travel, impact their health and productivity. Many are either reluctant to mention this to others or haven't been satisfied with what they have heard or read.

THE BOOK'S PLAN

This book has two main parts. Part 1 consists of five chapters and is entitled "Effective Leadership." It provides the reader with a conceptual framework to understand and appreciate the dynamics and determinants of executive leadership.

Chapter 1 describes the economic and emotional value of leadership effectiveness to corporations and their employees. It presents a continuum of leadership effectiveness—from derailment-proneness to highly effective or peak performance leadership—and illustrates the continuum with several case studies. Chapter 2 explains current models and theories of executive leadership. It summarizes and integrates these models with recent quantitative and qualitative research on leadership effectiveness and proposes an Integrative Model of Leadership Development. Chapter 3 focuses on the requisite skills and competencies of highly effective leaders. Chapter 4 covers common personality and leadership styles in executives. Chapter 5 describes the context for leadership, which includes organizational dynamics, family dynamics, and the dynamics of the job itself.

Part 2 consists of six chapters and is entitled "Strategies for Maximizing Productivity and Health." It provides the reader with detailed descriptions of several cutting-edge strategies for promoting executive and corporate effectiveness. Chapter 6 presents a practical approach to completing a comprehensive assessment of leadership effectiveness and the personal and contextual factors that facilitate or impede it. Chapter 7 surveys seven powerful strategies for increasing effectiveness. Four of these strategies are described and illustrated in separate chapters: Chapter 8 focuses on the practice of executive coaching, chapter 9 on the practice of executive counseling, chapter 10 on the practice of executive consultation, and chapter 11 on the practice of promoting executive health.

Part 1

The Effective Executive Leader

1

Profiles of Leadership Effectiveness

You see them every day in the office or in the community. They are executives who can and do wield considerable influence. Although they share a number of commonalities, they are also unique in many ways. One of the ways in which they differ is in leadership effectiveness, as noted in the following profiles.

Profile # 1: Wesley Saunders was surprised to learn that he had been passed over for promotion. For a week he had sulked and wondered why he had not been invited to join the top-management team. It was not for lack of credentials, he concluded, because his pedigree included an MBA from Wharton and 5 years at Price-Waterhouse prior to assuming his present position. So what else could it be? After 3 years in this smaller and less prestigious firm, he had expected to have no trouble moving into a senior leadership position. He knew that his unit had met its projections nearly every quarter, and he was confident that he got along well with his peers and direct reports. Nevertheless, he seemed unaware that his superior was being pressured to terminate him. Although the superior had some misgivings about the productivity of Saunders's unit, he was more dismayed by Saunders's attempts to be accepted by employees "as a regular guy" by second guessing and even mocking top-management decisions. Saunders appeared oblivious of the inappropriateness of his actions.

Profile # 2: Expectations were high that Alex Vasquez would accomplish big things as the new vice president of sales and marketing. After an exhaustive 18 month-search, it seemed that landing Vasquez was too good to be true. He had excellent credentials and references, he was handsome and friendly, and he had great chemistry with the CEO and the executive team, something that the other two candidates seemed to lack. From the moment he started, Vasquez seemed to be on the road at least 3 weeks a month, ostensibly rallying the sales forces in the South and on the West Coast. When he was in town, attending the weekly top-management meeting, he could provide only general answers about sales projections because he had delegated so many responsibilities to his staff. For the first 3 months the CEO did not press the matter, although he was concerned that some people in outlying offices had not yet met the new VP of sales and marketing. A month later the CEO announced that an off-site retreat for the executive team had been scheduled for the upcoming weekend and that it was top priority, given the significant downturn for the current quarter. Everyone showed up but Vasquez, and no one seemed to know where he could be reached. The day before the retreat, the COO had made an offhand comment to the CEO about being uneasy about sales and marketing and wondered if the new VP was really too good to be true. Immediately after the retreat, the CEO conducted his own review of sales and marketing, calling every district sales manager, and was deeply disappointed by what he heard about sales and about Vasquez. His first impulse was to terminate Vasquez immediately.

Profile # 3: Yesterday marked Wendy Jenz's first year as vice president of product development. She had quickly established a reputation as a steady performer with a no-nonsense style. She met or exceeded quarterly quotas, something that her predecessor had been unable to accomplish consistently. She was a welcome addition to the otherwise all-male top-management team. There were, however, some concerns about her. One was that recent data showed that turnover in her division was nearly 20% above the company-wide figure. Because the availability of engineers and other skilled workers in the regions was limited, and employee performance and developmental coaching were not priorities for her, the CEO had noted this observation in Wendy's first annual performance appraisal report. When the CEO approached the matter in their performance appraisal meeting, Wendy replied that she expected everyone to give 100% or else. Needless to say, morale was low in her division. The other concern was that she seemed to take more sick time than any other executive did. She dismissed these concerns as "necessary consequences of being a high-flying Type-A personality." Initially, after watching Wendy's performance in her first 3 months, the CEO was convinced that she would be able to succeed the current COO when he retired in 9 months. Now, he was not sure that Wendy would be a good fit for that position, given its additional stressors and interpersonal requirements. He hoped that things might still work out and wondered if coaching would be sufficient to make a difference.

Profile # 4: Wallace Quade had the enviable reputation of being a leader who made things happen. As CEO of an academic medical center, he was known and admired in the community for his vision, integrity, and charm. Despite the crisis in health-care reimbursement that impacted all medical centers, Quade had the distinction of maintaining balanced budgets for 10 of the 11 years he had been CEO. Only one other medical center in the nation had come close to matching this accomplishment. Annual staff turnover, which averaged 18 to 23% at many other medical centers, was a mere 4%, largely due to Quade's capacity to create a family atmosphere and a sense of commitment among his 2,200 employees. At age 57, Quade kept hours that none of his younger executive staff members could match. He had early breakfast and dinner meetings and receptions with stakeholders nearly every day of the week, except weekends. On weekends, when he was not in Washington testifying before Congress or attending professional meetings, he managed to get away from the medical center to spend time with his family, which included several grandchildren. Although he was amazingly active and energetic, one never got the impression that he was rushed or in a hurry. He exuded an unmistakable sense of harmony and centeredness, which positively influenced the rest of his top-management team. No one could remember his taking any sick time during his 11 years as CEO at the medical center. His colleagues insisted that he had to have a cast-iron stomach to continue to sample the various ethnic cuisines at the many receptions he regularly attended in the community. Not surprisingly, the chair of the medical center's board of directors is considering asking the board, at its next meeting, to approve Watson's contract for another 3 years.

These four profiles reflect varying degrees of leadership effectiveness. The purpose of this chapter is to provide the reader with an approach to understanding and analyzing or profiling leadership effectiveness. Accordingly, it describes a continuum of leadership effectiveness. Before that, it lists three basic premises regarding effectiveness, the nature of executive leadership, and the value of leadership effectiveness to corporations.

THREE BASIC PREMISES ABOUT LEADERSHIP EFFECTIVENESS

This is a book about leadership effectiveness and strategies for increasing it in executives. Some of the four profiles cry out for strategies to increase leadership effectiveness. Several questions may be asked at this point: What defines and characterizes leadership effectiveness? Is it high productivity or performance? What is the relationship of leadership effectiveness to corporate effectiveness? How can leadership effectiveness be increased?

Before I address these questions, a clarification of terms is necessary. Given that some of these terms are used synonymously, it is essential that they be defined and differentiated.

Productivity is a measure of outcomes and is the ratio of input to output. Increased productivity means higher profits, competitiveness, or market share.

Performance is a less precise term, in that it reflects both process—that is, how things get done and how long it takes—*and* outcome, that is, productivity and quality.

People refers to employees, leaders, and other stakeholders involved with a given corporation or organization. This term includes the skills, talents, competencies, and needs of these individuals.

Health, like productivity, is also a measure of outcome and is reflected in both individuals and the corporation. Health for individuals involves physical and psychological well-being. It includes health status, level of psychological functioning, job satisfaction, and so on. Health for the corporation includes absenteeism rates, turnover rates (particularly executive derailment), direct and indirect costs associated with disease management and disability management, return on investment for health promotion programs or initiatives, and commitment to the organization, to name some of the more obvious ones.

The effective leader operates concurrently on two tracks: one is the *performance track,* for which the end point is *productivity*; the other is the *people track,* for which the end point is *health*. The effective leader tracks both simultaneously. In other words, effectiveness involves both productivity and health.

The first basic premise of this book is that *leadership effectiveness is a function of both productivity and health*. In the past, the productivity track or dimension of leadership effectiveness was unduly emphasized. Management assumed that leaders only needed to focus on the productivity dimension; the people dimension really didn't matter. The price of this one-sided emphasis has been high—for example, low commitment and morale, high rates of burnout, and increasing health costs. Nevertheless, research data and firsthand corporate experience confirm the intricate link between productivity and health. I will repeatedly point out such research in this and subsequent chapters. In addition to leadership effectiveness, there is also corporate effectiveness. In fact, a close link exists between both.

The second basic premise of this book is that *leadership effectiveness significantly leverages and impacts corporate effectiveness*—in other words, corporate productivity and health. The reciprocal is also often true. That is, highly effective corporations tend to attract, hire, and retain highly effective executives. Such corporations are also very likely to transform executives with average levels of effectiveness into higher-functioning executives. This transformation occurs because of the influence of a corporate culture that prizes and rewards effectiveness, the allocation of significant resources for leadership-development initiatives, and the provision for easy access and regular mentoring by senior executives.

The book's third basic premise is that *corporations are continually searching for better strategies to increase leadership effectiveness in order to maximize corporate productivity and health*. As corporations have come to better recognize and appreciate this leverage, they have focused on increasing resources for leadership development and enhancement. The goal is to develop the potential of new executives and enhance the capacity of the corporations' existing executives.

THE NATURE OF EXECUTIVE LEADERSHIP

Wesley Saunders, Alex Vasquez, Wendy Jenz, and Wallace Quade share one thing in common: All four occupy executive leadership positions. Executive leadership, also called senior leadership or strategic leadership, is a unique type of leadership. It involves leadership at the systemic level, with primary responsibility for formulating strategy and ensuring the best possible alignment or "fit" between the organization and its external environment and stakeholders. Executive leadership differs considerably from leadership at the organizational or multiunit level, as well as from leadership at the unit level. Roles and tasks can be reasonably differentiated among these three levels of leadership. Notable differences exist in the type of strategic operational focus and time span at each level. Strategic focus refers to the specific role function of strategy formation at a given level; operational focus refers to the specific role function of strategy implementation at a given level; and time span refers to the frame of reference—from as short as 1 month to as long as 20 or more years—during which decisions about tasks and goals need to be conceptualized to optimize outcomes. Table 1.1 summarizes these differences.

THE VALUE-ADDED BENEFITS OF EXECUTIVE EFFECTIVENESS

Presumably, a leader's level of effectiveness can be quantified and translated into value for the corporation. Unfortunately, because it is much easier to quantify the value of production-line employees than senior executives,

TABLE 1.1
Levels and Focus of Leadership

Leadership Level	Strategic Focus	Operational Focus	Time Span
Systemic Level	Formulation of overall strategy: alignment with external environment	Strategy implementation system-wide via structural and cultural change	Short term to long term
Organizational Level	Translation of the overall strategy for multiunits	Resource allocation; empowerment, motivation, and coaching of personnel	Short term to medium term
Unit Level	Translation of the multiunit strategy to unit goals and tasks	Resource distribution, task assignment, motivation and coaching of personnel	Short term

considerably more data are available on the value added to corporations by highly effective leaders. That being said, some data and estimates suggest the value that effective leadership adds to an organization. For example, highly effective executives—also called peak performers—are noted to have productivity rates that are 25 to 50% higher than their minimally effective—also called poor performers—counterparts (Beatty, 1994, p. 19). Two large retrospective studies suggest some actual dollar values associated with the efforts of effective executives. In their study of 193 corporations over a 19-year period, Weiner and Mohoney (1981) reported that leadership accounted for nearly 44% of variance in profit margins as well as 47% of variance in stock prices. Similarly, Barrick, Day, Lord, and Alexander (1991) reported that in 132 corporations studied over a 15-year period, an executive added $25 million—after taxes—to a corporation. Because this data was collected and analyzed more than 10 years ago, the current value-added figure would likely be considerably higher.

Minimally effective executives are sometimes referred as derailment-prone. Derailment refers to executives who are "off track" when it comes to matters involving performance, people, or both. Reasons for derailment are described in a subsequent section. Derailment and other forms of poor productivity and health are very costly to corporations. At the present time, accurate data on the total costs to corporations are yet to be established. However, it is possible to provide some estimates, based on what it costs to replace an executive who has derailed. Beatty (1994) has calculated the direct cost of replacing a minimally effective lower-level executive in the early 1990s. Assuming that this executive commanded a salary of $75,000 in 1994, the direct costs for a severance package—including pay and benefits, outplacement assistance, and recruitment costs to refill the position, such as search firm fees, candidate travel expenses, and moving expenses—come to $165,000. In today's dollars, that would be over $200,000.

But this figure does not include the indirect costs associated with this termination. Indirect costs include a number of factors, such as lost productivity while the terminated manager was employed, lost productivity while the firm awaits replacement, training cost and lost productivity during the training period, lower morale and lower productivity of subordinates, increased difficulty and expense of recruiting others, higher unemployment insurance rates, lost credibility of the management function, possibly litigation costs associated with wrongful discharge, and so on. Beatty notes that many consider the indirect costs to be at least 5 to 10 times more than the direct cost. For the lower-level executive position, Beatty (1994) estimated the indirect replacement cost to be between $750,000 and $1.5 million (p. 29). In today's dollars that figure would more likely be $1–2 million. Thus, the combined indirect and direct replacement costs would be between $1.2 and $2.2 million. For a senior-level executive, below the level of CEO, with salary and benefits in the range of $400,000 to $500,000 per year, the combined indirect and direct replacement costs would be considerably higher. Given the golden parachute clauses that are common in executive employment agreements, the replacement costs are often in excess of $5 million for executives below the level of CEO and often over $10 million for low-profile CEOs.

If effective executives add $25 million over the course of the years they spend at a corporation, as noted in the study by Barrick et al. (1991), cited previously, what about the impact of minimally effective executives? Based on Beatty's (1994) estimate that effective individuals may be 50% more productive than minimally effective individuals, it could be argued that minimally effective individuals would produce 50% *less* value to a corporation. Thus, assuming that minimally effective executives remained in their positions for as long as effective executives, the minimally effective executive would add only about $12.5 million instead of $25 million to the corporation.

PATTERNS OF LEADERSHIP EFFECTIVENESS

Earlier, effectiveness was defined as a function of both productivity and health. The effective leader was described as simultaneously functioning on two tracks; the *performance track,* for which the end point is productivity; and the *people track,* for which the end point is health. *Productivity* was defined as a measure of task and people outcomes, whereas *perfor-*

mance was described as a more inclusive term that includes both *process*—that is, how an executive relates to others—and *outcome*, or productivity. Health reflects the people dimension and includes job satisfaction, commitment, morale, and personal well-being.

Thus, a leader may manifest high levels of productivity in the short run but might not be an effective leader. In the integrative model of effective leadership, which will be described in chapter 2, a productive leader may exhibit only one or two of the seven competencies that characterize the effective leader.

The Leadership Effectiveness Continuum

Efforts to study leadership effectiveness have provided important clues about the requisite attributes and competencies associated with effective leader functioning. One of the first and most interesting sets of studies of leader effectiveness was described by Luthans and colleagues (1985, 1988). Their initial efforts to isolate the attributes of successful leaders led them to operationally define different types of effectiveness. In a 1985 study they reported their findings on attributes of successful managers at various levels of an organization. They found that "success," operationally defined as salary increases and promotions, did not appear to be associated with traditional leadership attributes or functions, such as greater involvement with strategic planning and coordinating activities, as were associated with top management. Rather, success was associated with networking activity, particularly with outside constituencies.

In a subsequent study, Luthans (1988) further differentiated successful managers from those he called "effective" managers and "average" or traditional managers. *Effective managers* were defined as those who achieve the highest levels of productivity and quality by motivating workers. *Successful managers* were defined as those who achieve rapid career outcomes, in addition to above-average levels of productivity in their units. *Average managers*, by contrast, were defined as those who achieved low to average productivity, quality, and career advancement.

It is interesting to note that whereas those designated as effective managers spent more time with their own employees and networking with colleagues inside the corporation, those designated as successful managers spent more time networking with individuals outside the organization. Unfortunately, no measures of employee commitment were reported to differentiate the impact of the three different leadership patterns on long-term organizational effectiveness. It might be speculated that those designated as effective managers would be more likely to mobilize employee commitment to the organization than would the so-called successful or

<-------+--------------------------------+-----------------------------------+-------->

Minimally Moderately Maximally

FIGURE 1 1. The Leadership Effectiveness Continuum

average managers. Probably the most valuable insight from the Luthans research was the effort to operationally define leadership effectiveness. Of necessity, an integrative model of leadership development and effectiveness, described in chapter 2 of this book, must define and differentiate various levels or types of effectiveness.

This section delineates a continuum of three levels of leadership effectiveness and then briefly describes each of these three levels. The relationship of these three levels to the proposed integrative model will be further amplified in chapter 2. Figure 1.1 illustrates the continuum dimension of the integrative model.

Of the three descriptions that follow, only "Minimally Effective Leadership" will be described in detail. In many instances, executives functioning at this end of the continuum are unlikely to remain in their positions for long, because either they are forced to leave or they derail. Occasionally, these individuals may be offered coaching or another executive-development strategy. Usually, however, coaching is provided to executives who are functioning in the average to moderate range of effectiveness. They are more likely to be responsive to interventions aimed at maximizing their productivity and health than are executives with lower levels of effectiveness.

Minimally Effective Leadership

Approaching the far left of the Leadership Effectiveness Continuum is minimally effective leadership. Minimally effective leadership is characterized by productivity problems, health issues, relational behaviors, or all of these that are well below average functioning. Derailment reflects a form of minimally effective leadership. As noted earlier, derailment means "getting off track" because of disappointing performance. The derailed executive is someone who "either leaves the organization non-voluntarily (through resignation, being fired, or retiring early) or is plateaued as a result of a perceived lack of fit between personal characteristic and skills and demands of the job" (Leslie & Van Velsor, 1996). In the executive profiles that opened the chapter, Wesley Saunders and Alex Vasquez are examples of executives who function at this level. Although Saunders has been average on the productivity dimension, he appears to be only minimally effective on the people dimension. On the other hand, Vasquez appears to be only minimally effective on both dimensions.

Statistics and Reasons for Derailment: What are the chances of an executive derailing? Someone assuming a new or different executive position today has a 40% chance of derailment within 12 to 18 months (Betof & Harrison, 1996). An American Management Association study reported that 22% of employers surveyed had fired an executive from a position that person had occupied for less than 3 months (reported by Johnson, 2000). Johnson (2000) contends that underdeveloped "emotional intelligence" (Goleman, 1998) is a major reason for derailment.

Leslie and Van Velsor's research describes some of the factors contributing to derailment. These include poor working relations, excessive ambition, and excessive authoritarianism (Leslie & Van Velsor, 1996). A British survey indicated these reasons for executives' derailment: 82 % failed to build partnering relationships with subordinates or peers; 58% were confused or unclear about job expectations; and 50% lacked the necessary internal political savy (Manchester Consulting, 1997). Finally, a recent article in *Fortune* argued that executive failure and derailment are not matters of having the ability and vision to succeed, but are rather problems in execution. Derailed executives were characterized as indecisive, missing deadlines, and failing to keep commitments. The article suggested that the reason for derailment is a failure of the selection process—that is, a poor match or fit between executive and position, or not recognizing and addressing the problem soon enough (Anonymous, 1999).

Patterns of Derailment-Proneness: Hogan, Raskin, and Fazzini (1990) describe profiles of three patterns exhibited by ineffective or derailment-prone leaders. They contend that each of these patterns limits performance or precludes promotion to executive positions.

1. The first pattern is described as the high likability floater. Although individuals with this pattern are quite likable and congenial, they tend to have low achievement motivation, little sense of direction, and a limited capacity for assertiveness and confrontation. Consequently, they tend to placate others and avoid conflict, and predictably, the units they manage exhibit low to mediocre performance.
2. The second pattern is called the "homes de resentiment," which represents the leaders who, although appearing to be competent and charming, actually harbor deep resentment and seek retribution against others. These individuals cannot provide consistency or mobilize trust and commitment from employees.
3. The third pattern is described as the narcissist. Leaders who exhibit this pattern typically are overconfident in their abilities and display an exaggerated sense of self-importance. They are also likely

to avoid accepting responsibility for failure, to be hypersensitive to criticism, and to resist the suggestions and advice of others, believing that their judgment is superior to others', including that of their superiors. Unfortunately, though these individuals may make a very good first impression and may initially appear to perform quite well in a new assignment, a simple stressor such as a relatively innocuous criticism may trigger a rageful response.

Hogan's three patterns are a useful starting point for developing a typology of derailment-proneness, but they are, nevertheless, incomplete. Other characteristics of low effectiveness and derailment-proneness will be obvious in subsequent sections of this chapter. These include character deficits such as difficulty with self-directiveness or irresponsibility, uncooperativeness, and incapacity for self-transcendence. Other characteristics could be fearfulness, timidity, and a lack of authenticity, as well as low levels of cognitive complexity.

Moderately Effective Leadership

Moderately effective leadership is characterized by productivity, health, relational behaviors, or any of these in the average range of functioning. As noted earlier, executives at this level of functioning are the main target of initiatives aimed at maximizing their productivity and health.

In the executive profiles that opened the chapter, Jenz would likely be considered functioning closer to this point on the effectiveness continuum than would Vasquez or Saunders. Jenz has the potential for functioning at a much higher level of effectiveness. There is little question that she has high productivity, but the price paid for it in terms of her health (that is, excessive absenteeism) and that paid by her employees (for example, high turnover and low morale) may well be too high. Presumably, with the aid of coaching or another executive-development strategy, she might be assisted in achieving both high productivity and a higher level of health.

Maximally Effective Leadership

Approaching the far right of the Leadership Effectiveness Continuum is maximally effective or highly effective leadership. Highly effective leadership is characterized by productivity, health, relational behaviors, or any combination of these that well exceed moderate functioning. Very highly effective executives are sometimes referred to as "peak performers" (Lark & Richards, 2000). In the executive profiles that opened the chapter, Wallace Quade would be considered functioning at this level.

This level of leadership effectiveness is the ultimate goal of strategies for maximizing productivity and health. In my opinion, corporate effectiveness cannot be achieved unless a critical mass of executives are close to this end of the leadership effectiveness continuum. To the extent that this critical mass is reached and exceeded, the organization's culture will shift more in the direction of a culture of effectiveness, which will further shape and facilitate effectiveness behavior among other executives and employees.

CONCLUDING NOTE

The chapter began with profiles of four senior executives who had differing levels of leadership effectiveness. The organizational impact of each was different, as was the type of concern they evoked in their immediate superiors. Of the four, Wallace Quade is clearly functioning at a very high level of effectiveness. Accordingly, the concern of his superior, the chair of the board of directors, is rather straightforward. Because Quade is a very skilled and effective executive, apparently nothing warrants any action other than the superior recommending and approving Quade's contract renewal. The situations with Alex Vasquez, Wesley Saunders, and Wendy Jenz are decidedly more complex. A basic concern with Vasquez, who is functioning at a very low level of effectiveness, is determining whether he is salvageable and worth the effort of coaching or counseling, or whether termination is the better alternative. Similarly, with Saunders the question is whether the CEO has a feasible alternative to termination. The concern with Jenz is quite different. She is functioning at an above-average level of effectiveness, but appears to have the potential to function at a high level of effectiveness. The question is not simply whether she might become a viable candidate for COO, but how to address her performance in her current position. She seems to need executive coaching, but her receptivity and responsiveness to it appear uncertain. Executive consultants regularly face these considerations. Traditionally, external consultants have advised senior executives about such matters. In the past decade, however, internal consultants—usually, in-house human resources personnel who have additional training and experience in coaching, counseling, and consulting—increasingly advise senior leaders in their own corporations on how to handle such issues.

REFERENCES

Anonymous. (1999, June 21). Why CEOs fail and CEOs in denial. *Fortune,* 69–82.

Barrick, M., Day, D., Lord, R., & Alexander, R. (1991). Assessing the quality of executive leadership. *Leadership Quarterly, 2,* 9–22.

Beatty, R. (1994). *Interviewing and selecting high performers.* New York: Wiley.
Betof, E., & Harrison, R. (1996, Spring). The newly appointed leader dilemma: A significant change in today's organizational culture. *The Manchester Review*, 3.
Goleman, D. (1998). *Working with emotional intelligence*. New York: Bantam.
Hogan, R., Raskin, R., & Fazzini, D. (1990). The dark side of charisma. In K. Clark & M. Clark (Eds.), *Measures of leadership* (pp. 345–354). West Orange, NJ: Leadership Library of America.
Johnson, J. (2000). Learning strategies for newly appointed leaders. In M. Goldsmith, L. Lyons, & A. Freas (Eds.), *Coaching for leadership: How the world's greatest coaches help leaders learn* (pp. 209–217). San Francisco: Jossey-Bass/Pfeiffer.
Lark, S., & Richards, J. (2000). *The chemistry of success: Six secrets of peak performance*. San Francisco: Bay Books.
Leslie, J., & Van Velsor, E. (1996). *A look at derailment today: North America and Europe.* Greensboro, NC: Center for Creative Leadership.
Luthans, F. (1988). Successful vs. effective real managers. *Academy of Management Executives, 2,* 127–132.
Luthans, F., Rosenkrantez, S., & Nenessey, H. (1985). What do successful managers really do? An observational study of managerial activities. *Journal of Applied Behavioral Science, 21,* 225–270.
Manchester Consulting. (1997). Survey of 826 respondents. Reported in J. Johnson (2000), Learning strategies for newly appointed leaders. In M. Goldsmith, L. Lyons, & A. Freas (Eds.), *Coaching for leadership: How the world's greatest coaches help leaders learn* (pp. 209–217). San Francisco: Jossey-Bass/Pfeiffer.
Weiner, N., & Mahoney, T. (1981). A model of corporate performance as a function of environmental, organizational and leadership influences. *Academy of Management Journal, 24,* 453–470.

2

Leadership Models and Research

I noted in chapter 1 that the Continuum of Leadership Effectiveness is a key component of the Integrative Model of Leadership Effectiveness. Prior to introducing the Integrative Model, I will present the experiential and empirical bases from which the Integrative Model was derived. This chapter summarizes five theoretical models of leadership, as well as seminal findings from both qualitative and quantitative research on leadership effectiveness. The key contributions from the best theoretical, qualitative, and quantitative research on leadership are then synthesized in the Integrative Model of Leadership Effectiveness. As will be described in the second half of this book, this model provides a systematic basis for understanding, assessing, and maximizing leadership effectiveness.

CONTRIBUTIONS FROM LEADERSHIP MODELS AND THEORIES

From ancient times, scholars have propose theories of leadership to explain why certain leaders—that is, kings, religious leaders, and military leaders—were effective and successful, whereas others were not. Until the 20th century, these theories were largely "trait" theories. Such theories assumed that one or more specific temperament, character, or social trait, such as intelligence, speaking ability, energy level, or dominance, accounted for a leader's success or effectiveness. More recently, other leadership theories have been proposed that focus on the leader's behavior patterns, situational factors, and relational factors that ostensibly offer more potent and compelling explanations than do trait theories. However, in an extensive survey of historical and current theories, Yukl (1999) concludes that none of the several hundred leadership studies published so far has validated any leadership theory or model. Nevertheless, considerable research supports specific factors or dimensions of some theories. Accordingly, he and others suggest that it may be more useful and heuristic to develop integrative models of leadership that incorporate specific factors that are supported by empirical research. One main purpose of this book is to propose an integrative model of leadership that has clinical value and utility for executive consultation.

In the remainder of this section, five classes of leadership models that are currently in vogue and that have some measure of research support will be briefly reviewed. The five models described are attribute models, cognitive complexity models, behavioral complexity models, strategic decision-making models, and transformational models. The purpose of reviewing these models is to highlight specific contributions or factors that support and validate my proposed integrative model of leadership. The following section will likewise highlight specific contributions from large-scale qualitative and quantitative research that support and validate my integrative model.

Attribute Models

Attributes are the inner or personal qualities that are believed to constitute effective leadership. *Attributes* is an umbrella term that includes traits, skills, styles, abilities, and capabilities. The attributes model—and in particular, trait theory—is the oldest model of leadership. As noted earlier, trait theories premise that the possession of certain personal traits is a hallmark of a leader. Although trait theory espouses the view that "leaders are born, not made," other attribute model approaches, such as skill and competency training, take a broader view. Many research studies have failed to identify specific traits or skills that distinguish leaders from nonleaders and have concluded that leadership traits, like skills, can probably be learned.

Despite such research, attribute theories of leadership continue to remain in vogue today, as witnessed by the attention that the "emotional intelligence" approach has garnered in the corporate world. Similarly, interest is growing in the phenomenon called "peak performance." Both of these will be briefly described.

Emotional Intelligence

Possessing considerable intellectual and technical competencies is no guarantee that the leader possesses similar emotional and social competencies.

In fact, some researchers have found that "executives failed most often because of a 'an interpersonal flaw' rather than a technical ability" (quoted in Hiebert & Klatt, 2001, p. 455). Leadership-development programs that emphasize or include emotional intelligence focus on achieving a balance between leaders' cognitive and conceptual skills and competencies and their emotional, social, and relational skills and competencies.

Emotional intelligence is variously known as emotional quotient or EQ, emotional literacy, and emotional competence. Daniel Goleman (1998) has popularized the theory, and research on emotional intelligence was developed by two psychological researchers, Peter Salovey and John Mayer. In his book *Working with Emotional Intelligence*, Goleman defines emotional intelligence as "the capacity for recognizing our own feelings and those of others, for motivating ourselves, and for managing emotions well in ourselves and in our relationships" (p. 316). Emotional intelligence—or EQ, as some call it—complements intellectual intelligence, cognitive capacities measured by IQ. Goleman describes five basic emotional and social competencies. Self-awareness, self-regulation, and motivation are considered interior or emotional competencies, whereas empathy and social skills are considered exterior or social competencies.

1. *Self-awareness:* Self-awareness involves recognition of one's feelings in the moment, the capacity for realistically assessing one's own abilities and possessing sufficient self-confidence to take risks.
2. *Self-regulation*: Self-regulation involves sufficient mastery over one's emotions and impulses to cope effectively with emotional distress and changing circumstances. It also involves self-responsibility and the capacity to delay gratification in the pursuit of personal and professional goals.
3. *Motivation*: Motivation involves having a results orientation and the capacity to take initiative, to strive for improvement, and to persevere despite frustrations and setbacks. It also involves holding oneself accountable for one's goals.
4. *Empathy*: Empathy involves one's awareness of others' emotions and needs. An empathic individual can take on the perspective of others and establish rapport with them.
5. *Social skills*: Social skills involve the capacity to accurately read social cues, to cooperate and interact with others in a positive and effective manner, and to utilize these skills in persuading, negotiating, problem solving, and settling conflicts.

Peak Performance

Although research on peak performance on world-class athletes has been underway for at least 3 decades, only recently have researchers turned their attention to executive leaders. It seems that among very effective and successful executives, a certain subgroup exhibits special traits that the others do not. Such peak-performing leaders seem to possess unlimited energy and stamina, while being apparently immune to—and quickly recovering from—the minor illnesses and injuries that distress and account for reduced productivity among their peers. What's more, they can also eat and drink almost anything and remain energetic and productive despite grueling work conditions, deadlines, and travel schedules, as well as family demands. What are these special traits or attributes that distinguish the peak performers from their peers?

Medical research has identified a number of chemical functions essential for optimal health and resistance to disease that are present in peak performers. These functions include the optimal regulation of acid-base balance, chemical balance, and toxic substances in body organs, as well as optimal levels of digestive enzymes, oxygenation, and sex hormones. "The more of these functions an individual has intact and operating efficiently, the more capable of peak performance he or she will be" (Lark & Richards, 2000, p. 7). Research indicates that these chemical functions are critical in supporting the eight traits of peak performance.

1. *Vitality and stamina*: Possesses significant energy reserves, allowing the individual to achieve short-range goals despite grueling working conditions, deadlines, and long hours without caffeine or other energy boosters.
2. *Determination and perseverance*: Sustains a keen sense of focus and tenacity in accomplishing long-range goals despite distraction, lack of support from others, and adversity.
3. *Mental clarity and acuity*: Thinks clearly and analytically to solve problems efficiently and effectively, while at the same time demonstrating good judgment and impartiality. Tends to possess excellent short-term and long-term memory.
4. *Ability to get along with others*: Knows how to listen, receive feedback, and communicate verbally in an effective manner. Relates positively with peers, supervisors, and reports, as well as with family and friends.
5. *Ability to remain calm under pressure*: Maintains an air of confidence and calmness despite the stress of deadlines, unexpected circumstances, and critical negotiations.
6. *Optimism and vision*: Anticipates and visualizes future developments and revises strategies and tactics to accomplish goals. Maintains hope and meets or exceeds expectations, and inspires others to do so as well.
7. *Speedy recovery from illness, injury, and exertion*: If the individual sustains a minor injury or illness, will quickly heal or recover.

8. *Resistence to illness*: Able to maintain a high level of wellness despite adverse work demands and emotional stress. Unlikely to develop chronic health conditions that reduce productivity and work involvement.

Although some biochemical basis appears to exits for traits 1, 2, and 8, Lark and Richards contend that all eight traits are supported by the previously noted chemical functions. In addition, Lark and Richards cite several research studies from medical literature, as well as their own clinical experience, that indicate that it is possible to restore these chemical functions to peak or near-peak functioning levels with specialized nutritional and lifestyle-based therapies.

Finally, until approximately age 35 many executives appear to be peak performers, with their seemingly unlimited energy and stamina. Yet by the age of 40, most find themselves unable to maintain their fast pace and begin to find it harder to tolerate certain foods, recover quickly from jet lag, and retain the level of stamina of their 20s. However, real peak performers, either by genetic predisposition or by expert nutritional and lifestyle counseling, often continue to function at peak levels well into their 60s and 70s.

Conceptual Complexity Models

Today, organizations face rapidly changing and complex environmental circumstances, including globalization, rapidly shifting markets, and increased regulatory demands. The basic premise of the conceptual complexity models is that the complexity of a leader's cognitive capacity must correspond to the complexity of the organization and the environments with which it interacts. As a result of this environmental complexity, senior executives are faced with increasingly complex information-processing demands, as well as increasingly complex organizational issues and problems to solve. This means that effective executives must possess very high levels of *conceptual capacity* to cope with such complexities. Cognitive or conceptual capacity is more than intelligence, as measured by IQ tests. So what is conceptual capacity? Stratified systems theory is the best-known conceptual complexity model to address that question. It is briefly described in this section.

Stratified Systems Theory

Stratified systems theory (SST) was developed by Jacob and Jacques (1987). According to SST, conceptual capacity is the ability to think about and organize experiences in terms of time frame and conceptual patterns. With regard to time frames or time horizons, SST postulates that senior executives in more complex environments require more proactivity and planning, with longer time frames, than do more junior leaders. With regard to conceptual patterns or maps, SST assumes that these maps provide the leader with a rational basis for understanding and interpreting information and events encountered in the organization's operating environment. Accordingly, SST postulates that the complexity of the executive's conceptual map should correspond to the complexity of that individual's job environment. It is assumed that the conceptual maps of effective senior executives will be more complex than those of less effective senior executives and other executives at lower levels of the organization. The maps of effective senior executives are more complex for many reasons, including the novel and ill-specified nature of organizational-environmental issues facing senior executives today, the number of factors involved with these issues, the complexity of the interconnections of these various factors, and the multiple causal chains linking these and other factors. Furthermore, SST premises that the increasing complexity of tasks and problems requires organizations that are more stratified, rather than less stratified and flatter. Jacques describes the "requisite organization" as an intentionally hierarchical organization that has three functional levels—production, organizational, and strategic—systemic levels from which seven strata of leadership can be derived. The first three strata relate to the production level and include supervisory and middle-management; the next two strata relate to the organization level and include less senior executives; and the highest two strata relate to the strategic-systemic level and include top senior executives.

Studies on SST reported by Jacques and Clement (1991) confirm these premises and assumptions. The studies indicate that the longer an executive's time frame or time horizon and the more complex that individual's mental pattern or cognitive map of representing a given experience, the more likely that executive will be effective and successful in a senior leadership position. Furthermore, research supports the premise that whereas effective middle managers need only operate with a time horizon of at least 1 year and with conceptual maps that are minimally abstract, effective senior executives operate with time horizons of between 5 and 20 years and cognitive maps that are very abstract. Empirical evidence shows that higher conceptual capacities "are associated with higher executive leadership and organizational performance" (Zacarro, 2001, p. 118). Leadership-development programs have attempted to increase the level of cognitive complexity. At the present time, no research evidence supports the view that modification of either time frame or conceptual maps is possible.

In short, according to SST, as leaders move to higher levels of leadership "they are required to plan and think within longer time spans and incorporate more influences from outside the organization into their perspective" (Zacarro, 2001, p. 30). Finally, the reader may wonder why conceptual complexity was not subsumed under the Attributes Models because it appears to have features of a trait or an attribute and seems to be difficult to modify, which is a characteristic of traits. The answer is that by convention, conceptual complexity has developed as a line of research separate from what has traditionally been understood as trait theory. However it is classified, it may well be that conceptual complexity is the single most important factor in predicting leadership effectiveness.

Behavioral Complexity Models

Focusing on what the leader does, not on the traits that individual possesses, the behavioral complexity model emphasizes the leader's ability to manage various organizational orientations or roles that specify different, and possibly competing, leader behaviors. From this perspective, effective leadership involves dealing with the demands of multiple constituencies and requires leaders to respond differentially and to balance a number of competing roles—for example, task versus employee, mentor versus director, facilitator versus producer, and so on. Early research in these models emphasized the competing roles of employee-orientation versus task-orientation, which warranted the conclusions that leadership styles can be learned, they should be flexible, and no single style is appropriate for all situations.

More recent research has elucidated the link between cognitive complexity and behavioral complexity. Apparently, whereas the leader's cognitive complexity greatly facilitates the process of strategy formulation, behavioral complexity facilities strategic implementation within the organization and its external environment (Zacarro, 2001, p. 124). Denison et al., (1995) note that "cognitive complexity . . . may well be a necessary conditon for the effective practice of leadership. Behavioral complexity, however, must certainly be the sufficient condition" (p. 524).

Important studies of leadership behavior have expanded our knowledge. In the Ohio State studies, leadership researchers studied leadership function in terms of initiating structures (in other words, task orientation) and consideration (that is, employee orientation), finding that no one emphasis was always effective. Similar University of Michigan studies distinguished between job-centered and employee-centered approaches to leadership and found that although employee-centered leadership was more effective, other styles could also be effective and that leadership effectiveness must be judged by more than productivity. These studies formed the basis of the managerial grid theory of leadership.

Contingency theories of leadership are behavioral approaches that stress the needs and dynamics of the particular situation and the necessity of adapting leadership styles to the situation. Among the factors emphasized in the situational approach to leadership are the personal characteristics of the leader, the nature of the job itself, the nature of the organization, and the characteristics of subordinates. Perhaps the most well-known contingency theory of leadership is the situational leadership theory.

Managerial Grid Theory

One of the most well-known approaches to leadership is the managerial grid. Robert Blake and Jane Mouton (1964) derived the managerial grid from the premise that leaders tend to emphasize either a task-orientation or a people-orientation to their job. Five leadership styles or types can be derived from these two orientations.

1. *Laissez-faire management*: This leadership style is characterized by minimal concern for the people and minimal concern for the production. Such managers pass along orders and lack initiative. This style is sometimes known as impoverished management.
2. *Country club management*: This style is characterized by high concern for people but less attention to production.
3. *Task management*: Leadership characterized by high concern for production and low concern for people is called task management. Such managers typically set high production quotas for their subordinates.
4. *Middle-of-the-road management*: Leadership that is characterized by an adequate concern for both people and production and an attempt to balance the two is called middle-of-the-road management, for obvious reasons.
5. *Democratic (team) management*: This style is characterized by high concern for both people and production. Blake and Mouton believe it to be the ideal style.

Situational Leadership Theory

Another well-known behavioral complexity model of leadership is situational leadership. Paul Hersey and Kenneth Blanchard (1996) developed a leadership model that attempts to explain effective leadership as interplay among (1) the leader's relationship behavior, defined as the extent to which leaders maintain personal relationships with followers through open communication and by exhibiting supportive behaviors; (2) the leader's task behavior, which is the extent to which leaders organize and define roles of followers and guide and direct them; and (3) the followers' readiness level, which is defined as readiness to perform a task or function or to pursue an objective. This model focuses on followers as the key situational variable, specifically their readiness to perform. The basic premise is that the most effective leadership style is determined by the readiness level of the people whom the leader is attempting to influence. Even though their model focuses on only one situational variable, Hersey and Blanchard call it the situational leadership variable. This model involves two dimensions: leadership style and follower readiness.

Leadership Style: The relative presence (high–low) of task and relationship behaviors can be used to identify four distinct leadership styles, as follows:

1. *Telling* (high task–low relationship): The leader makes the decision. The leader defines roles and tells followers what, how, when, and where to do various tasks, emphasizing directive behavior.
2. *Selling* (high task–high relationship): The leader makes the decision and then explains it to followers. The leader provides both directive behavior and supportive behavior.
3. *Participating* (low task–high relationship): The leader and followers share decision making. The main role of the leader is to encourage and assist followers in contributing to sound decisions.
4. *Delegating* (low task–low relationship): The followers make the decision. The leader provides little direction or support.

Follower Readiness: Follower readiness refers to a person's readiness to perform a particular task. Readiness is assessed by two factors: ability and willingness. Ability refers to knowledge, experience, and skill that an individual or group possesses. Willingness is the extent to which an individual or group has the motivation, confidence, and commitment that is needed to accomplish a specific task.

Hershey and Blanchard (1996) use the *ability* of followers and their *willingness* to develop a four-stage continuum of follower readiness, from low to high.

1. *Followers are unable and unwilling to take responsibility for performing a task*—that is, they do not possess the necessary ability and they feel insecure about taking responsibility.
2. *Followers are unable but willing to do job tasks*—that is, they do not possess the necessary ability, but they are motivated and feel confident if the leader provides guidance.
3. *Followers are able but unwilling to do what the leader wants*—that is, they possess the necessary ability, but they feel insecure about doing what the leader wants.

4. *Followers are able and willing to do what is asked of them*—that is, they possess the necessary ability and feel confident about their ability to do what is asked of them.

Strategic Decision-Making Model

Strategic decision-making models are based on the premise that organizational effectiveness derives from the appropriateness of the "fit" or alignment between an organization and its environments (Zacarro, 2001). The executive's role is to create and manage this fit or alignment. The strategic decision-making process is essential in accomplishing this role. Though all executives are involved with the strategic formulation and implementation process, their responsibilities differ, depending on their position in the organization. Senior executives have primary responsibility for strategic decisions related to the organization's future and for tactical decisions regarding organization-wide policy implementation and control systems, whereas junior executives have primary responsibility for strategy implementation and operational decisions at the unit level. Accordingly, strategic decision-making models focus primarily on the involvement of senior executives. Although several theories of strategic planning and decision-making exit, this section will focus on the common features of these various theories.

The Strategic Decision-Making Process

As noted previously, senior executives utilize the strategy decision-making or formulation process to create and manage the best possible fit between their organization and its environments. The strategic decision-making process can be described as a three-step sequential process.

1. In the first step, the executive is involved in the process of environmental scanning. For the senior executive, such scanning is quite comprehensive and involves various sectors within the organization, as well as events and trends in the organization's environment.
2. The second step focuses on processes involving interpretation and meaning construction. Specifically, this involves an SWOT analysis, which includes assigning information to categories such as *strengths, weaknesses, opportunities,* and *threats*. Information in the categories of strengths and weaknesses is derived from scanning and analyzing organizational processes, whereas information on threats and opportunities is derived from environmental issues and events that are understood to have high-gain potential or high-loss potential.

3. The third step focuses on processes involving strategic choice and organizational responding. Decisions about the organization's direction and resources are based on the analysis and interpretation of potential loss or gain from Step 2. For example, "events labeled as threats may prompt defensive organizational reactions, whereas opportunities may lead to the adoption of more risky choices" (Zacarro, 2001, p. 175).

Transformational Models

Transformational models of leadership is a broad category that encompasses several theories of inspirational leadership, including charismatic leadership, visionary leadership, and transformational leadership. The common theme in these theories is that effective leaders develop a vision that both structures and motivates its implementation throughout the organization. Thus, successful strategic implementation requires that leaders galvanize support for the vision and strategy by empowering and inspiring employees.

Transformational Leadership

One of the best known of the transformational models is Bass's (1985) theory of "transformational leadership." For Bass, transformational leadership is best understood when it is contrasted with "transactional leadership." The term *transactional leadership* captures well what management and leadership mean to most people. Bass describes transactional leadership as an exchange process. That is to say, subordinates agree to accomplish a particular job in exchange for a pay check, job security, and other benefits from the superior or employer. A basic assumption underlying transactional leadership is that subordinates' basic and higher-level needs are met when these workers perform according to their exchange agreement. Therefore, they should not be expected to extend themselves in an altruistic or heroic manner.

Accordingly, transactional leaders function effectively when they: (1) recognize what actions subordinates must take to achieve organizational goals; (2) specify the actions; (3) recognize subordinates' needs; and (4) clarify the connection between subordinates' actions and needs.

In contrast, the transformational leader approaches leadership from an entirely different perspective or level of awareness. Rather than improvement resulting from a better application of the same principles, as proposed by the contingency theorists, improvement comes from the application of different principles. According to Bass, the transformational leader (1) raises levels of consciousness about the importance of certain goals or actions; (2) encourages subordinates to transcend self-interest for the good of the team; and (3) causes subordinates to focus on higher-order needs, such as self-actualization.

Table 2.1 provides a capsule summary of these leadership models, as well as illustrates their contribution to my integrated model of effective leadership.

CONTRIBUTIONS FROM QUALITATIVE RESEARCH

The last few years have witnessed a proliferation of published research reports on executive leadership. This research involves both qualitative and quantitative studies. This section reviews qualitative research studies whereas the next section reviews quantitative studies.

For the most part, recently published qualitative research utilizes the method of intensive interviews. Several of these interview studies were conducted with individual executives who are regarded by their peers and leadership researchers as highly effective executives. One study, called *Lessons*

TABLE 2.1
Key Contibutions of Contemporary Leadership Models

Leadership Model	Brief Description	Key Contribution
Attributes	Traits, skills, styles, character, competencies, or capabilities that constitute effective leadership; in vogue today are emotional competency (EQ) and peak performance.	Exhibit EQ and peak performance
Conceptual Complexity	Complex information processing and environmental demands require leaders to possess significant conceptual capacities to cope with such complexities.	Manifest cognitive complexity
Behavioral Complexity	Successfully dealing with the demands of multiple constituencies requires leaders to respond differentially and to balance a number of competing roles, such as, task versus people, mentor versus director, facilitator versus producer, and so on.	Balance "roles" of task versus people
Strategic Decision Making	Effective strategy formulation, and decision making requires leader to analyze, create, and manage the "fit" between the organization and its environments.	Manage organization and environment fit

From the Top (Neff & Citrin, 2001), will be reviewed in some detail in this section.

Thomas Neff and James Citrin (2001) studied 50 of the most effective and successful leaders of profit and nonprofit corporations in America. Study participants included Jack Welch, Bill Gates, Michael Dell, Michael Eisner, and Elizabeth Dole. Based on intensive, in-depth interviews with these leaders, Neff and Citrin noted that these leaders shared 10 common attributes and utilized 6 specific strategies in their leadership. The 10 attributes were passion, intelligence and clarity of thinking, great communication skills, high energy level, keeping their egos in check, inner peace, capitalizing on formative early experiences, strong family lives, positive attitude, and a focus on "doing the right things right" (pp. 380–387). The 6 core leadership strategies they elicited were to live with integrity and lead by example; develop a winning strategy or "big idea"; build a great management team; inspire employees to achieve greatness; creative a flexible, responsive organization; and tie it all together with reinforcing management and compensation systems (p. 362).

Similarly, Ullrich, Zenger, and Smallwood (2000) report the results of their qualitative research on highly effective leaders in their book *Results-Based Leadership*. They isolated four core leadership strategies among the leaders they studied. The four strategies are to demonstrate a personal character of integrity and trust, develop a corporate vision and a set direction, mobilize individual employee commitment, and engender organizational capability by building teams and managing change (pp. 8–13). A remarkable degree of correspondence exists between the core leadership strategies of these two studies.

Another noteworthy interview study is reported by Buckingham and Coffman (1999). This study, conducted by the Gallup Organization, involved taped 90-minute semistructured interviews with 80,000 managers. These researchers found that the most effective managers were characterized by four factors: they selected employees based on talent rather than on experience or other qualifications; they defined expectations and right outcomes for their employees, rather than the right steps; they motivated their employees by building on employee strengths, rather than by trying to fix weaknesses; and they developed their employees by emphasizing finding the right fit, rather than by promoting people to the next rung on the corporate ladder.

CONTRIBUTIONS FROM QUANTITATIVE RESEARCH

Several hundred quantitative research studies have been published on executive leadership in the past decade. As with the qualitative studies, many quantitative studies were conducted on leader attributes, but fewer focused on leader competencies. Of particular note is that some researchers are beginning to critically analyze these various studies, and at least one has attempted to synthesize the current research on executive leadership. Stephen Zaccaro, PhD, a social psychologist and leadership researcher, has recently published the results of his systematic review of several hundred quantitative research studies on executive leadership (Zaccaro, 2001). He has also proposed a model of executive leadership based on this systematic and critical review.

Zaccaro (2001) has analyzed and distilled the findings of these quantitative studies on leadership performance requirements. He posits six research-based propositions as the foundation for his generic leader performance requirements model. Four of these propositions are directly relevant to my Integrative Model of Effective Leadership. The four are

1. Executives engage in envisioning, strategy making, and direction setting, all of which require increased cognitive complexity.
2. Executives are responsible for strategy implementing and operational coordination and maintenance within the organization.
3. Executive effectiveness facilitates organizational effectiveness and success.
4. Organizational dynamics influence leader effectiveness.

Essentially, these research-based propositions profile the effective executive leader as being responsible for making and implementing strategy. In addition, these executives both influence corporate effectiveness and are in leadership-development programs influenced by corporate or organizational dynamics. Finally, it is noteworthy that the quantitative research findings are reasonably similar to the qualitative research findings.

COMPETENCIES OF EFFECTIVE EXECUTIVE LEADERSHIP

So far, leadership effectiveness has been described largely in terms of leadership attributes and strategies. Less research data seems to be reported on leadership competencies than on other topics. In their survey of major corporations with leadership-development programs, Giber, Carter, and Goldsmith (2000) found that the three highest-ranked leadership competencies cited were building and strengthening teamwork, business understanding, and conceptual thinking. Among the 15 corporations with the best leadership-development programs, 8 specified the leader competencies they believed were essential to effectiveness. These corporations include Abbott, BP Amoco, Bose Corporation, Barclays Global Investors, Colgate-

Palmolive, PECO Energy, SIAC, and Smith Kline Beecham. Smith Kline lists 21 leadership competencies, whereas Abbott lists 6 sets of competencies: setting vision and strategy, building the organization, inspiring people, possessing a drive for results, making difficult decisions, and encouraging open communication and knowledge sharing.

Table 2.2 summarizes the 7 core competencies I have found most useful in my recent consultation work. Chapter 3 will further describe these

TABLE 2.2
Core Competencies of Leadership Effectiveness

1. *Acts with Integrity and a Sense of Balance*
   The leader creates a committed organization that acts with unparalleled integrity, courage, and authenticity. Serves as a role model by acting in a consistent and fair manner. Manifests a high degree of stability and balance among corporate, personal, and family needs and demands.

2. *Develops a Winning Strategy*
   The leader creates and communicates a compelling vision of the future that reflects corporate values, resources, trends, and opportunities. Establishes and commits to strategies and a course of action that accomplish the vision.

3. *Mobilizes Employee Commitment*
   The leader inspires and motivates individuals to achieve and remain loyal to the organization's strategy, vision, and goals. Develops and maintains a strong talent pool by continuously developing individuals' skills, knowledge, and capacities.

4. *Possesses Requisite Job Capabilities and Corporate Understanding*
   The leader possesses requisite job capabilities and a keen understanding of customers, markets, operations, and emerging issues to accomplish the corporate vision. Makes and accepts decisions based on facts, experience, and warranted assumptions about changes in markets, resources, or regulations.

5. *Engenders Corporate Capability*
   The leader sets high goals for organizational and personal performance and commits the organization's resources to achieve these goals. Utilizes performance monitoring to hold self and others accountable for achieving high-quality results.

6. *Communicates Effectively and Encourages Knowledge Sharing*
   The leader creates a culture of open, honest communication and knowledge sharing. Regularly solicits ideas, provides honest feedback, and shares information with staff and others. Practices effective listening, as well as excellent verbal and written communication skills.

7. *Exhibits a High Level of Energy and Health Status*
   The leader manifests significant energy reserves to achieve short- and long-range goals, despite arduous working conditions, and maintains a high level of physical and psychological well-being, despite adverse circumstances, demands, and emotional stress.

competencies and specify them with behavioral indicators or markers in terms of high, moderate, and low levels of effectiveness.

THE NEED FOR AN INTEGRATIVE MODEL OF EXECUTIVE LEADERSHIP

Executive leadership as a field of study is relatively new. Although leadership has been studied formally for over 60 years, most of this research has been on supervisory and middle-level management. Only in the last 5 years has executive leadership become an important focus of theory development and empirical research in the field of leadership studies.

The mark of a discipline's maturity is reflected by the presence of validated theories. Theory development can be described in terms of a sequence of stages that proceeds from observation to taxonomy to model and finally to full-fledged theory.

A taxonomy is a formal way of classifying and ordering observations of phenomena. For example, disordered human behavior can be classified in a taxonomy such as *The Diagnostic and Statistical Manual, Fourth Edition* (*DSM-IV*). The value and viability of a taxonomy of executive leadership are determined by the extent to which that taxonomy is comprehensive in ordering observation. Models are simplified representations of reality. They are a means of specifying relationships between and among ordered observations—taxonomies—of ideas, concepts, or methods. The diagnostic system of *DSM-IV* is an example of a model of psychopathology. The value and viability of a model of executive leadership are determined by the extent to which the model represents these relationships. The final progression in theory development is a full-fledged theory. Theory is defined as a means to explain a wide set of observations and the relationships among these observations. The value and viability of a theory are determined by the adequacy and validity of its explanations. Currently, there is no widely accepted, empirically based theory of leadership—or of psychology, for that matter. Accordingly, many researchers and theorists are now focusing on developing taxonomies and models as a prelude to theory development. For example, the *DSM-IV* is described as a theoretical model of psychopathology. It will remain a model based on taxonomies until sufficient empirical validation exists for a full-fledged theory of psychopathology. Although considerable scientific progress has been made in recent years, such a theory is not anticipated to be forthcoming for quite some time.

At this stage of theory development, it is premature to expect that an empirically based, full-fledged theory of executive leadership will emerge soon. Rather, it is more realistic to focus efforts on the development of comprehensive and integrative taxonomies and models. In this spirit, the following model of executive leadership effectiveness is proposed.

AN INTEGRATIVE MODEL OF LEADERSHIP EFFECTIVENESS

At this point in time, a number of taxonomies of executive leadership skills, talents, and competencies have been forthcoming. A critical next step is the development of models of executive leadership. A significant step in model building in executive leadership is Zacarro's (2000) leader performance requirements model, which focuses on a broad-scale view of executive leadership. The model proposed in this book is more narrowly focused on executive leadership effectiveness and leadership development.

The model proposed here incorporates some insights from the theoretical models of leadership and from both the quantitative and qualitative research on determinants and outcomes of leadership effectiveness. It is based on various taxonomies of leadership skills, talents, and competencies, as will be described in chapter 3. It is also based on my experience consulting with senior executives and incorporates concepts previously described in two of my previous books, *Psychiatric Consultation in the Workplace* and *Corporate Therapy and Consulting*. Basic concepts in this model are what I have called the "Four Ss": situation, style, skills, and synchronism or "fit" (Sperry, 1996).

The Integrative Model of Leadership Effectiveness is composed of six interrelated components.

Situation, 1, 2, and 3 (boxes 1—3), which refer to the organizational and family system dynamics that impact, positively and negatively, the executive's thoughts, feelings, and behavior. The executive's job/position (4) includes all the demands, such as job functions, performance standards, decisional authority, and attendant stressors and stress buffers associated with the position—for example, access and relations with peers and superiors, mentoring, and so on.

Styles/Skills (box 4) includes the impact of the executive's values and leadership and personality style, as well as leadership skills and competencies and other qualifications.

Synchronism (box 5) refers to the degree of "fit" among the three key components and constituencies, which can be the source of considerable distress, on one hand, or of overall effectiveness, well-being, and job and life satisfaction, on the other hand.

Leadership Effectiveness (box 6) is the outcome of the other components (boxes 1–5).

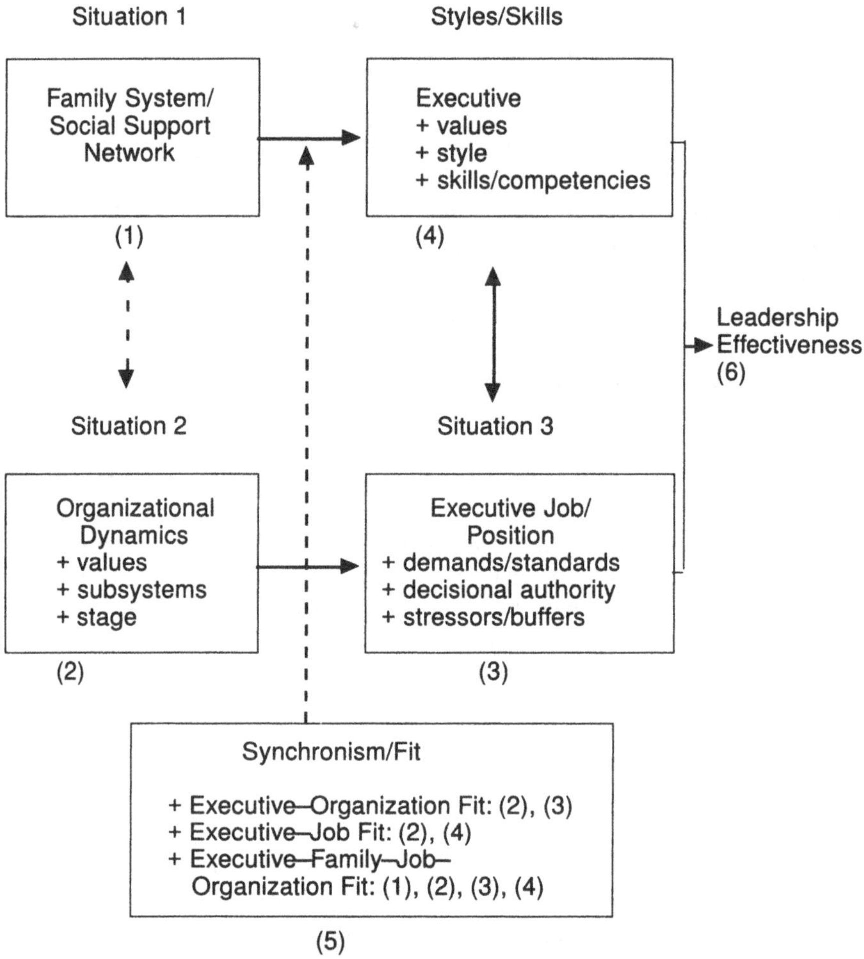

FIGURE 2.1. An Integrative Model of Leadership Effectiveness

The seven leadership competencies, described in the previous section and detailed in chapter 3, can be used as specific behavioral indicators or markers of the executive's level of overall leadership effectiveness. Figure 2.1 illustrates these components. The arrows indicate the type of interaction or impact, unidirectional or bidirectional; the solid lines indicate direct influence; whereas the broken line points indicate indirect influence.

The remaining chapters of this book elaborate these components and their relationships, with chapter 6 providing a systematic method for assessing these components and establishing tailored intervention strategies.

CONCLUDING NOTE

The purpose of this chapter was to establish a foundation for an integrative model of leadership based on the characteristics and competencies of exceptional and effective leaders. It began by overviewing five major models of leadership, and highlighting critical elements relevant to leadership effectiveness. It then selectively reviewed recent qualitative and quantitative research of effectiveness in executive leadership and highlighted key determinants of leadership effectiveness. I proposed an Integrative Model of Leadership Effectiveness, based on this analysis and synthesis. Presumably, this model provides a useful framework for understanding and assessing leadership effectiveness, as well as for guiding decisions about selection, termination, or intervention planning to increase and maximize leadership effectiveness.

REFERENCES

Bass, B. (1985). *Leadership and performance beyond expectations.* New York: Free Press.

Blake, R., & Mouton, J. (1964). *The managerial grid.* Houston, TX: Gulf.

Buckingham, M., & Coffman, C. (1999). *First, break all the rules: What the world's greatest managers do differently*. New York: Simon & Schuster.

Dennsion, D., Hooijberg, R., & Quinn, R. (1995). Paradox and performance: Toward a theory of behavioral complexity in managerial leadership. *Organization Science, 6,* 524–540.

Giber, D., Carter, L., & Goldsmith, M. (2000). *Linkage, Inc.'s best practices in leadership development handbook.* San Francisco: Jossey-Bass/Pfeiffer.

Goleman, D. (1998). *Working with emotional intelligence*. New York: Bantam.

Hersey, P., & Blanchard, K. (1996). *Management of organizational behavior: Utilizing human resources*. Englewood Cliffs, NJ: Prentice-Hall.

Hiebert, M., & Klatt, B. (2001). *The encyclopedia of leadership*. New York: McGraw-Hill.

Jacob, T., & Jacques, E. (1987). Leadership in complex systems. In J. Zeidner (Ed.), *Human productivity enhancement*. New York: Praeger.

Jacques, E., & Clement, S. (1991). *Executive leadership: A practical guide to managing complexity.* Arlington, VA: Cason Hall.

Lark, S., & Richards, J. (2000). *The chemistry of success: Six secrets of peak performance*. San Francisco: Bay Books.

Neff, T., & Citrin, J. (2001). *Lessons from the top: The 50 most successful business leaders in America and what you can learn from them*. New York: Currency/Doubleday.

Sperry, L. (1993). *Psychiatric consultation in the workplace*. Washington, DC: American Psychiatric Press.

Sperry, L. (1996). *Corporate therapy and consulting*. New York: Brunner/Mazel.

Ulrich, D., Zenger, J., & Smallwood, N. (2000). *Results-based leadership*. Cambridge, MA: Harvard Business School Press.

Yukl, G. (1999). *Leadership in organizations* (4th ed). Englewood Cliffs, NJ: Prentice-Hall.

Zaccaro, S. (2001). *The nature of executive leadership: A conceptual and empirical analysis of success*. Washington, DC: American Psychological Association.

3

Leadership Skills and Competencies

A key component of the Integrative Leadership Effectiveness Model is leadership skills and competencies. This chapter describes skills and competencies of leadership. Next, skills, talents, and competencies are defined and differentiated. This is followed by a listing and description of 5 sets of core leadership skills, involving 22 subskills. Then talents associated with executive leadership are briefly described. Finally, a set of core competencies of executive leadership are listed in three levels of effectiveness. Because talents, by definition, cannot be learned through training or coaching, the emphasis in this chapter is on leadership skills and competencies.

SKILLS, KNOWLEDGE, TALENTS, AND COMPETENCIES

Unfortunately, the terms *skills*, *knowledge*, *talents*, and *competencies* are used interchangeably. Because of their importance in our understanding of effective leadership, it is helpful to distinguish them. This sections defines and differentiates these key terms.

Skills are defined by Buckingham and Coffman (1999) as "the how-to's of a role" (p. 82). Skills are capabilities that can be transferred from one person to another. For example, reading a balance sheet is a financial management skill. Similar to skills is the term *knowledge*, which is "what you are aware of" (p. 82). Knowledge can be differentiated into factual—that is, concepts or ideas available to anyone—and experiential knowledge, such as what is learned subjectively through firsthand experience. Both types can be learned and transferred from one person to another. For example, for human resources managers, provisions of the Americans for Disability Act are pertinent factual knowledge.

Talents are natural abilities that influence an individual's "recurring patterns of thought, feeling, or behavior" (Buckingham & Coffman, 1999, p. 83). These abilities are inborn traits, which means that they cannot be learned. For example, "precision" is a talent associated with effective accountants and computer programmers. It is possible to train someone—who does not have this talent—to follow a protocol that may increase that person's attention to detail, which is one aspect of precision; nevertheless, the outcome of this training will never instill precision in an individual.

Take the talent of good judgment. In my 30+ years as both an executive and a consultant, I have learned that good judgment is really an inborn talent that cannot be easily approximated. I have observed that individuals with good judgment can intuitively make split-second decisions under duress that turn out to be excellent assessments of people or tasks. Individuals lacking innate good judgment, who have been taught a problem-solving protocol, may be able to follow the protocol and systematically think through a problem reasonably well when there is sufficient time and little or no duress; however, these individuals are at a great disadvantage when they are forced to make quick decisions under fire.

Buckingham and Coffman indicate, based on their leadership research, that the capacity to discover talent in others is an important ability for executives. They note that "the best managers are adept at spotting a glimpse of talent in someone and then repositioning him so that he can play to that talent more effectively" (p. 83). Such leaders are talent hunters and talent developers and do not confuse talents with skills. Jack Welch, the recently retired CEO of General Electric who described himself as GE's best talent scout, exemplifies this view of leadership.

Competencies, on the other hand, can be defined as capabilities that many corporations use to describe expected behavior in leaders. Unfortunately, Buckingham and Coffman note that some competencies may actually be talents such as "remaining calm when under fire," whereas other competencies may actually be skills, such as "implements basic operational systems." Yet others may be "part skills, part knowledge and part talent" (p. 89). They urge executives to be very clear about the actual requirements of specific competencies, because if a talent-based competency is specified for a given individual, unless the individual possesses that talent, it cannot be learned.

The ideal is to establish "pure" competencies—those that are primarily skill-based and not talent-based. Over the past several years, I have observed that the most discerning and effective executives were those who could establish skill-based competencies. It is critically important for leaders to clearly distinguish talents from skills and competencies when selecting individuals for positions and when coaching or planning leadership-development activities. In other words, the best leaders are those who know how to search out needed talents in others and coach for needed skills and competencies.

LEADERSHIP SKILLS

Robert Katz, in a 1974 classic *Harvard Business Review* article entitled "Skills of an Effective Administrator," suggested that all managers need three basic skills to be successful. He described them as technical, human relations, and conceptual skills. Today, these three skills are more commonly referred to as technical/analytic, relational, and strategic skills

These core leadership skills are requisite behaviors of all leaders—from supervisors to CEOs—in their everyday functioning. Demands of leadership at the supervisory level focus primarily on technical/analytic skills, and secondarily on relational skills, and to a lesser extent on strategic skills. The demands of leadership at the middle-management level primarily involve both technical/analytical and relational skill sets. Ponder (1998) has described three categories of basic leadership skills: technical/analytic, relational, and strategic. Demands of leadership at the executive level are primarily on strategic skills and relational skills and secondarily on technical/analytic.

Based on my experience as an executive consultant, as well as my experience as an executive, I have noted that although these three skill sets encompassed perhaps 90% of a manager's daily demands in the past, they no longer are sufficient. In the last 10 years, three phenomena have significantly impacted the practice of leaders. These are the information revolution; accountability, particularly accountability requiring financial analysis; and job stress. Increases in these demands have prompted the addition of two other skills sets, which I call "financial/information skills" and "personal development skills." Table 3.1 lists the skills and subskills. The remainder of this section briefly describes the value of each skill in effective leadership. Those interested in further discussion can turn to appendix A, which details the requisite skills for each skill set.

Technical/Analytic Skills

Mastering Job-Specific Skills: Job-specific skills are the basic competencies related to a job position—that is, computer literacy, preparing a production schedule, budgeting, and so on. They are specified by a job

TABLE 3.1
Essential Leadership Skills

Technical/Analytic Skills
- Mastering job-specific skills
- Problem solving and decision making
- Time and priorities management
- Project management
- Performance monitoring
- Training and development

Relational Skills
- Communication
- Team development
- Diversity
- Motivation
- Conflict resolution
- Coaching

Strategic Skills
- Visioning and strategy formulation
- Strategic implementation and management
- Guiding change

Financial/Information Technology Skills
- Mastering the budgeting process
- Understanding balance sheets and financial reports
- Monitoring financial and human resources
- Using data to guide management decisions

Personal and Self-Development Skills
- Stress and lifestyle management
- Balancing family, work, and personal life
- Developing/utilizing a personal mission statement and a career plan

description, job analysis, and job specifications. These specific skills can be learned in several ways: management training program, apprenticeship, and so forth.

Problem Solving and Decision Making: Both decision making and problem solving are action processes that overlap—in other words, decision making is a step and a skill in the problem-solving process.

Time and Priorities Management: Managing priorities is irrefutably linked with being a successful leader. Effective management of priorities is related to time management.

Project Management: Unlike day-to-day responsibilities, projects are one-time undertakings that are divided into specific sections that can be sequenced and independently evaluated. Effective project management is a sure-fire test of both project team and leader performance.

Performance Monitoring: Monitoring is the continuous process of checking progress on performance and goal outcomes. It involves both formal and informal checks, and when the leader renders feedback based on performance monitoring, the process becomes proactive.

Training and Development: Training provides individuals with the necessary knowledge and skills to perform a job, whereas development prepares individuals for increasingly responsible or complex jobs or careers.

Relational Skills

Communication: Communication is considered the most important of the leadership skills. It is the "bridge" for transferring knowledge and guidance, as well as for receiving information from inside and outside the organization.

Team Development: A team is a group of individuals that collaboratively accomplishes specified goals; effective leaders promote optimal teamwork.

Diversity: Diversity in a work team may involve gender, age, race, ethnicity, religion, and lifestyle factors. Effective leaders have the capacity of facilitating subordinates to work together as a team—despite their diversity—and to perform optimally.

Motivation: Motivating subordinates to function effectively is essential for both individual and team productivity. Leaders need to be sufficiently competent in understanding and utilizing motivation and recognizing and eliminating sources of job dissatisfaction.

Conflict Resolution: Resolving conflict is essential for both efficient and effective team performance. Most leaders would do well to increase their skill level in preventing and resolving conflict.

Coaching: Coaching is a process of guiding and encouraging subordinates to achieve optimal performance. It is considered the pinnacle of the relational skills, requiring a high degree of competence in the other relational skills. Assuming that the subordinate and the leader/coach have previously developed and agreed upon job standards and goals, coaching can proceed.

Strategic Skills

Visioning and Strategy Formulation: Vision is the capacity to perceive possibilities and to create an ideal depiction of where an organization will be or needs to be at a future time. It involves setting a clear, focused, desirable direction that points toward and energizes an organization toward a specific destination.

Strategic Implementation and Management: Strategy is an integrated, long-term way of perceiving, thinking, deciding, and acting that produces viable plans for achieving an organization's vision.

Guiding Change: Guiding change involves preparing for, initiating, and implementing the change process.

Financial/Information Technology Skills

Mastering the Budgeting Process: This skill permits the leader to effectively plan, implement, and then evaluate a unit budget.

Understanding Balance Sheets and Financial Reports: Financial performance analysis and decision making that involves financial considerations both require sufficient understanding of financial statements.

Monitoring Financial and Human Resources: It is essential for leaders to have their own ongoing, informal measures and indicators of performance and financial indicators to compare with formal quarterly reports from finance, operations, human resources, and so on. These measures permit leaders to quickly and easily monitor and analyze critical financial and performance indicators.

Using Data to Guide Management Decisions: Managerial decision making can be greatly enhanced when data are appropriately utilized. The capacity to effectively utilize data in such decision making is essential for leadership effectiveness.

Personal and Self-Development Skills

Stress and Lifestyle Management: This skill set enhances the leader's capacity to control and cope with stress, on and off the job.

Balancing Family, Work, and Personal Life: Because individuals who can effectively balance job, family, and personal dimensions tend to be healthier and more productive, leaders need to develop the skill of balancing competing expectations and demands on them.

Developing/Utilizing a Personal Mission Statement and a Career Plan: The trajectories of personal development and career development tend to remain in parallel and in sync with job/organizational goals for highly effective individuals. Establishing a personal mission statement can facilitate both personal and career development.

LEADERSHIP TALENTS

Earlier, it was noted that talents are inborn abilities and cannot be learned or coached like skills or "pure" competencies. In their in-depth research on highly effective leaders, Buckingham and Coffman (1999) isolated 39 talents that individuals manifested to excel in their leadership role. These talents can be classified in three categories: striving talents, thinking talents, and relating talents. A few of these in each category will be noted and briefly defined.

Striving Talents: These talents "explain the *why* of a person. They explain *why* he gets out of bed every day, *why* he is motived to push and push just that little bit harder" (Buckingham & Coffman, 1999, p. 85). Stamina and vision are 2 of the 11 striving talents. Stamina is defined as the capacity for physical endurance, whereas vision is the "drive to paint valued-based word pictures about the future" (p. 251).

Thinking Talents: These talents "explain the *how* of a person. They explain *how* he thinks, *how* he weighs up alternatives, *how* he comes to his decisions" (p. 85). Strategic thinking, formulations, and creativity are 3 of the 14 thinking talents.

Strategic thinking is defined as the ability to specify alternative scenarios in the future, whereas formulation is the ability to find coherent patterns amid incoherent data sets. Creativity is defined as the ability "to break existing configurations in favor of more effective/appealing ones" (p. 252). Anyone who has worked with a group involved in strategic planning quickly recognizes that some individuals, with this talent, can quickly envision future alternatives, whereas others—without the talent—struggle with some or all of the process.

Relating Talents: These talents "explain the *who* of a person. They explain *whom* he trusts, *whom* he builds relationships with, *whom* he confronts, and *whom* he ignores" (p. 85). Empathy, positivity, and ability to be an activator are 3 of the 14 relating talents studied by Buckingham and Coffman. Empathy is the ability to identify feelings and perspectives in others, whereas positivity is the ability to see the bright side. Being an activator is defined as the "impatience to move others to action" (p. 252).

LEADERSHIP COMPETENCIES

So far, leader competencies have been described in general terms. But how would they be manifested in the workplace on a day-to-day basis? More specifically, how would they be manifested by leaders at different levels of effectiveness? This section articulates these seven core competencies of executive leadership. The reader will note that these competencies were derived from the review of quantitative and qualitative research presented in chapter 2. These seven competencies are listed with regard to three levels of effectiveness—highly, moderately, and minimally effective—with each level specified in behavioral terms. These levels of effectiveness correspond to the three levels of effectiveness in the Integrative Model of Leadership Effectiveness. A somewhat similar approach to competencies and information on how competencies can be incorporated into a leadership-development program are discussed by Giber, Carter, and Goldsmith (2000). Table 3.2 lists these competencies and general behavioral indicators. These seven competencies are briefly described in narrative form as follows. The interested reader will find a detailed set of specific behavioral indicators for each of the three levels of functioning for all seven competencies in appendix A.

1. Acts with Integrity and a Sense of Balance

The leader creates a committed organization that acts with full unparalleled integrity, courage, and authenticity. He serves as a role model by acting in a consistent and fair manner. He manifests a high degree of stability and balance among corporate, personal, and family needs and demands.

2. Develops a Winning Strategy

The leader creates and communicates a compelling vision of the future that reflects corporate values, resources, trends, and opportunities. Establishes and commits to strategies and a course of action that will accomplish the vision.

3. Mobilizes Employee Commitment

The leader inspires and motivates individuals to achieve and remain loyal to the organization's strategy, vision, and goals. Develops and maintains a

TABLE 3.2
Leadership Competencies: Behavioral Indicators

1. Acts with Integrity and a Sense of Balance
   - Genuinely lives with integrity and courage
   - Consistently keeps ego in check
   - Leads by example and models fairness, courage, and honesty
   - Balances among corporate, personal, and family demands
2. Develops a Winning Strategy
   - Scans environment and develops long-term approaches
   - Envisions the future when developing strategy
   - Anticipates potential obstacles, competition, and alternate scenarios
   - Fosters internal and external commitment for strategy
   - Effectively implements strategy throughout the organization
3. Mobilizes Employee Commitment
   - Identifies and develops organization strengths to match opportunities
   - Anticipates needed competencies and actively develops them in others
   - Effectively demonstrates how the organization meets customers' needs
   - Is significantly involved in coaching, developing, and supporting staff
   - Increases employees' commitment by developing a culture of trust
4. Possesses Requisite Job Capabilities and Understands Corporate Dynamics
   - Thoroughly and systematically analyzes strategic initiatives
   - Achieves an equitable outcome in a negotiation
   - Demonstrates the capacity to make and accept difficult decisions
   - Proactively develops contingency plans re: changing market, regulations, or resources
5. Engenders Corporate Capability
   - Proactively develops partnerships for achieving goals throughout the organization
   - Consistently sets the bar higher and searches for new tactics to improve results
   - Challenges current perceptions that limit effectiveness and results
   - Effectively maintains and manages organizational boundaries to deliver results
6. Communicates Effectively and Encourages Knowledge Sharing
   - Encourages and rewards diversity of opinion in discussing issues
   - Redesigns structure to support effective corporate communication
   - Seeks, quantifies, and responds to employee input in large and small issues
   - Utilizes communication networks for corporate exchange of best practices
7. Exhibits a High Level of Energy and Health Status
   - Exhibits and sustains a high level of energy and stamina
   - Has unlimited capacity to effectively entertain business clients
   - Recovers rapidly from minor illnesses, injury, exertion, and emotional stress
   - Retains excellent health, despite arduous job demands and deadlines

strong talent pool by continuously developing individuals' skills, knowledge, and capacities.

4. Possesses Requisite Job Capabilities and Understands Corporate Dynamics

The leader possesses requisite job capabilities and a keen understanding of customers, markets, operations, and emerging issues to accomplish the corporate vision. The leader makes and accepts decisions based on facts, experience, and warranted assumptions about changes in markets, resources, or regulations.

5. Engenders Corporate Capability

The leader sets high goals for organizational and personal performance and commits the organization's resources to achieve these goals. This individual utilizes performance monitoring to hold self and others accountable for achieving high-quality results.

6. Communicates Effectively and Encourages Knowledge Sharing

The leader creates a culture of open, honest communication and knowledge sharing. This individual regularly solicits ideas, provides honest feedback, and shares information with staff and others. The leader regularly practices effective listening and manifests good verbal and written communication skills.

7. Exhibits a High Level of Energy and Health Status

The leader manifests significant energy reserves to achieve short- and long-range goals, despite arduous working conditions. This person also maintains a high level of physical and psychological well-being, despite adverse circumstances, demands, and emotional stress.

LEADERSHIP COMPETENCIES IN THE LEADER PROFILES

Let's return to the four profiles described at the beginning of chapter 1. At the end of that chapter a global rating on the Leadership Effectiveness Continuum was offered for each profile. Now we are in a position to analyze these profiles more precisely utilizing the seven leadership competencies. The reader is referred to figure 6.2, the "Leadership Competency Rating Scale," in Chapter 6. This rating scale is based on the leadership competencies presented in this chapter.

As noted in Chapter 1, the profile of Wallace Quade was designated as *highly effective*. A review of his profile against the leadership competencies confirms this, in that Quade rates as functioning at highly effective levels in all seven leadership competencies. In addition, Quade also merits the designation "peak performer" because, in addition to high ratings in the first six competencies, he also receives high ratings on the seventh competency: "High Level of Energy and Health Status."

The profile of Wesley Saunders would be designated *minimally effective*. This overall rating reflects the assessment on ratings of minimum levels in six executive competencies. The exception was the rating for competency: "engenders corporate capability," in which he was assessed at the moderate level of functioning. The profile of Alex Vasquez would also be designated *minimally effective*. This overall rating reflects the assessment on ratings of minimum levels in all seven executive competencies.

Finally, the profile of Wendy Jenz would be designated between the *minimally effective* to *the moderately effective* range. This overall rating reflects the assessment on ratings of minimal levels in five of the executive competencies and moderate levels on the two other competencies: "engenders corporate capability" and "possesses requisite job capabilities and a keen understanding of corporate capability."

Some consultants might take the results of these competency ratings and establish specific goals and target an intervention strategy—that is, coaching—in order to increase leadership effectiveness. Although this is a common practice in executive coaching, I believe it is premature and potentially problematic. Though it is true that leadership competencies reflect—that is, they are observable markers of—overall leadership effectiveness, these competencies are only one of several determinants of leadership effectiveness. The value of the Integrative Model of Leadership Effectiveness is in systematically guiding the executive or consultant to consider reasons why functioning is low, moderate, or high on specific competencies. A strategy for assessing these reasons, called "executive profiling," is described in detail in chapter 6.

CONCLUDING NOTE

Because leadership skills and competencies are a key component of the Integrative Model of Leadership Effectiveness, they were described in some detail in this chapter. These leadership skills and competencies will be revisited again, this time as assessment instruments, in chapter 6 in the section entitled "Executive Profiling." Another component of the Integrative Model of Leadership Effectiveness, personal styles, is the focus of the next chapter.

REFERENCES

Buckingham, M., & Coffman, C. (1999). *First, break all the rules: What the world's greatest managers do differently*. New York: Simon & Schuster.

Giber, D., Carter, L., & Goldsmith, M. (2000). *Linkage, Inc.'s best practices in leadership development handbook.* San Francisco: Jossey-Bass/Pfeiffer.

Ponder, R. (1998). *Leader's guide: Fifteen essential skills.* Central Point, OR: Oasis Press.

4

Personality and Leadership Styles

Style is one of the six components of the Integrative Model of Leadership Effectiveness. Style refers to personal dynamics—that is, the executive's personality dynamics and leadership style, in contrast to organizational dynamics. Two types of personal styles are covered in this chapter: leadership styles and character and personality styles. The character dimension of leadership is given first. This is followed by an extended description of six common personality styles in executives. Each is explained in terms of the three development levels: healthy, average, and disordered. Finally, three approaches to leadership styles are described. This chapter provides the conceptual basis for "executive profiling," which is discussed and illustrated in chapter 7.

CHARACTER AND LEADERSHIP

Character is defined in various ways. Here are a few definitions and descriptions. Renshon (1996), a psychoanalyst and political scientist, defines character as the individual's basic psychological stance in relation to three elements: *ambition*, which is the consolidated capacity to strive, persist, and accomplish goals; *integrity*, which is the consolidated sense of one's ideals, values, aspirations, and worth, and the ability to remain committed to them; and *relatedness*, which is the consolidated capacity to develop mutually satisfying relationships with others. Josephson (1998a) describes three elements of character: (1) *good principles,* such as honesty, integrity, and duty; (2) *conscience*—the internalized sense of right and wrong, and courage or the will power to act on one's principles; and (3) *"do the right thing even when it's costly, risky, or unpleasant"* (p. 4).

My view is that character is the dimension of personality that describes how individuals conduct themselves in interpersonal and organizational situations and is shaped through the simultaneous development of self-identity and self-regulation. When this learning or socialization process is reasonably adequate and without significant developmental arrests, adaptive, creative, and socially responsible or virtuous behavior—called "good character"—can be expected. Generally speaking, an individual with a good character or reputation is considered to be responsible, trustworthy, respectful, fair, caring, and a good citizen, meaning that the person is cooperative and plays by the rules (Josephson, 1998b).

Dimensions of Character

Currently, personality is conceptualized in a broad perspective that includes the interdependent components of temperament *and* character (Sperry, 1999). Recently, some important developments in the scientific study of character have been reported. One very promising line of research that may have significant implications and applications to the field of consulting psychology will be described.

Extensive research, which integrates psychometric and neurobiological methodologies, finds that individuals with mature character structures tend to be self-reliant or responsible, cooperative, and self-transcendent (Cloninger, Svrakic, & Przybeck, 1993). In contrast, those with immature character structures—also referred to as personality disorders—were noted to have difficulty with self-acceptance, were intolerant and revengeful toward others, and felt self-conscious and unfulfilled. These three dimensions of character—self-responsibility, cooperativeness, and self-transcendence—were subsequently incorporated into Cloninger's seven-factor model of temperament and character and are measured by the Temperament Character Inventory (TCI) (Cloninger, Svrakic, & Przybeck, 1993). A healthy personality or matured character reflects positive or elevated scores on these three character dimensions, whereas negative or low scores reflect the presence of character or personality disorders. Each of these three dimensions will be briefly described.

Self-Responsibility: Self-responsibility and self-directedness refer to self-determination, which is one's ability to control, regulate, and adapt behavior in accord with one's chosen goals and values. Individuals differ in their capacity for self-determination. Individuals with moderate to high levels of self-determination are considered to be mature, effective, and well-organized; they exhibit self-esteem, are able to admit faults and accept themselves as they are, feel that their lives have meaning and purpose, can delay gratification in order to achieve their goals, and take initiative in overcoming challenges. On the other hand, individuals with lower levels of self-determination have low self-esteem, blame others for their problems, feel uncertain of their identity or purpose, and are often reactive, dependent, and resourceless. Self-responsibility can be considered to have various subcomponents, such as internal locus of control, purposefulness, resourcefulness, and self-efficacy. Furthermore, positive self-esteem and the ability to accept individual limitations are strongly correlated with self-responsibility (Cloninger et al., 1993).

Cooperativeness: The character factor of cooperativeness was formulated to account for individual differences in identification with and acceptance of other people. Cooperative individuals tend to be socially tolerant, empathic, helpful, and compassionate, whereas uncooperative individuals tend to be socially intolerant, disinterested in other people, unhelpful, and revengeful. In addition, cooperative individuals are likely to show unconditional acceptance of others, empathy with others' feelings, and a willingness, without selfish domination, to help others achieve their goals. Not surprisingly, social acceptance, helpfulness, and concern for the rights of others are correlated with positive self-esteem. Cooperativeness is a developmental process with several dimensions. These include social acceptance versus intolerance; empathy versus social disinterest; helpfulness versus unhelpfulness; compassion versus revengefulness; and pure-hearted principles versus self-advantage (Cloninger et al., 1993).

Self-Transcendence: Self-transcendence and character traits associated with spirituality have largely been neglected in systematic research and omitted from personality inventories. Nevertheless, self-transcendence may be the feature of personality that most people associate with the character traits of respect, caring, and good citizenship. Self-transcendence is essentially the polar opposite of self-interest. Josephson (1998b) points out that the real test of integrity is doing the right thing even when it is not in our own limited self-interest.

Considered a developmental process, self-transcendence has various stages. According to Cloninger's research, the basic stage is self-forgetfulness, which contrasts with self-consciousness; the intermediate stage is transpersonal identification, which contrasts with self-differentiation; and the third stage is spiritual acceptance, which contrasts with rational materialism (Cloninger et al., 1993).

When the three components of self-responsibility, cooperativeness, and self-transcendence are reasonably well developed in executives, I contend

TABLE 4.1
Comparison of Mature versus Immature Character

Mature Character Structure	Immature Character Structure
Self-directing, responsible behavior	**Difficulty with self-acceptance; irresponsible behavior**
They have self-esteem, admit faults, accept themselves as they are, feel their lives have meaning and purpose, delay gratification in order to achieve their goals, and take initiative in overcoming challenges.	They have low self-esteem, blame others for their problems, feel uncertain of their identity or purpose, and are often reactive, dependent, and resourceless.
Cooperative and collaborative	**Actively or passively uncooperative**
They are socially tolerant, empathic, helpful, and compassionate.	They are socially intolerant, disinterested in other people, unhelpful, and revengeful.
Self-transcendent	**Self-interest**
They manifest self-forgetfulness, Transpersonal identification, and spiritual acceptance.	They manifest self-consciousness, and unfulfilled self-differentiation, as well as rational materialism.

that such executives will act with integrity and manifest good judgment in all situations and circumstances, even when under considerable duress or temptation, or when doing the right thing is not in their immediate self-interest. Table 4.1 summarizes the differences between mature and immature character (personality disorder).

Character as a Key Dimension of Leadership

The relationship between character and leadership is complex and has been described in various ways. Bennis (1998), describing the connection between leadership and character, notes that effective leaders manifest vision and a strong sense of purpose, inspire trust, and accomplish change; then he defines leadership as "character in action" (p. 144). Another provocative definition is offered by Levinson (1997). He describes character as the moral component of personality that evolves out of a "genetic temperament posture" (p. 247) and is characterized by the skills of emotional intelligence, a consistency in behavior over time, and recognizability of this consistent pattern by others. Parenthetically, Levinson notes that organizations, like individuals, manifest a recognizable character.

Character reflects an enduring and consistent way of functioning, in both private and public spheres. Yet hidden aspects of character tend to emerge under stress, fatigue, or temptation. Usually, individuals attempt to hide or disown their "dark side"—that is, the more unflattering aspects of their character—and instead, emphasize their "bright side," their personality or persona. This phenomenon of "impression management," or the ability to manifest different personas in response to the press of circumstances, has been called "post-modern identity" (Gergen, 1991). Unfortunately, success in the art of impression management is highly regarded by some in corporate America. The trade-off for this success is diminished or absent personal integrity and difficulty in establishing and maintaining the trust of peers and superiors. Presumably, an individual with a mature character would not be a master of impression management, but instead would present a consistent style of being. "Leaders have vision and a strongly defined sense of purpose, they inspire trust, and they work for change. Thus, one way to define leadership is character in action" (Bennis, 1998, p. 142).

PERSONALITY STYLES OF EXECUTIVES

Considerable interest has arisen in the personality dynamics of executives. Kets de Vries (1989; Kets de Vries & Miller, 1987) has written widely about the personality dynamics of senior executives. He believes that individuals with narcissistic, controlling, paranoid, and aggressive styles or combinations of these styles tend to gravitate toward top leadership positions, whereas individuals with histrionic, dependent, passive-aggressive, and masochistic styles do not. He also noted that a combination of healthy narcissism and control creates a complementarity that is quite effective and successful in business, whereas the paranoid and detached styles are a poor combination for effective leadership. A perusal of Kets de Vries's descriptions of unhealthy executive personalities suggests that whereas the character trait of self-directiveness may be high, the traits of cooperativeness and self-transcendence are low.

Although Kets de Vries's characterizations of executive personality in clinical terms—narcissistic, paranoid, histrionic, and so on—accurately portray the functioning of leaders, many executives and consultants are uncomfortable with the use of such seemingly diagnostic and pathological designations to describe healthy, adaptive workplace functioning. Therefore, the following descriptions of six executive personality styles utilize the nonclinical designations suggested by Millon and Everly (1985), Oldham and Morris (1990, 1995), and Sperry (1996). Basic to these descriptions of healthy executive personality style are relatively high degrees of the traits of self-directedness, cooperativeness, and self-transcendence.

The Self-Confident Personality

Executives with this personality style are energetic, outgoing, and competitive. They can be visionary, hardworking, and decisive. In addition, they can set priorities, plan, delegate, and galvanize the commitment of subordinates. They present themselves as interested, interesting, and impassioned. They possess considerable politically savvy, in that they can size up the power structure and informal networks within a group or organization and will proceed to establish power alliances that are personally advantageous to them. Generally, they can work comfortably and productively with others. Nevertheless, they view others as the means to the successful ends they constantly seek. Though they may be deferential and cooperative to those in authority or from whom they seek gain, they can be generous in their financial and other types of support to loyal subordinates. In short, they can be extraordinarily effective and efficient persons and make excellent leaders.

As executives, they will allow subordinates sufficient autonomy and leeway to get the job done or accomplish a shared vision. They are quite skilled at team building, of which they must clearly be the source and center. They demand loyalty to the job and to team goals, as well as to themselves. Furthermore, they can be jealous of those in power and can be quite skillful in unseating an "opponent." They are innately competitive and relish staying one step ahead of their nearest competitor. Although they are the acknowledged leader when things are going as planned, they seldom insist on a hierarchical structure. And, as long as no one criticizes, competes, or attempts to share their glory, they can be encouraging, supportive, and fun to work with and for. However, if this unwritten agreement is breached, they can react with vengefulness. Finally, they can function effectively in the mentor role, provided that those under their tutelage are perceived as loyal and noncompetitive. The *DSM-IV* clinical counterpart to this personality style is the narcissistic personality disorder or, in less extreme form, narcissistic trait disturbance.

The Adventurous Personality

Executives with this personality style reflexively seek out challenges. When they perceive work to be such a challenge, they are likely to approach it with excitement and anticipation. They will then function in a disciplined, focused, and responsible manner. Their efforts are not only energetic, but can also be resourceful and innovative. In time, however, they may become bored with the task and, if they no longer find it stimulating and challenging, are likely to drop it and move on to another project or even another job. On the other hand, if this style is combined with sufficient compulsivity, these individuals are more likely to persevere and see the task through to completion. They don't particularly like authority figures and may resist those who attempt to control them. Not surprisingly, these individuals tend to gravitate to occupations that combine risk and challenge with skill. They tend to see themselves as "top guns," whether they are fighter pilots, ski instructors, heart surgeons, trial attorneys, salespeople, or venture capitalists. They energize themselves by thinking of ways to outwit conventional wisdom and standards. Being inner-directed, they may bend rules for expediency, if they believe the rules don't make sense or don't apply to them.

As executives, they may build corporate empires through wheeling and dealing. They can function exceedingly well as entrepreneurs, but when it comes to professionalizing an organization they often have neither the skills nor the desire to attend to such managerial functioning as initiating strategic planning and management systems, budgeting and control systems, and the like. Generally, they prefer to operate on ingenuity and instinct, rather than on the basis of rational thinking and long-range planning. Because of their tendency to resist authority and external constraints and regulations, they may run aground of state and federal regulating agencies or even of their board of directors.

Although the *DSM-IV* clinical counterpart to this personality style is the antisocial personality disorder, few executives would fully meet criteria for this diagnosis. On the other hand, some executives will likely manifest a few of these criteria or behavioral indicators. This less extreme form is known as antisocial trait disturbance.

The Dramatic Personality

Executives with this personality style tend to avoid repetitive, routine jobs and technical careers. Instead they are attracted to exciting and creative work settings and careers. These individuals tend to be broad stroke, idea people who operate on hunches and intuition, rather than detail persons who use reasoned, deductive thinking. They tend to be creative, emotional, persuasive, energetic, and fun to be around. Not surprisingly, they can promote, sell, and wheel and deal when it comes to a product line or service. They may have difficulty following strategic plans, instructions, and protocols. Staying on budget and keeping accurate records are alien to their free-spirited approach to life; thus, they look for others to take care of administrative details. They seem to be happy and content in job settings that can accommodate their creative flair, in terms of work habits, dress code, and working hours. Accordingly, these individuals often choose careers in teaching, sales, marketing, and the various entertainment industries.

As executives, dramatic individuals tend to be strong managers. They can be inspiring bosses to work with and for and are usually appreciative and generous in rewarding the efforts of their subordinates. Likewise, they can show their anger and displeasure at a subordinate's shortcomings. They may be gruff, make threats, and be uncommunicative one day, only to forget it all and be enthusiastic and cheerful the next day. Successful managers with this personality style may be able to assemble a strong organization to complement their creative flair. Usually, this means hiring assistants and staff members who are more compulsive than they are, to handle finances, legal issues, regulation, and paperwork. The *DSM-IV* clinical counterpart to the dramatic personality style is the histrionic personality disorder.

The Leisurely Personality

Executives with this personality style approach work for purely financial reasons, such as paying bills, ensuring a pension, or financing their hobbies and recreation. Rather than being attracted by the possibilities of fame or success, they are attracted by security. These individuals can be good workers and adequate team players, but they are quick to draw the line between work time and personal time. They won't take work home with them, they don't worry about job matters in off hours, and they'll refuse to do more than is required of them. When the job demands efforts beyond their stated responsibilities, they balk. They have little need to please their boss or co-workers or to feel better about themselves for being altruistic and dedicated. Rather, they will meet their stated job requirements, but will not allow themselves to be exploited by anyone. Generally, they don't seek meaning or fulfillment in their jobs or in the workplace, but rather in their personal lives. Not surprising, these individuals are not driven or achievement-oriented. They work slowly and comfortably, and they tend to chafe when deadlines are imposed. When it comes to authority figures, they will likely be mildly suspicious and wary. When asked to work faster or do more, they will likely feel they are being treated unfairly. These individuals are keenly aware of their rights and avenues of redress for perceived wrongs or exploitation. Consequently, if their supervisor insists and demands, they are likely to threaten to file a grievance. Furthermore, they can tolerate a considerable amount of routine and tedium. Individuals with leisurely work personalities are likely to be found in a wide range of job classifications and careers, but because of their need for security, they gravitate toward jobs in union shops, the military, civil service, and other bureaucracies. They may attain promotions, but are unlikely to achieve the top slots.

Because they are not inherently ambitious in the careers, they do not usually gravitate to top management. Their reluctance to sacrifice personal time, energy, and effort appears to be incompatible with corporate demands on executives. Nevertheless, consultants occasionally come across individuals with this personality style in executive suites. As executives, they may have no higher expectations for their subordinates' performance than they have for themselves. Consequently, they expect their staff to follow protocol and meet quotas, but they don't make unreasonable demands. At best, they are average and competent managers, but not leaders per se: They don't or can't develop and hold up a vision of how things could be, galvanize motivation and support for it, or muster the dedication and energy to achieve it. But they are able to keep the wheels of industry turning. The *DSM-IV* clinical counterpart to this personality style is the passive-aggressive personality disorder.

The Conscientious Personality

Executives with this personality style like to do things the right way, as compared to individuals with the obsessive-compulsive personality disorder who must do things perfectly. The need of those with the conscientious style to do things right is likely to result in uncompleted or delayed projects because the finished product may not be good enough. Thus, the conscientious individual who is writing a report will edit and re-edit sentences, laboring under the belief that there must be a better way to say it. These individuals figuratively drown themselves in a sea of never-ending possibilities and details, doubts that cannot be stilled, and decisions that seldom seem to get made. They can become so obsessed with minor details that they leave the most important tasks to the end, when time is at a premium. All sense of priority is lost. Having misplaced a list of things to be done, they spend an inordinate amount of time looking for the list rather than taking a moment or two to reconstruct it. Or, they may expend an inordinate amount of time and energy filling out reminders and schedules, which could better be directed toward completing the scheduled task. These individuals avoid opportunities to relax. They invest most of their energy in their work, but over time lose most of their enthusiasm for it. They are tense, anxious, and overwhelmed by the amount of work before them, whether it involves their job, their profession, or their hobbies and vacations.

Conscientious executives tend to be critical, demanding, and even tyrannical in the face of small errors made by subordinates. They demand more attention to small details, neatness, and perfection than do executives with other personality styles. Conscientious executives cannot recognize that their staff admirably completed a rush job, because they keep spotting minor imperfections—a few minor typographical errors or a computer terminal that wasn't turned off. Furthermore, they tend to equate overtime with job commitment and loyalty. Thus, they are likely to believe that subordinates or colleagues who leave the office at the regular quitting time are leaving early. Though these executives may be rigid and may lack interpersonal skills and political savvy, they tend to be extremely competent. They expect tasks to be accomplished thoroughly and to follow standard protocol. They frown upon creative and innovative approaches. They expect loyalty and consistent performances, but may find it difficult to offer reassurance and praise. They are likely to form quick judgments of others that are long-lasting and difficult to change. And they may hold grudges. They tend to dress conservatively and conventionally. As mentors, they may be quite talented and knowledgeable, but tend to be emotionally distant, proper, unspontaneous, and only minimally encouraging. The *DSM-IV* clinical counterpart to this personality style is the obsessive-compulsive personality disorder.

The Vigilant Personality

Executives with this personality style tend to gravitate to work settings and careers that are a good "fit" with their talents and style. They tend to be perceptive, alert, sensitive to subtle cues, and not easily misled. Their ability to attend to a variety of cues and multiple levels of meaning and communication suggests an exquisite sensitivity to people and situations. They tend to be ambitious and hardworking. But the degree to which they are successful in their work is often a function of their relationship with bosses and co-workers. These individuals are likely to be sensitive to an organization's power structure. Furthermore, they dislike and are uncomfortable with subordination to, and dependence on, others. And, because of their belief that power can be used against them, they might find it hard to trust authority figures and feel comfortable within particular organizations. Accordingly, they may work best in careers and occupations in which they can operate with considerable leeway and independence, or with limited oversight from a superior. Many individuals with this style may be able to tolerate their boss and peers, but are quite aware of inequities in corporate policies and practices and may be quick to point these out. It shouldn't be surprising that corporate watchdogs and whistle blowers tend to have this personality style. These individuals may be excellent investigative reporters, diagnosticians, critics, and researchers. Others may prefer to work with technologies, rather than with people, being well served by their unique ability to concentrate. Although some individuals with this personality covet the rise through the ranks, others choose to function more independently and gravitate to roles in which they can perform their duties without worrying about managing subordinates.

As executives, these individuals require the assurance of loyalty from their subordinates. Suspecting disloyalty, they can be angry, unforgiving, and grudging. In some instances they may mistake a subordinate's ambition for disloyalty and subsequently thwart that subordinate's movement within the company. Generally, these managers tend to take particularly good care of their staff. In certain situations, these managers may even protect their subordinates against corporate policies or actions they perceive as demeaning or unfair. Because they need to feel in complete charge of their units, they may find delegating important—especially politically sensitive—responsibilities to be most difficult. They don't mind putting in longer hours or being out "among the troops," as this provides them with an opportunity to closely monitor people and the situation. The *DSM-IV* clinical counterpart to this personality style is the paranoid personality disorder, though it should be noted that most working executives would unlikely meet full criteria for this disorder. Instead, some executives will manifest a few of these criteria or behavioral indicators. This less extreme form is known as paranoid trait disturbance.

EXECUTIVE PERSONALITY STYLES BY LEVEL OF FUNCTIONING

The brief sketches of the six common personality styles in executives in the previous section provide a general description. These descriptions may be too global to be useful for consultants working with executives or even for executives seeking increased self-knowledge. Various levels of psychological health or functioning are possible for each personality style. Table 4.2 briefly characterizes three levels of functioning for each of the six executive personality styles. The interested reader can find more detailed descriptions of each of the three levels of functioning in the appendix.

LEADERSHIP STYLES OF EXECUTIVES

Individual differences are apparent in an executive's style or manner of approaching job-related concerns, just as individual differences exist in personality structure—that is, personality styles. Although the topic has considerable interest among executives and consultants, leadership styles are considerably less interesting to leadership researchers. Three approaches to leadership styles are briefly described in this section.

TABLE 4.2
Executive Personality Styles by Level of Functioning

CONSCIENTIOUS	
Healthy	These conscientious, hopeful, and kind individuals balance integrity with generosity.
Average	These no-nonsense individuals perform tasks without emotional expenditure or error.
Disorder	They manifest perfectionism and feeling-avoidance that interferes with task completion and relationships.
DRAMATIC	
Healthy	Having found the love they seek within themselves, they are altruistic and giving, without expecting reciprocity.
Average	Though fun-loving and often impulsive, they can delay gratification and be emotionally appropriate much of the time.
Disorder	They are uncomfortable in situations in which they are not the center of attention.
SELF-CONFIDENT	
Healthy	These individuals are energetic and self-assured without expecting special treatment or privilege.
Average	These people are confident, yet emotionally vulnerable, and favor special treatment or privilege.
Disorder	They manifest a grandiose sense of self-importance and demand special privilege.
ADVENTUROUS	
Healthy	These executives have the gift of gab and easily befriend others, although they may not offer much depth to these relationships.
Average	These individuals earn respect by acting honorably and with compassion, by using power constructively, and by promoting worthwhile causes.
Disorder	They exhibit aggressive, impulsive, self-serving, and irresponsible behavior.
LEISURELY	
Healthy	Easy going, with a positive outlook on life, they can act decisively and courageously when the situation demands.
Average	They are somewhat pessimistic about life and the future and function at or below their ability.
Disorder	They express a consistently pessimistic attitude toward self, others, and life.
VIGILANT	
Healthy	Highly observant and discerning, they can defend themselves without losing control or becoming aggressive.
Average	Thin-skinned, they are rather sensitive to and hurt by criticism.
Disorder	These individuals are suspicious, without sufficient basis, that others are exploiting, harming, or deceiving them.

The Managerial Grid Approach

The managerial grid (Blake & Mouton, 1964) is a well-recognized and widely used classification of leadership styles. It relates the two main tracks or concerns of leadership: productivity and people. Leadership style is classified in terms of an emphasis on people, productivity, or both. According to the theory underlying this approach, the ideal leadership style has an equal emphasis on people and on productivity. Executives with this ideal style would endeavor to develop their employees in such as way as to achieve both high productivity and high job satisfaction, commitment, and health and well-being. These five leadership styles were previously described in an earlier chapter and are noted again here.

1. *Laissez-Faire Leadership Style:* At the lower left corner of the grid is the leadership style characterized by minimal concern for people and minimal concern for production. Such executives pass along orders and lack initiative.
2. *Country Club Leadership Style:* This style is characterized by high concern for people, but less attention to production.
3. *Task-Oriented Leadership Style:* This leadership style is characterized by high concern for production and low concern for people.
4. *Middle-of-the-Road Leadership Style:* This leadership style is characterized by an adequate concern for both people and production and an attempt to balance the two.
5. *Democratic Leadership Style*: This leadership style is characterized by a high concern for both people and production.

The Dual-Dimensional Approach

An interesting variant of the managerial grid is described by Stephenson (2000). To the dimension of people-orientation versus productivity-orientation, Stephenson adds the dimension of control versus creativity. This dimension accounts for the extent to which some leaders seek to be in control or to impose control on others, as compared to leaders who foster divergent thinking—"thinking outside the box"—and favor a hands-off and creative environment. Four leadership styles can be derived from comparing the polar opposites of each dimension.

1. *Production Controller*: The leadership style with a high emphasis on productivity and control
2. *Benevolent Autocrat*: The leadership style with a high emphasis on control and people

3. *Inspirational Leader:* The leadership style with a high emphasis on people and creativity
4. *Visionary Strategist*: The leadership style with a high emphasis on creativity and productivity

The Values Approach

Based on extensive research with executives, Maccoby (1988) articulated five leadership styles that reflect changing societal values: the expert, the helper, the defender, the innovator, and the self-developer. Maccoby believes that the self-developer is the leadership style most congruent with the changing organizational scene. He notes that work has various meanings for individuals and that individuals are most strongly motivated to work when the work demands made on them fit their dominant values.

1. *Experts* represent specialized technical excellence and professional knowledge and reflect the dominant value of mastery. Approximately 50% of the managers studied by Maccoby reflected this style.
2. *Helpers* are service-focused and seek to make the workplace a family atmosphere. They made up about 22% of Maccoby's leaders and reflect the value of relatedness.
3. *Defenders* are most concerned with policies, survival, protection, and defending human dignity. They composed only 1% of Maccoby's sample.
4. *Innovators* are enterprising, creative executives who made up about 8% of the sample. They have made a significant impact on the character of business and the economy.
5. *Self-developers* focus on facilitating problem solving with customers and clients and emphasize dominant values such as personal growth and participatory management. They demand that work be balanced with personal and family needs. Self-developers represented 20% of the executives studied and up to 90% of business students and interns.

CONCLUDING NOTE

Executive style, particularly character and personality styles and leadership styles, is a key component of the Integrative Model of Leadership Effectiveness. Recognizing and assessing these two styles can be particularly valuable in planning and implementing such executive-development strategies as executive counseling, executive coaching, or executive consultation. Specific information on style assessment is discussed in chapter 6, in the section entitled "Executive Profiling." Styles represent personal dynamics, in contrast to organizational dynamics. Chapter 5 deals with organizational dynamics as one aspect of the context of leadership.

REFERENCES

Bennis, W. (1998). The character of leadership. In M. Josephson & W. Hanson (Eds.), *The power of character: Prominent Americans talk about life, family, work, values and more* (pp. 142–149). San Francisco: Jossey-Bass.

Blake, R., & Mouton, J. (1964). *The managerial grid*. Houston, TX: Gulf.

Cloninger, R., Svrakic, D., & Przybeck, T. (1993). A psychobiological model of temperament and character. *Archives of General Psychiatry, 50,* 975–990.

Gergen, K. (1991). *The saturated self*. New York: Basic Books.

Josephson, M. (1998a). Introduction. In M. Josephson & W. Hanson (Eds.), *The power of character: Prominent Americans talk about life, family, work, values and more* (pp. 1–4). San Francisco: Jossey-Bass.

Josephson, M. (1998b). Being good: Easier said than done. In M. Josephson & W. Hanson (Eds.), *The power of character: Prominent Americans talk about life, family, work, values and more* (pp. 7–15). San Francisco: Jossey-Bass.

Kets de Vries, M. (1989). *Prisoners of leadership*. New York: Wiley.

Kets de Vries, M., & Miller, D. (1988). *Unstable at the top: Inside the troubled organization*. New York: New American Library.

Levinson, H. (1997). Organizational character. *Consulting Psychology Journal, 49*(4), 246–255.

Maccoby, M. (1988). *Why work: Leading the new generation*. New York: Simon & Schuster.

Millon, T., & Everly, G. (1985). *Personality and its disorders*. New York: Wiley.

Oldham, J., & Morris, L. (1990). *Personality self-portrait*. New York: Bantam Books.

Renshon, S. (1996). *The psychological assessment of presidential candidates*. New York: New York University Press.

Sperry, L. (1996). Leadership dynamics: Character and character structure in executives. *Consulting Psychology Journal, 49*(4), 268–280.

Sperry, L. (1999). *Cognitive behavior therapy of DSM-IV personality disorders*. New York: Brunner/Mazel.

Stephenson, P. (2000). *Executive coaching: Lead, develop, retain motivated talented people*. Frenchs Forest, NSW: Pearson Education Australia.

5
The Context of Leadership

The focus of the previous four chapters was exclusively on the executive. The dynamics of leadership, as well as leadership skills and competencies, were addressed in chapters 1–3, and the executive's personal dynamics were addressed in chapter 4. The present chapter focuses on the context or situational factors that influence the executive's functioning on the job and in the organization. This context includes organizational and family dynamics as these impact executives in their position in the organization. This chapter addresses organizational dynamics and family dynamics. Organizational dynamics refers to the composition and functioning of an organization. Family and social dynamics refers to the influences that family members and other social support systems have on the executive's values, attitudes, and behaviors. This chapter begins with an overview of the contextual factors impacting the executive. An extended discussion of organizational dynamics follows next. Then five sub-systems of corporate organizations are described, as well as the stages or processes by which organizations develop, adapt, and decline. The chapter concludes with a brief discussion of the strategies utilized by extraordinarily effective corporations to achieve high levels of productivity and health.

CONTEXTUAL COMPONENTS IMPACTING THE EXECUTIVE

The Integrative Model of Leadership Effectiveness presented in chapter 2 portrays four components that impact leadership effectiveness: the executive, and three situational or contextual components. The three contextual

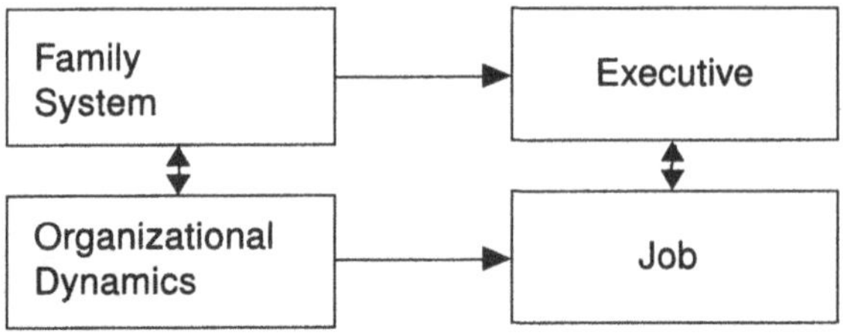

FIGURE 5 1. Contextual Components Impacting the Executive

components are family/social support system, organizational dynamics, and job. Figure 5.1 illustrates the type of interaction of these three components on the executive. The arrows indicate the type of interaction or impact, unidirectional or bidirectional; the solid lines indicate direct influence; and the broken line points indicate indirect influence.

This section describes the interacting relationship among these components. We'll use Charlie Chaplin's award-winning film *Modern Times* to highlight and explain these interactions. The storyline of the film is straightforward. Chaplin portrays a hapless worker who tightens bolts on an assembly line that is arbitrarily speeded up by a "big brother" company president, who monitors his employees on a video screen in his office while he amuses himself assembling kid's puzzles. Chaplin's work team consists of contentious and unsupportive assembly workers, supervised by a demanding and critical line foreman. That day, a device is field-tested during the lunch break, which automatically pours food into the worker so that his hands are free to continue working the assembly line. The president "volunteers" Chaplin for the demonstration. In slapstick fashion, the device malfunctions and literally assaults Chaplin, who later that day becomes so traumatized that "men in white coats" are called to carry him off to an insane asylum. In many respects, this film reflects a contemporary view of the impact of organizational change on worker health and well-being: that stress engendered by organizational changes—such as a merger or downsizing—can combine with already stressful job demands and low supervisory and peer support to result in impaired physical and psychological health.

Job

Chaplin's job was inherently stressful and impairing, given its unrealistically high demands for production, with very little control or decision-making input about this. Recall that the company president controlled the speed of the assembly line. Job demand and control decisions are two factors in the job strain model researched by Karasak and Theorell (1990). Job strain is defined as the short-term physiological, psychological, and behavioral manifestations of stress resulting from a job where psychological demands are high and control over the job is low. All job classifications can be thought of in terms of the degree of demand and control. Essentially, the demand/control model articulates a 2 × 2 contingency table of high and low demand on the horizontal axis and high and low control on the vertical axis.

Thus, job classifications such as telephone lineman and machinist, which have low demand and high control, are considered low-strain jobs, whereas assembly worker and telephone operator are considered high-demand, low-control jobs. However, even though job demands are high, the extent to which workers can make decisions about how to plan and execute their jobs attenuates the extent of stress and impairment they experience. For example, a study of over 5,000 Swedish and American men found that the lower tenth of workers, measured by their ability to control their own jobs, were five times more likely to develop heart disease than the top tenth of the workplace hierarchy, which had the greatest control over their jobs (Karasek & Theorell, 1990). Other job factors that have been related to health problems are occupational and safety hazards and shift workers. Shift work, particularly rotating shift work, can significantly impact physical, as well as psychological, well-being. Workers who choose fixed shift work experience better health than do those on rotating shifts, where choice is limited and social and physiological adjustment is difficult (Jamal & Jamal, 1982).

Organizational Dynamics

Chaplin's company epitomized Taylor's "scientific management" approach, wherein workers were trained to be efficient and productive "cogs in the corporate machine," and managers assumed all planning and decisional responsibilities. Subsequently, when organizational change was considered, management had total responsibility for its implementation. Chaplin was literally the victim of the president's decision to implement the automatic "feeding machine."

Prevalent forms of organizational change today are downsizing, layoffs, and mergers. To the extent that workers are not active participants in the change process, they experience varying degrees of victimization that range from stress symptoms, such as insomnia, irritability, and anxiety, to anxiety disorders, including posttraumatic stress syndrome. Marks and Mirvis (1998) describe the "merger syndrome," which consists of anxiety, dysphoria, stress reactions, worry and preoccupation, constricted communications, "we–theyism," crisis management, and culture clash. They suggest three strategies to reduce merger syndrome. First, during the initial deliberations for corporate mergers, top management must carefully consider the human implications, along with the financial and business aspects. A transition team, with members focusing on the people side of the merger, is then formed. Second, emotional preparation of workers is accomplished through pre-merger workshops. Third, counseling is made available for workers at all levels who have experienced difficulty coping with the syndrome. McCann and Gilkey (1988) found that establishing effective two-way communications—upward and downward—is of paramount importance in short-circuiting the merger syndrome.

Worker or Executive

Chaplin's character showed a marked degree of vulnerability, and thus his "nervous breakdown" was not unexpected. Several descriptors or markers describe individual vulnerability. Two of the most widely studied markers are hardiness and optimism. Hardiness is a marker of personality that reflects how individuals view themselves and the world. Stress-hardy individuals show high levels of control, commitment, and challenge. Those who are high in control have a strong belief that they can exert influence on their surroundings. Those high in commitment tend to fully engage themselves in what they are doing, whereas those high in challenge see change as a natural part of life that affords opportunities for growth. Maddi and Kobasa (1984) found that high levels of hardiness are more important than a strong body constitution in buffering stress and impairment. In a prospective study, 259 workers were rated on their level of hardiness and were followed for 5 years. Under equal amounts of stress those with hardy personalities experienced half the illness episodes of those with little hardiness (Maddi & Kobasa, 1984). Additional data reported by these same researchers show that hardiness could be bolstered by exercise, diet, and a nurturing support system.

Optimism is related to hardiness, in that although optimists tend to attribute or explain bad events as externally caused, time-limited, and having minimal impact on their lives, pessimists tend to explain the same events as internally caused—they blame themselves—and as stable and global in impact. The pessimistic explanation can result in helplessness, depression, and physical illness. Seligman's (1998) research shows that workers with a pessimistic style have a compromised immune function and subsequently more illness than those with an optimistic style. Similarly, those with a pessimistic style develop chronic degenerative illnesses, such as hypertension and heart disease, earlier in life and die at a younger age than do those with an optimistic style (Seligman, 1989). Like hardiness, a more optimistic style can be learned.

Family Social System

In addition to having little peer support on the job, the Chaplin character had no family support. Research shows a link between the presence of social support and health maintenance, particularly among married men (Bjorksten & Steward, 1985). McCubbin and Thompson's (1989) extensive study of stockbrokers and their families showed that workers' health and well-being could be maintained under great duress when workers experienced job supervisors' support as well as nurturing, supportive communication from their spouses, and high levels of family hardiness and optimism. On the other hand, workers' health deteriorated when there was little or no job supervisors' support; an incendiary, harsh, critical, and blaming spousal communication pattern; and low levels of family hardiness.

Gottman (1991) reports another type of spousal communication pattern that can greatly impact health. He describes something akin to the "pursuer–distancer" interaction pattern (Guerin et al., 1987), wherein physiological arousal predicated marital dissatisfaction, separation, and divorce. To the extent that the pursuing spouse "attacked," the distancing spouse experienced high physiological reactivity and engaged in "stonewalling" (avoiding eye contact, limited vocalization, and refraining from other indications of response). From this behavior pattern, the researchers were able to predict not only separation or divorce within a 4-year period, but also deterioration of the distancer's physical health (Gottman & Levinson, 1988).

In closing, research data now support the clinical observation that corporate change can greatly impact worker health and well-being and that job factors, workers' characteristics, and family factors can either exacerbate or buffer the extent of distress and impairment experienced by workers. It is fascinating that a movie produced 66 years ago so clearly captured a truth that behavioral science literature is now documenting.

ORGANIZATIONAL DYNAMICS: ORGANIZATIONAL SUBSYSTEMS

Imagine an organizational system as a set of five overlapping concentric circles, representing the subsystems of structure, culture, strategy, leaders, and members, within a larger circle representing the suprasystem or the organization's external environment. Each of these six will be described in this section. Table 5.1 provides a capsule summary of these subsystems.

TABLE 5.1
Organizational Dynamics: Subsystems of an Organization

Subsystems	Description
Structure	The mechanisms (roles, reporting relationships, policies and procedures, reward and sanction systems, etc.) that aid the organization in achieving its intended mission and goals.
Culture	The constellation of shared experiences, beliefs, assumptions, stories, customs, and actions that characterize the organization. Defines the organization's identity to those inside and outside the organization.
Leadership	The process of inspiring, guiding, and coordinating others to achieve the mission and goals of the corporation. Effective leadership matches mission, followership styles, and organizational stage of development.
Followership	The individuals and work teams who, in relationship with leadership, accomplish the organization's mission. A good match between the leader and followers usually results in better productivity and health.
Strategy	The organization's overall plan or course of action for achieving its mission and goals. Whereas mission specifies "what will be done," strategy specifies "how it will be done."
Environment	This subsystem includes factors outside the organization system (shareholders, competitors, customer demands, community, government regulations, etc.) that influence it and interact with it.

Structure

Structure refers to mechanisms that aid an organization to achieve its intended task and goals. The task is divided into smaller, person-sized jobs or roles and clustered into larger sets labeled teams, departments, or divisions. Structure specifies the reporting relationship of all roles, their span of control and scope of authority, and their location in a hierarchy of roles—called an organizational chart. Structure specifies the expectations of each role, along with policies, procedures, and routines for interacting and communicating with others in the performance of the task (Miller, 1990). Roles prescribe the boundaries of acceptable behavior for a particular job, whereas norms define group behavior. Norms are shared group expectations about what constitutes appropriate behavior. Role ambiguity, meaning the lack of clarity as to how an individual in a role is expected to behave, and role conflict—the inconsistency or contradiction in the messages about a role that an individual plays in the work context—are often major sources of stress in an organization.

Structure specifies the ways in which the person in a role performs. A formal means of measuring role performance is called performance appraisal. Structure defines decision-making procedures, such as which information will be utilized and how routine decisions are made and reviewed, particularly the degree of control and participation of the person in a certain role or job title (Leavitt & Bahrami, 1987). Another basic function of structure is to control and coordinate information among the other subsystems, as well as in the suprasystem.

An organization's structure might be thought of as a "snapshot" of an organization's work process, frozen in time so that it can be viewed. That snapshot could show a structure that is orderly or rigid, organic or chaotic, decentralized or overly bureaucratic, or divisionalized or fractured. Because of the interrelated nature of the subsystems, structure molds culture and strongly influences the decisions of corporate leaders (Miller, 1990). It can greatly account for a worker's job productivity and satisfaction, as well as significantly impact health and well-being.

Culture

Culture refers to the constellation of shared experiences, beliefs, assumptions, stories, customs, and actions that characterize an organization. The major determinants of culture are the values held by senior executives, the history of the corporation, and the senior executive's vision of the organization. These translate into culture through the shared experiences, memories, stories, and actions of employees. The corporate culture provides a guide to action for new situations and for new employees. Culture is to the organization what personality and temperament are to the individual. Thus, culture defines an organization's identity, to those both inside and outside the organization. In their classic book *Corporate Cultures*, Deal and Kennedy (1982) list five aspects of culture: corporate relations or business environment, corporate values, corporate heroes, corporate rules and rituals, and the "secret" network: the rumor mongers, spies, cliques, and whispers that form the "hidden hierarchy of power" in the organization. The culture of a corporation may be difficult to describe in words, but everyone senses it. It gives an organization its unique "flavor" and essentially is "just the way we do things around here."

This subsystem subtly controls the behavior of its members. Accordingly, management can influence its workers by effectively managing the organization's culture. Stable organizations have strong, clear cultures that are consistent with other subsystems. The general character of a corporation's culture tends to remain the same, but its manifestations may be healthy or dysfunctional. The concept of "core cultures" is useful in understanding the character or personality of an organization.

The concept of core culture was developed by Schneider (1994), a psychological consultant. Core culture refers to the innermost essence of an organization's culture. It is the nucleus of the culture. As one moves from the nucleus to the periphery, however, one finds a myriad of different-looking organizations. Indeed, a single organization has characteristics of all four core features. Like individual character, core culture develops naturally in the course of human events. No core culture is better than another. Each has its own mix of strengths and weaknesses and its own role to play in the structure and conduct of organizational life. Nevertheless, a particular core culture may be better suited to a particular organization's mission than another would be. Core culture is intimately tied to leadership. How leaders of an organization believe things should be done drives the kind of culture that is established. Finally, the foundation of each core culture is reflected in its focus and its decision making. In other words, each core culture is uniquely defined by the kind of input that is important to it and by the processes it utilizes to form judgments and make decisions. According to Schneider, there are four core cultures: control, collaboration, competence, and cultivation.

Control Culture

The control culture focuses its attention primarily on the tangible, the practical, and the utilitarian. Its decision-making process is analytically detached, formula oriented, and prescriptive. The best occupational counterpart for this culture would be a surgeon. A surgeon has to get control, to stay in command of the situation, and to be very thorough and methodical. Surgeons must stay attentive to the realities of their task, and they must be analytically detached and impersonal when deciding what to do. It is a no-nonsense and matter-of-fact culture. It is a serious and highly realistic world. Considerable emphasis is placed on objective certainty and on having information and methods that can be relied upon. Discipline and predictability are very important.

Given its content and process nature, this culture is highly task-oriented, particularly concerning daily tasks. Getting the job done on a consistent, regular, and current basis is very important. Strong emphasis is placed on rules and adherence to them. Although production is clearly important for every culture, it holds center stage in a control culture.

The epistemology, or view of how something becomes known or believed, for this culture is quite distinct from those of the other three cultures. In the control culture something is believed when the organization's goals and reality coincide. Furthermore, the well-being of the organization as a system comes first, before that of the customer or the employee. Accordingly, the design and framework for information and knowledge in the control culture are built around the goals of the organization and the extent to which those goals are met. Objectivity lies at the very center of the control culture. How decisions get made hinges on content and methods that exist outside people. In the control culture, reality lies outside people. As a result, people are used essentially in the service of externals: what gets worked out and how the work is done.

Collaboration Culture

The collaboration culture focuses a great deal of attention on concrete, tangible reality; actual experience; and matters of practicality and utility. However, its decision-making process is people-driven, organic, and informal. Whereas the surgeon best represents the control culture, a nurse best embodies the working-person counterpart in a collaboration culture. Nurses are focused on the immediate, real, and physical matters that pertain to their patients. Serving the sick, infirm, or injured has immediacy. Patients need to be treated now, not down the road. In addition, a nurse typically works as part of a medical team. Judgments about what treatment is needed and how to conduct it usually come from the team. The process is dynamic and highly participative. The relationship between the patient and the nurse is extremely important. What the two accomplish together—the synergy created—contributes considerably to the effectiveness of the outcome.

Synergy is the natural definition of success in the collaboration culture. Synergy itself captures the content and process of this culture. Involvement and empowerment are important in this culture. There is no place for the helpless, detached, or overly independent employee here. The dynamic process enables people to empower one another and deliver what is within each to the other, in order to bring about something more. Interaction and involvement are central elements. Harmony and cooperation are essential elements in this "can-do" culture.

This culture probably puts more trust in its people than any of the other three do. Because its content is immediate reality and actual experience, and its process is driven by connections between people, the risk of the organization being surprised by problems is higher in this culture than in any other. Though the cultivation culture is also people-driven, its focus on the future and on possibilities gives it more time to deal with unforeseen events. The collaboration culture must be more adaptive, ready, and able to make adjustments than the other three cultures are.

Although the epistemology of a control culture involves the connection between the organization's goals and reality, in a collaboration culture the connection is between people's experience and reality. The organization moves ahead through the collective experience of people from inside and outside the organization. Collaboration culture people know something when collective experience has been fully utilized.

Competence Culture

The competence culture focuses attention on potentiality, imagined alternatives, creative options, and theoretical concepts. Its decision-making process is analytically detached, formula-oriented, scientific, and prescriptive. The best occupational counterpart to the competence culture is the research scientist. A research scientist focuses on what might be and looks at data, information, patterns, and underlying meanings and relationships. Anticipated outcomes or hypotheses drive scientists' work. They investigate insights. The essence of science itself is to go beyond what we already know or have learned and to determine what else is possible. Theoretical development is often at stake. The scientist's process is the scientific method. This means that the scientist must stay analytically detached and objective and must follow prescribed formulas for making judgments. Possibility is determined objectively by the relevant scientific principles.

This is a world of external verification and merit, in which objective feedback is probably more critical than in any other culture. Feedback provides external verification and tells the competence culture whether its output has merit. Life in a competence culture is intense and high-strung. People always have standards to reach and go beyond. The work is rigorous and carries a sense of urgency. The norms are excellence, superiority, and challenge.

The competence culture has a unique epistemology. People believe something when conceptual system goals and reality connect. As a result, the framework for information and knowledge is built essentially around the conceptual system goals of the organization and the extent to which those goals are met. The competence culture has competition at its center. People compete with one another in a highly competitive world, which has more stringent standards and problems that stand in the way of getting the job done. The more competent you are, the more effective you are at competing. In contrast to the collaboration culture, this culture is often a win–lose world, in which discord is present and less competent people fail. Because superiority is paramount, inferiority stands out and is discredited. An organization whose goal is to create one-of-a-kind products or services instinctively fills the organization with one-of-a-kind people—specialists—to achieve that goal.

Cultivation Culture

The cultivation culture focuses attention on possibilities, inspirations, and creative options. Its decision-making method is people-driven, organic, open-minded, and subjective. The best occupation counterpart for this culture would be the religious steward, such as a minister, priest, or rabbi.

Religious stewards focus on catalyzing and cultivating growth and development among their people. They strive to help people fulfill their potential, particularly their spiritual potential. They focus on people's inspirations and aspirations and herald ideals and higher-level purposes. The content of the steward is possibilities and potentialities. The process used is highly subjective, organic, and frequently emotional. A religious steward emphasizes empowering people and unleashing that which is internal to them. This occurs both in the steward's own organization and with outside constituents.

The cultivation culture is very much a world of purpose, evolution, and change. Its organizations are magnetic, wherein the magnetism is caused essentially by the level of commitment that its people can attain. The cultivation culture gets results because its people believe in the purpose of the organization, in themselves and their leaders, in enriching their customers or constituents, and especially, in their own willpower and determination. This culture is value-centered. Self-expression is highly encouraged—indeed, nourished. Employees are given every opportunity to be all that they can be. They identify strongly with their organization.

The epistemology in the cultivation culture is determined by the values at its center. People know or believe something when there is a connection between reality and what they value, when what is espoused is put into operation. Whereas knowledge making in the collaboration culture is based on experience, in the cultivation culture it is based on what people value or hold as ideal. Change is perhaps more automatic and natural in this culture than in any of the other three. Growing, creating, and developing are essentially matters of change. In clear contrast to the objectivity of control cultures, the cultivation culture is one of subjectivity. Decision making hinges on content and processes that exist within people. Organic, evolutionary, and emotional judgment making rests within people. As a result, people within a cultivation culture work in the service of internals: what is worked on and how it is done.

Leadership

Leadership refers to a process of influence whereby a leader persuades, enables, or empowers others to pursue and achieve the intended goals of the organization. *Leadership* and *management* were terms that were used synonymously until recently. Today, many authors want to distinguish the two. They contend that management involves the five functions of planning, organizing, staffing, directing, and controlling, whereas leadership involves only one component of the directing function. Rather, an effective leader creates a vision that tells members where the corporation is going and how it will get there. The leader then galvanizes members' commitment to the vision by being ethical, open, empowering, and inspiring (Bennis & Nanus 1986). Not all agree with this bifurcation. Jacques and Clement (1991) contend that good leaders must be good managers and vice versa.

There are several ways of conceptualizing the leadership process. One is to assume that effective leaders have the flexibility to shift their style from being "boss-centered"—called the autocratic style—to "employee-centered," or the participative style, to accommodate the needs of specific situations (Tannenbaum & Schmidt, 1958). Another way is to think of leadership as combining two orientations simultaneously, but in different proportions. One orientation is task-centered, the other is person-centered. By elaborating the possible combinations of these two orientations, Blake and Mouton (1964) derived five prototypical leadership styles. A third way of thinking about leadership considers three factors. Called "situational leadership," the best form of leadership is based on situational needs: the personal characteristics of the leaders, the nature of the organization, and workers' characteristics. In contrast, "task-oriented leadership" is most effective in situations where all three of the situational needs or factors are favorable and, conversely, in situations wherein the factors are relatively unfavorable. "Relations-oriented leadership" is most effective when the three factors are only moderately favorable and in situations where only some factors are favorable (Fielder, 1967).

The leadership subsystems play a critical role in shaping themes that harmonize with the subsystems of structure, culture, and strategy (Kets de Vries & Miller, 1984). In Miller's aforementioned research, leadership style was characterized as either "craftsman," "builder," "pioneer," or "salesman" in the successful firms he studied, and later as "tinkerer," "imperialist," "escapist," or "drifter," when these same corporations began to decline (Miller, 1990). These ways of conceptualizing leadership are described in more detail in chapter 2, "Leadership Dynamics," whereas leadership styles are more fully described in chapter 4, "Personal Dynamics."

Followership

Organizational researchers have largely neglected the attitudes of those in the organization who are led—the workers. Because an important key to most leaders' success is the behavior of their subordinates, this is an unfortunate oversight. Uris (1964) has studied "followership" style and concluded that subordinates have a preference for either the autocratic, democratic, or "free-rein"—participative—leadership style. He found that workers function best with leadership that corresponds with their followership style. For example, a subordinate with an affinity for the autocratic approach will respond favorably to the autocratic leadership style. The lack of match between leadership and followership styles probably accounts for conflict, stress, and decreased worker productivity and performance.

Individuals do not work in isolation, but for memberships in small groups as a way to increase their adaptability within the organizational system. These groups may be a formal part of the structural subsystem, such as work teams, or they may be informal. The informal group, also called the informal organization (Leavitt & Bahrami, 1987), is formed by workers, usually around a workplace issue or an outside activity. Actually, these groups accomplish much of the organization's work. Chance meetings at the coffee machine, impromptu lunch meetings, and informal telephone calls go a long way toward defining and achieving the organization's intended goals. Needless to say, the presence of a disaffiliative or hostile informal organization can also seriously undermine the organization's objective.

Strategy

Strategy refers to the organization's overall plan or course of action for achieving its identified goals (Pfeiffer, Goodstein, & Nolan, 1989). Corporate strategy is based on the organization's vision and mission statements. The vision statement answers the question "What can the organization become, and why?" whereas the mission statement answers "What business are we in, and who is our customer?" Strategy answers "How do we do it?" There are three levels of strategy: the corporate strategy, which charts the course for the entire organization; the business strategy, which is charted for each individual business or division within the corporation; and the functional strategy, which deals with the basic functional areas—marketing, finance, personnel, and so on—within the firm.

Strategy takes the form of a strategic plan, and the process of developing and implementing the strategy is called strategic planning and management. This process will be described in some detail later in the chapter. An important consideration in strategic planning is achieving a good fit between the strategic and structural subsystems, because a given strategy can best be carried out by a given structure (Miller, 1990).

Most organizations believe that strategic planning is essential for corporate success. A key function of strategic planning is helping the corporation achieve its goals by effectively organizing its people. Yet many firms struggle to achieve their goals, often because of a failure to link their business strategies with the ways in which people are managed. For that reason, the workplace psychiatric consultant can impact the organization by advocating that the corporate strategy include both a business plan and a people plan (Sperry, 1991).

Just as a business plan describes targeted business goals and results in measurable terms, the people plan must also detail people "results" in measurable terms. It is insufficient to state slogans such as "People are our most important asset" or "Our employees make the difference." Targeted people goals must be specified, just as targeted business goals are specified. Examples of targeted business goals are "We will increase our market share by 15%," and "We will increase sales by 20%." Examples of targeted people goals might be "We will have the highest productivity and cost containment scores in the industry," "Ninety percent of our employees will rate their supervisors as good or excellent on showing respect to subordinates," or "Ninety percent of our employees will state that they are proud to work here." Such "people results" can be articulated, quantified, and assessed through surveys, interviews, or formal third-party observation. These results will also be manifested in job productivity, satisfaction, and morale, noted on a daily basis (Busch, 1990).

By attempting to incorporate both a people plan and a business plan in the corporate strategy, corporate leadership may need to change past management practices that resulted in high levels of stress, distrust, or dissatisfaction. The goal of integrating both plans is to achieve a reasonable balance and synergy between people and production (Sperry, 1991). An effective integrative corporate strategy should positively impact all the other subsystems and probably will require changes in the structural subsystem.

Environment

These five internal subsystems interact and mutually influence one another. The configuration of these sub-systems is also greatly affected by the corporation's external subsystem, the environment. The environmental subsystem refers to those factors outside the organization's internal subsystems that influence it and interact with it. The environment includes economic, legal, political, and socio-cultural factors. It also includes technological factors such as community relations, workforce availability, competitors, shareholders and other stakeholders, market saturation, customers' demands and changes, government statutes, environmental policies, other regulatory requirements, and standard industrial practices. In times of turbulence and rapid social and technological changes, the environmental subsystem may exert as much or more influence on organizational direction and functioning as other subsystems. This is particularly evident during economic recessions, war or even the threat of war, drought, and other natural disasters.

The Design of an Organization

The design of an organization can be likened to the skeletal subsystem of a person, which provides a framework that supports the other subsystems. Organizational design refers to the overall configuration and interrelationships, particularly among the roles and positions in the structural subsystem, but it also reflects the configuration of all the subsystems and the suprasystem (Morgan, 1986). An organizational chart illustrates these positions and relationships.

The continuum of organizational designs ranges from the hierarchical or bureaucratic at one end to the adaptive at the other end. The *hierarchical design* takes a pyramidal shape, with a clear chain of command, strict division of specialized jobs, and a comprehensive set of rational rules and rigid guidelines. Communication and decision sending proceed from the top—the senior executive level—of the pyramid down through middle management and then to the worker at the bottom of the pyramid. Hierarchical organizations are designed for stable times and conditions and seem particularly suited for a manufacturing or industrial economy.

The *adaptive design,* on the other hand, emphasizes flexibility, horizontal communication, a low level of specialization and standardization, and high levels of cooperation (Forisha-Kovach, 1984). The adaptive design can be likened to a network where managers function much as switchboard operators, coordinating the activities of employees, suppliers, customers, and other stockholders. Large construction firms like Bechtel function in ways similar to the adaptive organization. They handpick crews of employees and outside contractors with the skills appropriate for each new dam, refinery, or airport project. In an adaptive organization, a skilled scientist or marketer who is a leader on one project may switch to the role of follower on a subsequent project. Obviously, the adaptive organization design is useful in fast-changing markets such as computers, telecommunications, and publishing.

In between these two polar designs are the matrix design, the divisional design, and the "flat" organization. The *matrix design* is common in medical schools with major hospital affiliates, where the staff and faculty report to both institutions. The *field organization* refers to a hierarchical design, consisting of a layer of executives and a layer of workers, with few, if any, layers of middle managers (Dumaine, 1991).

Organizational Processes

Describing how organizations work is no small undertaking. The field of organizational behavior is devoted to describing and explaining how organizations work. This chapter focuses on four processes related to organizations: (1) the concept of "fit"; (2) the stages of development and decline in organizations; (3) the process of adaptation or strategic planning; and (4) health and pathogenesis in organizations.

The Concept of "Fit"

Achieving and maintaining a sense of balance and harmony are central to organizational well-being. In the organizational literature, balance is usually described by the concept of "person–environment fit," also called "person–organization fit" (Levinson, 1981). Achieving balance and a good fit between person and organization is a challenge to corporate leadership and the consultants whom leaders engage. A basic assumption is that not all persons are equally suited for all organizations.

A second assumption is that a good fit or balance results in higher job performance, higher job satisfaction, increased self-esteem, and less stress. Similarly, dysfunctional responses to poor fit include an increased level of stress, burnout (defined as a syndrome of emotional exhaustion and cynicism among employees who engage in "people work"), role ambiguity, and role conflict (Muchinsky, 1990).

A third assumption is that indications of poor fit do not necessarily reflect deficits within either the person or the organization. Rather, problems are usually functions of the lack of fit between the needs and resources of the person and those of the setting.

This view is in stark contrast with the more common perception among many in management and leadership, who assume that problems experienced by individuals are primarily due to their own constitutional or character deficits. Because an organization can significantly influence an individual's attitudes, behavior, and overall health, this view implies a "blaming the victim" philosophy. Similarly, the view that organizations totally control how a person thinks and behaves is one-sided. The person–organization fit model assumes some measure of joint responsibility. With regard to achieving change, the model involves matching individuals with suitable subsystems, rather than a modifying of the individual or the subsystem (French et al., 1974).

A fourth assumption is that fit between a person and an organization is dependent on matching each party's developmental needs. Arthur and Kram (1989) suggested that fit or reciprocity between the two parties is best understood in terms of their developmental stages and the representative needs of those stages. Synthesizing a wide variety of research on individual and organizational development, these authors specify three stages of personal-organizational development: (1) exploring-exuberance (the expansion and entrepreneurial stage), (2) advancing-directedness (the professionalization stage), and (3) protecting-stewardship (the consolidation stage).

A fifth assumption is that person–organization fit can also be improved or enhanced by altering the person—for example, coaching, training, or even psychotherapy—by altering the organization, such as by job redesign, or some combination of the two. If the environment is assumed to be fixed or balanced, corporate leaders might consider modifying their selection process or the type of employees they hire and train. Alternatively, if the leaders assume that people are fixed, they might attempt to modify the organization.

Representative of studies that examine the construct of fit between an individual and an organization is the work of Matteson and Ivancevich (1982). These researchers studied the fit or lack thereof between Type A or Type B behavior patterns in employees and Type A or Type B patterns in the organizations in which these employees worked. Dependent measures consisted of various health indices. As predicted, Type B employees in Type B organizations reported the fewest negative health symptoms, whereas Type A employees in Type A organizations reported the most negative health symptoms. Type B employees in Type A organizations and Type A employees in Type B organizations reported an intermediate level of symptoms, as hypothesized, thus supporting the "fit" model.

ORGANIZATIONAL DYNAMICS: DEVELOPMENTAL STAGES

Just as an organism develops and declines, so do organizations. Six stages of organizational growth and decline are described here: new venture, expansion, professionalization, consolidation, early bureaucratization, and late bureaucratization. These stages are adapted from Sperry (1990) and are based on the work of Greiner (1972), Adizes (1988/2000), and Miller (1990). Table 5.2 provides a capsule summary of these stages.

Stage 1: *New Venture*

Stage 1 of an organization involves the conception of a new venture. The critical tasks at this stage include defining a target group (e.g., hospital patients, high school seniors, middle managers) and developing a service that targets such a group. Accomplishing these tasks requires the ability to extend or create a market need; the willingness to make a risky investment of time, energy, and money to create an organization that satisfies the unmet need; and the ability to create an embryonic organizational structure that

TABLE 5.2
Organizational Dynamics: Developmental Stages

Stage	Description
New Venture	A new organization, or unit of it, is launched to meet an unmet need. Tasks at this stage are to define a targeted market, to develop a product/service targeted to it, and to inspire worker effort and loyalty.
Expansion	During this stage of rapid growth, the task is to develop a basic operating system and infrastructure that fosters efficiency and effectiveness and to deal with "growing pains"—for example, high turnover.
Professionalization	As it grows and stabilizes, the organization must now implement a strategic management system and shift from entrepreneurial leadership—effective for earlier stages—to professional leadership.
Consolidation	The challenge here is to maintain growth and worker and customer commitment; develop a consistent, healthy corporate culture; emphasize product/service quality; and avoid risky expansion.
Early Bureaucratization	Blurring of corporate vision and erosion of commitment results in inefficiency, demoralization, passive-aggressivity, and loss of talented personnel. Task is to maintain operating systems.
Late Bureaucratization	Impaired communication and productivity and a culture marked by hand-wringing and hopelessness prevails. The organization is terminal and can only be maintained by external life-support systems.

can provide that service to the target group. These abilities are characteristic of the entrepreneurial leader, and the entrepreneurial leadership style is most compatible with this stage.

Adizes (1988) noted three distinct leadership roles and patterns: entrepreneur, performance, and administration. Gerber (1986) similarly referred to these roles as entrepreneur, technician, and manager. The *entrepreneur* is the visionary and risk-taker who is creative and innovative. The entrepreneur craves change and control over people and events. The entrepreneur can easily transform an idea into reality and can singlehandedly give birth to an organization. The *performer* is the doer or task-focused leader. The performer is diligent, dedicated, and loyal to the assigned task. The performer focuses exclusively on what needs to be done. The *administrator* focuses on how things should be done. The administrator craves order and the status quo. The administrator manages operating systems better than either the entrepreneur or the performer and is comfortable with bureaucratic matters. The more leaders are able to adapt their leadership style to the needs of the organization, the more valuable and effective leaders are.

At first, the organization is likely to be quite small in terms of members and clientele, and its structure can be flexible and informal. Thus,

Stage 1 involves developing a basic system for day-to-day operations and finding individuals to staff the organization. Often little role differentiation exists among leaders and followers. The planning and development functions do not need to be formalized at first, and on-the-job training is prevalent. Entrepreneurial leadership, especially when combined with performance-style leadership, is particularly effective in keeping the vision and embryonic organizational structure viable (Flambolz & Randle, 2000). The entrepreneurial leadership pattern lends itself to the autocratic or benevolent organizational style. Because of their visionary and risk-taking stance and their hard-won success, entrepreneur-performer leaders easily become the object of admiration. They tend to attract members who are in awe of the founder's success (Sperry, 1990). These members readily accept a dependent stance and easily acquiesce to the demands of the entrepreneur-performer leader.

Stage 2: *Expansion*

Stage 2 is the stage of rapid growth. Stage 2 either commences very quickly or after the organization has been in Stage 1 for a number of years. The major problems that occur in Stage 2 involve growth, rather than survival. Organizational resources are stretched to their limits, as a new wave of members joins the organization, as demands for services increase, and as the organization's rather primitive day-to-day operating system becomes overwhelmed. Organizational "growing pains" are painfully present. Growing pains signal that changes are needed and cannot be ignored; they imply that the organization has not been fully successful in developing the internal system it needs at a given stage of growth.

If the founder of the organization is unable to cope with the management problems that arise in Stage 2, the organization is likely to flounder and even fail (Flambolz & Randle, 2000). Not surprisingly, the critical task at this stage is to develop an infrastructure of operating systems that results in efficiency and effectiveness. As this more complex operating system develops, the organizational structure becomes more differentiated. Basic human resources and management training become a necessity at this stage. Whereas little formal management structure beyond "doing what the owner said" was needed in Stage 1, more managerial structure is needed in Stage 2, particularly with delegation of authority. Entrepreneurs tend to be less interested in the nonglamorous challenge provided by Stage 2, as compared with Stage 1. Thus, a need arises at Stage 2 for the administration dimensions of leadership to blend with the entrepreneurial. The entrepreneur-administrator style and the turmoil wrought by growing pains at this stage almost guarantee that members will become disenchanted with leadership and dissatisfied with the organization itself. Member turnover and rebelliousness are manifestations of counterdependency, particularly when leaders are slow to decentralize and share power or when they vacillate by proposing and then rejecting initiatives to delegate and decentralize the process (Sperry, 1996).

Stage 3: Professionalization

Stages 1 and 2 represent the entrepreneurial organization. Even though they may have lacked well-defined goals, policies, plans, or controls, these organizations prospered. However, as this critical size is being achieved, the organization begins experiencing "growing pains" as it outgrowns its initial structure and operating systems (Flambolz & Randle, 2000). New structures and operating systems must be implemented. Another wave of new members requires more formal planning, defined roles and responsibilities, performance standards, and control systems. Developing a strategic planning and management system then becomes the critical task at Stage 3. This, in turn, requires organizational development efforts that provide the concurrent level of skill training needed to implement this management system.

Those in leadership must change and increase their skills and capabilities. The challenge for the founder, entrepreneurial leader, or both is to transition from an entrepreneurial style of operation to a more professional style of management (Flambolz & Randle, 2000). Optimal leadership at Stage 3 involves an integration of the administrative expertise with a sensitivity toward employee needs and development. Not surprisingly, an organizational climate that encourages consultative and participative management matches well with people who are able to function relatively interdependently.

Stage 4: Consolidation

After transitioning to a professionally managed system, the organization can focus its efforts on consolidation. Consolidation means maintaining a reasonable increase in growth, while developing organizational culture. In Stage 1, the organization's culture was transmitted by contact between the founder(s) and the members. In Stages 2 and 3, the first wave of members transmitted the culture to the next wave or generation. But this informal mode of socialization became much less effective and less adequate with the subsequent waves of members. Culture becomes a critical concern in Stage 4.

Thus, in Stage 4, a more conscious and formal method of transmission is needed. Otherwise, members may no longer share a vision of what the organization is or where it is going. As a result, members begin interpreting culture in ways that meet their own needs but not those of the organization. First, in Stage 4, the organization's culture must be assessed. The underlying beliefs and norms of the particular organization must be elicited. Examples of unhealthy beliefs and norms include "Avoid conflict," "Set unrealistic performance expectations, "Avoid accountability," or "Poor performance is tolerated." Next, the organization must decide on a more appropriate and healthy cultural form—for example, "Two-way communication and conflict-reclamation are high priorities," "Set realistic performance expectations," "Quality is a concern," "Innovation is encouraged," and "Poor performance is not tolerated."

The organizational structural of Stage 4 is a further enhancement and articulation of the organizational structure of Stage 3. Knowledge of, and commitment to, the organization's mission statement and implementation strategies must be widespread throughout the organization. The mission statement must be reflected in both the orientation for new members and the newsletters to existing members. Members are respected and prized and thus human resources development and employee assistance programs (EAPs) will become integrated parts of the organization. Members' horizons, knowledge base, and skills are regularly upgraded. Leadership that combines entrepreneurship and integration is most compatible with Stage 4 functioning. Note that whereas administrative leadership professionalized the organization in Stage 3, now entrepreneurial leadership is needed to rekindle and augment the original dream and to motivate and challenge the organization, especially the fourth wave of new members. At Stage 4, individual members who are able to function interdependently with superiors, co-workers, and subordinates are most compatible with the organization's collaborative or participative styles.

The challenge of effective leadership is to assist the organization in arriving at this stage and in remaining there. This requires considerable effort to grow and adapt to the constantly changing external environment—the suprasystem—in which the organization finds itself. Self-renewal becomes the organization's basic strategy. Failure to strategically plan and manage the corporation can result in the organization's downward trend and decline. Stages 5 and 6 describe this downward trend, which can result in the eventual death of the organization.

Stage 5: Early Bureaucratization

As the organization transitions to Stage 5, a subtle but clear shift occurs from substance to form. Status-seeking, "business as usual," and appearances characterize the behavior of members. The organization is usually well endowed at this stage and may be cash-rich for the first time in its history.

Later in Stage 5, the focus shifts to internal turf wars. Backbiting, coalition building, and paranoia are common. Growing pains are particularly intense as members' dissatisfaction mounts. In some organizations, negativity threatens to poison the organization's climate. Leadership at first was content to rest on the organization's laurels, but now shifts to a self-protective mode. Cliques become the usual mode of communication. The best and brightest start leaving the organization. The emphasis has clearly shifted from growth and maintenance to decline. The structures and the planning and development functions are much less responsive than in previous stages. Leadership is marked by administration and, in the later part of this stage, by inefficient administration. Decentralization and delegation become increasingly threatening to leadership, and efforts to re-centralize power are expected behaviors. Counterdependency behavior, including passive-aggressivity, becomes commonplace, reflecting demoralization among workers, as well as among managers.

Stage 6: Late Bureaucratization

Many of the subunits and subsystems of the organization become clearly dysfunctional during Stage 6. Miscommunication is commonplace, and two-way communication is limited or nonexistent. Coordination and follow-through are the exception, rather than the rule. The right hand is seldom aware that a left hand exists, much less knows what it is doing. New members are no longer informed of the mission statement and strategy, and, for all members, the organizational culture reflects a sense of helplessness and a lack of common direction. "Come late, leave early," "Do as little as you have to," "Don't try to change anything," and "Protect job security at all costs" are attitudes reflecting the organizational culture in Stage 6. The critical function at this stage is to forestall and avoid extinction, as the organization is figuratively in intensive care and is being maintained by external life-support systems. The corporate subsystems are conflictual and nonresponsive to the needs of both members and clientele. Little, if any, training and development occur. Administrators struggle to buy time and prolong the organization's life. But inefficiency and ineffectiveness are to be expected. Clients find access to responsive subsystems the exception, rather than the rule. Not surprisingly, the re-emergence of dependency among members complements the autocratic style of leaders.

The eventual demise of the organization seems inevitable, and consultants report that the prognosis for organizations in Stage 6, even after heroic interventions, is poor (Adizes, 1988).

As noted earlier, organizational decline and poor person–organization fit are not inevitable. A strategically managed corporation is able to adapt to changing times and circumstances and is able to renew itself and achieve a new level of homeostasis.

HIGHLY EFFECTIVE ORGANIZATIONS

Much of the discussion in previous chapters has focused on describing the skills, competencies, and styles of effective and highly effective leaders. This section will briefly note the strategies utilized by effective organizations in achieving high levels of productivity and health. As a result of their extensive analysis of corporations such as Southwest Airlines, Cisco Systems, Men's Wearhouse, and Cypress Semiconductors, O'Reilly and Pfeffer (2000) noted three common themes and several common strategies.

The three common themes shared by all these corporations are (1) a clear, well-articulated set of shared values that serves as the foundation for "management practices that build the core capabilities that in turn provide a basis for the company's competitive success" (O'Reilly & Pfeffer, 2000, p. 232); (2) a high degree of alignment and consistency in corporate practices that express its core values; and (3) in addition to founders and CEOs, senior executives "ensure that corporate values are maintained and constantly made real to all of the people who work in the organization" (p. 232).

Here are the common corporate strategies they noted: (1) a strong culture that aligns norms, attitudes, and behaviors to core corporate values; (2) a screening process that identifies and hires only individuals who share corporate values; (3) a major commitment and investment in employee health by providing opportunities for development and career growth; (4) "absolute" consistency between corporate values and all corporate practices that express these values; (5) widespread information sharing, including corporate operational and financial data, throughout the organization; (6) team-based systems that promote a sense of purpose and belonging among all employees; (7) the conviction that the primary role of senior executives is to set and reinforce the vision, values, and culture of the organization, whereas strategic planning, decision making, and operational oversight are secondary roles (pp. 238–245).

CONCLUDING NOTE

Having a highly effective or peak-performing executive in charge is no guarantee that high levels of corporate productivity and health will be achieved. However, if an executive, with the potential for high-level effectiveness, functions within a context that not only expects but supports and facilitates productivity and health, a very high probability exists that high levels of corporate productivity and health will be achieved. In other words, a mutual interaction occurs between the values, skills, and competencies of the executive and the values, vision, mission, and resources of an organization. The better the "fit"' or match between these, the better the outcome. As this chapter points out, another factor influences the executive–organization fit, and that is family and social support.

REFERENCES

Adizes, I. (1988/2000). *Managing corporate lifecycles*. Englewood Cliffs, NJ: Prentice-Hall.

Bennis, W., & Nanus, B. (1985). *Leaders: The strategies for taking charge*. New York: Harper & Row.

Bjorksten, O., & Steward, T. (1985). Marital status and health. In O. Bjorksten (Ed.), *New clinical concepts in martial therapy* (pp. 81–110). Washington, DC: American Psychiatric Press.

Blake, R., & Mouton, J. (1964). *The managerial grid*. Houston, TX: Gulf.

Busch, M. (1990). Linking strategic planning to the management of people. In J. Pfeiffer & J. Jones (Eds.), *The 1990 Annual: Developing Human Resources* (pp. 265–270). San Diego, CA: University Associates.

Deal, J., & Kennedy, A. (1982). *Corporate cultures: The rites and rituals of corporate life*. Reading, MA: Addison-Wesley.

Dumaine, B. (1991). The bureaucracy busters. *Fortune, 123*(13), 37–50.

Fielder, F. (1967). *A theory of leadership effectiveness*. New York: McGraw-Hill.

Forisha-Kovach, B. (1984). *The flexible organization*. Englewood Cliffs, NJ: Prentice-Hall.

Flambolz, E., & Randle, Y. (2000). *Growing pains: Transitioning from an entrepreneurship to a professionally managed firm*. San Francisco: Jossey-Bass.

French, J., Rogers, W., & Cobb, S. (1974). A model of person–environment fit. In G. Goehlo, D. Harnburgh, & J. Adams (Eds.), *Coping and adaptation* (pp. 316–333). New York: Basic Books.

Gerber, M. (1986). *The e-myth: Why most businesses don't work and what to do about it*. San Francisco, CA: Harper Business.

Gottman, J. (1991). Predicting the longitudinal course of marriage. *Journal of Marital and Family Therapy, 17,* 3–7.

Gottman, J., & Levinson, R. (1988). The social psychology of marriage. In P. Noler & M. Fitzpatrick (Eds.), *Perspectives on marital interaction*. Philadelphia: Multilingual Matters.

Greiner, L. (1972). Evolution and revolution. *Harvard Business Review, 50,* 37–46.
Guerin, P., Fay, L., Burden, S., & Kautto, J. (1987). *The evaluation and treatment of marital conflict.* New York: Basic Books.
Jamal, M., & Jamal, S. (1982). Work and non-work experiences of employees on fixed and rotating shifts: An empirical assessment. *Journal of Vocational Behavior, 20,* 282–293.
Jacques, E., & Clement, S. (1991). *Executive leadership: A practical guide to managing complexity*. Cambridge, MA: Blackwell Business.
Karasek, R., & Theorell, T. (1990). *Healthy work: Stress, productivity and the reconstruction of working life*. New York: Basic Books.
Kets de Vries, M., & Miller, D. (1984). *The neurotic organization: Diagnosing and changing counterproductive styles of management*. San Francisco, CA: Jossey-Bass.
Leavitt, H., & Bahrami, H. (1987). *Managerial psychology: Managing behavior in organizations* (5th ed.). Chicago: University of Chicago Press.
Levinson, H. (1981). *Executive*. Cambridge, MA: Harvard University Press.
Maddi, S., & Kobasa, S. (1984). *The hardy executive: Health under stress*. Chicago: Dorsey.
Marks, M. (1994). *From turmoil to triumph: New life after mergers, acquisitions, and downsizing*. New York: Lexington Books.
Marks, M., & Mirvis. (1994). *Joining forces: Making one plus one equal three in mergers, acquisitions, and alliances.* San Francisco: Jossey-Bass.
Matteson, M., & Ivancevich, J. (1982). *Job stress and health*. New York: Free Press.
McCann, J., & Gilkey, R. (1988). *Joining forces: Creating and managing successful mergers and acquisitions*. Englewood Cliffs, NJ: Prentice-Hall.
McCubbin, H., & Thompson, A. (1989). *Balancing work and family life on Wall Street.* Edina, MN: Burgess International Group.
Miller, D. (1990). *The Icarus paradox: How exceptional companies bring about their own downfall.* San Francisco, CA: Harper Business.
Morgan, G. (1986). *Images of organization*. Beverly Hills, CA: Sage.
Muchinsky, P. (1990). *Psychology applied to work* (3rd ed.). Pacific Grove, CA: Brooks/Cole.
O'Reilly, C., & Pfeffer, J. (2000). *Hidden value: How great companies achieve extraordinary results with ordinary people*. Boston: Harvard Business School Press.
Pfeiffer, J., Goodstein, L., & Nolan, J. (1989). *Understanding applied strategic planning: A manager's guide.* Glenview, IL: Scott, Foresman.
Schneider, W. (1994). *The reengineering alternative: A plan for making your current culture work*. Burr Ridge, IL: Irwin Professional Publishing.
Seligman, M. (1998). *Learned optimism: How to change your mind and life*. New York: Pocket Books.
Sperry, L. (1990). Development of organizations. *Human Development, 10*(2), 26–31.
Sperry, L. (1991). Enhancing corporate health, mental health, and productivity. *Individual Psychology, 47*(2), 247–254.
Sperry, L. (1996). *Corporate therapy and consulting*. New York: Brunner/Mazel.
Tannenbaum, R., & Schmidt, W. (1958). How to choose a leadership pattern. *Harvard Business Review, 36*(2), 95–101.
Uris, A. (1964). *Techniques of leadership*. New York: McGraw-Hill.

Part 2

Strategies for Maximizing Productivity and Health

6
Assessment Strategies

The first five chapters have provided a comprehensive perspective on the dynamics and determinants of leadership and executive performance. Presumably, this perspective provides leaders, as well as those who consult to them, with accurate and current information and with a useful cognitive map for understanding current models and research on leader effectiveness and executive performance. Chapters 6 to 11 apply this perspective to the process of assessing, planning, and implementing strategies for enhancing and maximizing executive performance. This chapter focuses on the assessment of leadership and the components of leadership effectiveness. A strategy is provided for developing a profile of executive functioning, including leadership effectiveness. This assessment strategy, called "executive profiling," consists of four components: skills, styles, situation, and synchronism or "fit." The assessment of each of these components is described. The chapter concludes with a case report of executive profiling.

EXECUTIVE PROFILING

Executive profiling is a comprehensive and contextual representation of an executive's capacity and potential for leadership effectiveness. This can include leadership style, dynamics, and experience; talents, skills, and competencies; person–job–organizational fit; personality, temperament, and character; family and social supports; and overall health status. Executive profiling is more than an individual profile or portrait of the executive. It is, rather, a contextual profile or a portrait of the executive in relation to job, family, and organizational dynamics, and includes all the problems and potentials involved. This section describes some key components of this profile. Assessing the various dimensions of this profile can be facilitated by a four-part strategy. The strategy focuses on an in-depth appraisal of four critical components impacting executive effectiveness and performance. These components are (1) skills and competencies; (2) styles; (3) situation (i.e., family, organizational subsystems, and stages); and (4) synchronism or "fit." Specific suggestions are offered for assessing these four components. These include instruments, interview formats, and observation. The final part of this section, entitled "Formulating an Assessment and Intervention Strategy," briefly describes how to conceptualize this profile with regard to specific problems and concerns facing the executive.

ASSESSING LEADERSHIP SKILLS AND COMPETENCIES

Two basic elements of the profile are the leader's skills and competencies. Chapter 3 has described 22 essential skills and 7 competencies necessary for leadership effectiveness. These skills and competencies are usually assessed with inventories or rating instruments. Although numerous instruments and surveys for assessing most dimensions of leadership are commercially available, relatively few assess for skills and competencies. Accordingly, I have included two instruments that I developed for your consideration and use. Both instruments incorporate the concepts and criteria presented in chapter 3.

360-Degree Feedback

An alternative approach is 360-degree feedback. Unlike traditional types of assessment instruments and surveys that provide unilateral or single-dimensional feedback, 360-degree surveys provide feedback from multiple sources. The surveys are called 360-degree because feedback comes from all directions: self, superior, peers, subordinates, and even customers. More accurately, 360-degree assessment is a multiple-feedback methodology, rather than a special or new kind of survey or instrument. Nearly any survey or instrument can be utilized. The methodology involves collecting data on identical surveys or instruments, from at least three different sources or directions of feedback, to assess the specified individual.

This method of assessment is commonplace in business today and has become an essential part of leadership assessment. This 360-degree methodology is typically used to assess overall leadership performance or effectiveness, or specific skills and competencies. For example, the "Assessment of Leadership Skills" (in Figure 6.1) and the "Assessment of Leadership Competencies" (in Figure 6. 2) can be used to collect 360-degree feedback on a given executive.

Ratings of Technical/Analytic Skills (1 = low, 3 = average, 5 = high)

_____Mastering Job-Specific Skills
_____Problem Solving and Decision Making
_____Priorities Management
_____Project Management
_____Progress Monitoring
_____Training and Development
_____ Composite Rating of Technical/Analytic Skills

Ratings of Relational Skills (1 = low, 3 = average, 5 = high)

_____Communication
_____Team Development
_____Motivation
_____Conflict Resolution
_____Coaching
_____Diversity
_____ Composite Rating of Relational Skills

Ratings of Strategic Skills (1 = low, 3 = average, 5 = high)

_____Visioning and Strategy Formulation
_____Strategic Implementation and Management
_____Guiding Change
_____Composite Rating of Strategic Skills

Ratings of Financial/Information Technology Skills (1 = low, 3 = average, 5 = high)

_____Mastering the Budgeting Process
_____Understanding Balance Sheets and Financial Reports
_____Monitoring Financial and Human Resources
_____Using Data to Guide Management Decisions
_____Composite Rating of Financial/Information Skills

Ratings of Personal and Self-Development Skills (1 = low, 3 = average, 5 = high)

_____Stress and Lifestyle Management
_____Balancing Family, Work, and Personal Life
_____Developing/Utilizing a Personal Mission Statement and a Career Plan
_____Composite Rating of Personal Development Skills

FIGURE 6.1. Inventory of Leadership Skills

LEADER STYLES ASSESSMENT

Assessing Personality Style

Several standard personality inventories are commercially available for assessing the executive's personality. These include the California Personality Inventory, the NEO Personality Inventory, the Sixteen PF Test, and the Millon Clinical Multiaxial Inventory. Some psychological consultants

1. Acts with Integrity and a Sense of Balance

Minimally Effective			Moderately Effective		Highly Effective	
1	2	3	4	5	6	7

- Genuinely lives with integrity and courage
- Consistently keeps ego in check
- Leads by example and models fairness, courage, and honesty
- Balances among corporate, personal, and family

2. Develops a Winning Strategy

Minimally Effective			Moderately Effective		Highly Effective	
1	2	3	4	5	6	7

- Scans environment and develops long-term approaches
- Envisions the future when developing strategy
- Anticipates potential obstacles, competition, and alternate scenarios
- Fosters internal and external commitment for strategy
- Effectively implements strategy throughout the organization

3. Mobilizes Employee Commitment

Minimally Effective			Moderately Effective		Highly Effective	
1	2	3	4	5	6	7

- Identifies and develops organization strengths to match opportunities
- Anticipates needed competencies and actively develops them in others
- Effectively demonstrates how the organization meets customers' needs
- Is significantly involved in coaching, developing, and supporting staff
- Increases employees' commitment by developing a culture of trust

4. Possesses Requisite Job Capabilities and Understands Corporate Dynamics

Minimally Effective			Moderately Effective		Highly Effective	
1	2	3	4	5	6	7

- Thoroughly and systematically analyzes strategic initiatives
- Achieves an equitable outcome in a negotiation
- Demonstrates the capacity to make and accept difficult decisions
- Proactively develops contingency plans re: changing market, regulations, or resources

5. Engenders Corporate Capability

Minimally Effective			Moderately Effective		Highly Effective	
1	2	3	4	5	6	7

- Proactively develops partnerships for achieving goals throughout the organization
- Consistently sets the bar higher and searches for new tactics to improve results
- Challenges current perceptions that limit effectiveness and results
- Effectively maintains and manages organizational boundaries to deliver results

FIGURE 6.2. Inventory of Leadership Competencies

6. Communicates Effectively and Encourages Knowledge Sharing

Minimally Effective			Moderately Effective		Highly Effective	
1	2	3	4	5	6	7

- Encourages and rewards diversity of opinion in discussing issues
- Redesigns structure to support effective corporate communication
- Seeks, quantifies, and responds to employee input on large and small issues
- Utilizes communication networks for corporate exchange of best practices

7. Exhibits a High Level of Energy and Health Status

Minimally Effective			Moderately Effective		Highly Effective	
1	2	3	4	5	6	7

- Exhibits and sustains a high level of energy and stamina
- Has unlimited capacity to effectively entertain business clients
- Recovers rapidly from minor illnesses, injury, exertion, and emotional stress
- Retains excellent health, despite arduous job demands and deadlines

FIGURE 6.2. Continued

may also utilize additional methods, such as the Thematic Apperception Test (TAT). Despite some concerns about reliability and construct validity, the Myers-Briggs Type Indicator (MBTI) is often used with executives, particularly in leadership-development programs and team-building contexts. For example, the MBTI is a basic assessment instrument in the leadership-development program of the Army Management Staff College (Giber, Carter, & Goldsmith, 2000). Other psychological assessment methods include incomplete sentence forms, certain cards from the Rorschach test, and intensive interviews.

I have developed and used an instrument to assess personality styles in my consultation work. Each personality style will manifest differently, depending on an individual's level of psychological health and development. These levels span the continuum from healthy to disordered. Accordingly, my Personality Styles-Health Indicator (Table 6.1) incorporates three levels of health: healthy, average, and disordered, specified by behavioral indicators. The disordered level reflects *DSM-IV* criteria of personality disorders that correspond to each of the six personality styles in my indicator. For example, the criteria for the *DSM-IV* Narcissistic Personality Disorder are reflected in the behavioral indicators for the disordered level of the Self-Confident personality style.

TABLE 6.1
Personality Styles-Health Indicator

CONSCIENTIOUS	
Healthy	These conscientious, hopeful, and kind individuals balance integrity with generosity.
Average	These no-nonsense individuals perform tasks without emotional expenditure or error.
Disorder	These people are prone to perfectionism and feeling avoidance, which interferes with task completion and relationships.
DRAMATIC	
Healthy	Having found the love they seek within themselves, they are altruistic and giving without expecting reciprocity.
Average	Though fun-loving and often impulsive, they can delay gratification and be emotionally appropriate much of the time.
Disorder	These individuals are uncomfortable where they are is not the center of attention.
SELF-CONFIDENT	
Healthy	They are energetic and self-assured, without expecting special treatment or privilege.
Average	These individuals are confident, yet emotionally vulnerable, and favor special treatment or privilege.
Disorder	They manifest a grandiose sense of self-importance and demand special privilege.
ADVENTUROUS	
Healthy	They have the gift of gab and easily befriend others, although they may not offer much depth to these relationships.
Average	They earn respect by acting honorably and with compassion, by using power constructively, and by promoting worthwhile causes.
Disorder	These people exhibit aggressive, impulsive, self-serving, and irresponsible behavior.
LEISURELY	
Healthy	Easy-going, with a positive outlook on life, they can act decisively and courageously when the situation demands.
Average	Somewhat pessimistic about life and the future, they function at or below their ability.
Disorder	They express a consistently pessimistic attitude toward self, others, and life.
VIGILANT	
Healthy	Highly observant and discerning, they can defend themselves without losing control or becoming aggressive.
Average	Thin-skinned, they are rather sensitive to and hurt by criticism.
Disorder	They are suspicious, without sufficient basis, that others are exploiting, harming, or deceiving them.

Assessing Character

Lately, corporations increasingly are questioning the efficacy and predictive value of psychological assessment methods in screening candidates for executive positions. Besides knowing if a specific candidate will be a good "fit" with the corporation, corporate officers need to know if the candidate's work performance will be consistent over time, and if the individual will demonstrate sound judgment when threatened, when tempted, or when doing the right thing may not be in that person's own best interest. In other words, corporations need to know about executives' basic character dynamics. Of course, the second and third considerations are not addressed in traditional personality assessment. This section describes the relationship of character to personality and the process of assessing the character dimension it complements.

In short, character refers to good judgment, self-regulation, consistency, and acting in a responsible, cooperative, and self-transcendent fashion. Leonard (1997) suggests that the assessment of character in executive candidates essentially revolves around a single question: "Will a manager be able to demonstrate sound judgment when under stress, when threatened, when tempted, or when doing the right thing is not in his or her best interest?" (pp. 243–244).

So, what constitutes a reasonable and valid assessment of the character dimension? A considerable amount of research and development effort will be needed to design and field-test such an assessment protocol, a process that may take years. It must begin with an integrative operational model of character and its components, which can be systematically studied. Perhaps it will include or be based on the exciting research of Cloninger and colleagues. Inevitably, one of the core components will be good judgment. Well, what is "good judgment" and which behavioral indicators would assess it? Renshon's (1996) work on good judgment is noteworthy. He has developed a detailed operational analysis of the phenomenon of "good judgment" consisting of three dimensions: analysis, reflection, and enactment.

Inventories: Currently, some validated inventories purport to measure the construct of character. The Hogan Personality Inventory (Hogan & Hogan, 1995), according to its authors, is a measure of the "bright side" of personality. It includes three scales that reportedly describe how moral an individual appears to others. The Hogan Development Survey is a revision of the Hogan Profile and is, reportedly, a measure of the "dark side" of personality. Individuals with high scores are described are selfish, deceitful, self-absorbed, and unable to garner the trust of others. Cloninger's Temperament and Character Inventory (TCI; Cloninger, Svrakic, & Przybeck, 1993) seems quite promising. Extensive research suggests that individuals with mature character structures tend to be self-reliant or responsible, cooperative, and self-transcendent (Cloninger, Svrakic, & Przybeck, 1993). In contrast, those with immature character structures—also referred to as personality disorders—were noted to have difficulty with self-acceptance, were intolerant and revengeful toward others, and felt self-conscious and unfulfilled. These three dimensions of character—self-responsibility, cooperativeness, and self-transcendence—were described in some detail in chapter 4. They can be measured by the Temperament Character Inventory (TCI), a paper and pencil inventory (Cloninger, Svrakic, & Przybeck, 1993). A healthy personality or a mature character reflects positive or elevated scores on these three character dimensions, whereas negative or low scores reflect the presence of character or personality disorders.

Interview: Though convenient, interviewing is the most reactive measure in the assessment protocol. Direct questioning about the candidate's judgment and consistency in stressful and trying circumstances is unlikely to yield an accurate portrayal of character with savvy, street-wise, interview-smart candidates. Therefore, utilizing indirect inquiry and "testing the limits" of candidates' narratives of their efforts in actual complex situations can be more valuable than hypothetical questions. Nevertheless, Cloninger has found that a focused interview can effectively elicit information on the dimensions of self-directedness, cooperation, and self-transcendence.

Simulations: Ultimately, simulations might prove to be the most useful in assessing executive character. However, Leonard (1997) points to some inherent difficulties in assessing character through simulation or role playing. He notes that although well-crafted simulations can provide a measure of the intensity that executives face in making judgments under real-life pressures and circumstances, the development of adequate behavioral indicators of an individual's capacity to contain disruptive emotions has yet to be accomplished. The challenge for consultants is to directly assess behavioral evidence of sound judgment, as well as "additional indicators, often nonverbal, contextual, and historical, or the ability to manage emotions as well as to apply good reasoning in solving problems. The ability to think effectively while emotions of fear, greed, pity, disappointment, and so forth, are raging identifies those individuals who will be able to demonstrate sound judgment and character consistently over time and a wide variety of situations" (Leonard, 1997, p. 242).

Character and Derailment

When a promising senior executive fails to live up to expectation, top management and the corporate officers who hired the executive want an explanation. Often such executives were assessed as possessing superior ability and technical and interpersonal skills and succeeded in impressing top management during the interview process, yet they subsequently derailed within the first year of employment. In other words, these executives were unable to sustain their winning impression of being skilled and effective over time and under certain circumstances. The fact is, up to 50% of recently appointed executives "derail" (Hogan & Sinclair, 1997). As noted in chapter 1, there are many reasons for derailment, one of them being character deficits. Accordingly, character assessment should be a critical consideration in selection and promotion considerations.

Three basic questions need to be answered about a candidate for an executive position: (1) Will the individual be a "good fit" in working with a given team or manager?; (2) Will the individual demonstrate sound judgment under duress or when doing the right thing is not in that person's own best interest?; and (3) Will the individual's winning initial impression be sustained over time? (Leonard, 1997). Because the first question reflects the personality dimension, personality assessment strategies are useful and appropriate in addressing "goodness of fit" concerns, whereas character assessment strategies are more useful and appropriate in addressing the second and the third questions.

ASSESSING SITUATION: ORGANIZATIONAL AND FAMILY DYNAMICS

Assessing Organizational System and Stage

Chapter 5 described the powerful impact that organization dynamics can exert on executives. Accordingly, a key part of executive profiling is to assess this impact. As noted in chapter 5, the two basic dimensions of organizational dynamics are organizational subsystems and organizational stage.

Organizational Subsystems: Assessment of organizational subsystems is possible through observation and thorough focused interviews. Sperry (1996) provides a detailed interview format for assessing organizational subsystems in the chapter entitled "Organizational Diagnosis." The interview format consists of several focused questions for each of the six organizational subsystems. A cross-section of managers and employees is interviewed, individually or in focus groups, with the same questions. Figure 6.3 contains a few representative questions for each subsystem from that full interview format.

Organizational Stage: Assessing organizational stage can be accomplished by instrument or observation. Flambolz (1990, 2000) provides a 10-item instrument, called the "Organizational Growing Pains Questionnaire," which may be useful in the assessment of stage. He also describes six key tasks or sequential steps that must be performed in an integrated fashion

Subsystem	Interview Questions
Strategy	What would you say is the overall mission or purpose of this organization? What percentage of employees knows it and follows it?
Structure	Who reports to whom in your unit? How close does this match the official organizational chart?
Culture	If you were telling a friend what it is really like to work here, how would you describe the atmosphere of the organization?
	What is more valued here: speed, quantity, or quality?
Leader	What is it like to work with your superior? What does this person do to help you in your job? Your career?
Worker	How do employees feel about working here? What are their main concerns? What are your main concerns?
Environment	What is the competition for your product (service)? What is the community's attitude toward this organization?

FIGURE 6.3. Questions for Assessing Organizational Subsystems

for an organization to develop properly and function successfully. All six are essential or requisite to the functioning of the organization at any given time, but each develops to a different degree at different stages in an organization's growth process. Observing and asking a few pertinent questions about these tasks can be useful in assessing organizational stage (Flambolz, 1990, 2000).

These six tasks can be correlated with the stages of an organization's development, as described in chapter 5. At Stage 1, New Venture, the critical task is markets and products. At Stage 2, Expansion, the critical task is the development of resources and operational systems. At Stage 3, Professionalization, the key task is the development of management systems. At Stage 4, Consolidation, the critical tasks involve management of the organization's culture. Finally, at Stages 5 and 6, Early Bureaucratization and Late Bureaucratization, the critical tasks involve organizational revitalization. If consultants understand the framework, they will be able to orient their organizational development efforts to the appropriate focus. Table 6.2 summarizes specific tasks for each developmental stage.

ASSESSING SYNCHRONISM OR "FIT"

Assessing "fit" is the last component of an integrative leadership assessment. It may also be the most important. Several dimensions of a leader's job, career, organizational, family and personal needs, demands, and val-

TABLE 6.2
Organizational Stage and Requisite Tasks

Stage	Task
1. New Venture	Develop product/service and market
2. Expansion	Develop operational systems
3. Professionalization	Develop management system
4. Consolidation	Transform culture
5. Early Bureaucratization	Revitalize strategy, structure, culture
6. Late Bureaucratization	Forestall demise or plan for dissolution

ues impact performance and effectiveness. A number of these will be highlighted in this section. Because fit, or synchronism, is central to this assessment strategy, a brief discussion of fit is in order.

As noted in chapter 5, organizational subsystems are interrelated and influence one another. For instance, environment shapes strategy, but organizations are also shaped by their environments. The organization's structure and culture affect members' behavior—for example, productivity, satisfaction, and health—but their behavior also impacts structure and culture. Similarly, a reasonable degree of fit should exist between the stage of an organization's development and the subsystems. An obvious example is fit between an entrepreneurial leadership style and an organization in the Birth and Expansion Stage. On the other hand, a poor fit would be that leadership style in the Consolidation Stage.

Thus, consultants need to carefully assess the relationship and degree of fit between and among these subsystems and stages. With such a perspective, the consultant should be able to anticipate the impact of a change of one or more subsystems on the organization at different stages of development and decline. For example, management's plan to acquire a new information system to enhance accountability could be perceived as a threat to job security and labor–management relations in an organization in Early Bureaucratization, but would be applauded as consistent with the organization's strategy for facilitating communications in an organization moving into Professionalization.

A corporation's success and viability depend largely on its ability to adapt to its internal and external environment at a particular stage. Fit refers to the compatibility of requirements of subsystem components and stages. The better the fit, the higher the productivity, job satisfaction, and overall health, whereas decreased productivity, satisfaction, and health induce higher job stress, which is associated with poor fit (Beer, 1980; Muchinsky, 1993).

Here are some of the more useful dimensions of "fit" to assess. Strategy–culture fit is the degree to which shared norms, beliefs, values, symbols, and rituals positively support and reflect the organization's vision, mission, and strategy. Strategy–leader fit is the degree to which the executive's behavior responsibly supports and facilitates the accomplishment of the organization's strategy. Strategy–member fit is the degree to which members are aware of, are committed to, and actually achieve the organization's mission and strategy. Strategy–environment fit is the degree to which the organization interfaces with its internal and external environment in accomplishing its strategy.

The degree of strategy–structure fit can be very revealing, because strategy involves the organization's long-term goals and objectives, whereas structure is the way the organization is put together to administer the strategy. Chandler (1962) was one of the first to insist that structure must follow strategy. By this, he meant that an organization must establish its strategic plan prior to forming its organizational structures, and that whenever corporate strategy changes, structural changes must also take place. The assumption is that a good match between strategy and structure will result in increased organizational performance and decreased problems, whereas a mismatch results in more problems and less productivity. Such a mismatch is called an incompatible organizational design. Certain strategies lend themselves to certain structural designs. For example, a high-tech manufacturing corporation in a fast-changing market would fare better with a more flexible, organic structural design than with a hierarchical bureaucratic structural design.

Executive–Organization Fit

Levinson (1980) considers "executive–organization fit" critical to an executive's professional effectiveness and personal well-being. Essentially, the better the "fit" between the executive's values and beliefs and the organization's values and mission, the greater the likelihood of high job performance, commitment, satisfaction, and personal self-esteem. On the other hand, the poorer the "fit," the higher the likelihood of disillusion, distress, and derailment (Muchinsky, 1990).

Executive–Job Fit

The presence of high executive–organization fit is no guarantee that there will be a high level of executive–job fit, and vice versa. However, generally speaking, the better the match between worker talents, competencies, skills, and experience and the job's requirements, the more likely the executive will be productive and satisfied (Lowman, 1993). The poorer the fit, the greater the likelihood of distress, role ambiguity, role conflicts, and derailment. Several job-related factors can negatively or positively impact the degree of fit.

Work schedules can impact job productivity, commitment, and job satisfaction, as well as worker health. For some workers, flexible work hours offer an alternative to the traditional fixed working schedule and provide workers with some choice in arrival and departure times. For other workers, work scheduling might require second shift, night shift, or rotating shift work. Research indicates that many shift workers experience problems with health and social adjustment. Because of an interruption in the circadian rhythm, shift workers often complain of lack of sleep, fatigue, appetite loss, and constipation. They also experience family and marital difficulties (Muchinsky, 1993). In short, such job-related factors can not only affect worker productivity, health, and interpersonal relationships, it can impact family relations.

Executive–Family–Job–Organization Fit

Despite the potential for a good or high fit among the executive, job, and organization, family dynamics or the social support network can negatively—or positively—impact the executive's job performance, satisfaction, and overall sense of well-being. For this reason, the degree of fit with family dynamics and social support networks needs to be considered. McCubbin (McCubbin & Thompson, 1989; McCubbin et al., 1992) has presented convincing data that family factors—that is, illness, conflicts, and other problems—can significantly impact a worker's productivity and health. These outcomes are more likely with female workers. Similarly, this and other research confirms that high satisfaction with marriage, relationship with a significant other, family members, or a social network can effectively buffer job-related stress. In short, this dimension of fit should be assessed or evaluated.

PRE-INTERVENTION STRATEGY

As noted earlier, executive profiling is more than an individual profile or portrait of the executive. It is rather a contextual profile or a portrait of the executive in relation to job, family, and organizational dynamics and includes all the problems and potentials involved. Executive profiling can be even more helpful if the organizational dynamics, problems, and concerns impacting the executive can be succinctly formulated or conceptualized. Problem formulation is a necessary pre-intervention strategy.

How does one develop such a problem formulation? In my experience, there are only a few basic domains of organizational functioning around which a problem formulation and intervention plan can be derived. The first domain involves the exercise of power/authority, whereas the second relates to morale/cohesion. The third is centered on problems arising from norms/standards of conduct, and the fourth consists of any issue involving the goals/objectives of the organization. Blake and Mouton (1976, 1983) have contended that all organizational problems can be subsumed in one of these four domains. Goodstein (1978) disagrees and contends that the domain of roles/communication is an additional necessary and distinct domain of organizational functioning. I have found that these five problem areas/intervention targets are exceedingly useful in formulating an assessment and intervention strategy.

Power/authority, morale/cohesion, norms/standards, goals/objectives, and roles/communication are actually interdependent phenomena. This means that initiating a change in one domain will subsequently result in changes in the other domains as well. For instance, a reduction of a manager's unilateral use of authority may increase morale/cohesion among staff members. In short, the focal target is the domain of the organization that is causing or exacerbating a particular problem or concern. Though these five domains are interdependent, it is important that the clinician-consultant identifies the underlying problem and domain so that interventions can be effectively focused. It is equally important for the consultant not to confuse surface problems with underlying problems.

Power/Authority

Power refers to the capability of having an effect, and authority refers to the right to exercise power. Power/authority issues revolve around whether power and authority are used effectively in both formal and informal manners within the organization. Power/authority issues can arise over the ways that power and authority are in fact used or over the ways their use is perceived by those who are not in positions of power within the organization. Power/authority issues are the most common focal targets, outnumbering others by a frequency of about three to one (Blake & Mouton, 1983).

Morale and Cohesion

Morale is a state of high, positive mental energy among members of an organization. Cohesion refers to the degree to which members of a group experience a positive sense of togetherness and unity. Morale/cohesion issues concern how members perceive the organization and its direction, as well as the degree to which members see themselves as part of a "team."

Norms and Standards

Standards are the criteria organizations use for measuring quality. Norms are the "rules" that govern appropriate behavior by members of all or some part of the organization. Standards/norms issues are frequently raised when an organization is forced to cope with internal changes, external changes, or both. Standards and norms are usually difficult to change.

Goals and Objectives

Goals are the aims and purposes of an organization, and objectives are those things that are accomplished when goals are met. Goals/objectives issues are frequently related to standards and norms issues and typically arise when goals and objectives are either poorly defined or have not been achieved. Goals/objectives issues frequently surface during an investigation of standards/norms issues.

Roles and Communication

Roles are expected behavior patterns attributed to a particular position in an organization. The structure of an organization specifies the reporting relationship of all roles within a given organization. Roles, along with the policies and procedures for communication, are essential to achieving the organization's task and goals. Communication is the transmission of information and understanding among individuals in various roles in the organization. Roles/communication issues arise as roles become less clear and boundaries blur, particularly the roles of manager and subordinate. When compared with power/authority, other focal targets might seem less important, but such a conclusion would be unwarranted. Expecting that all organizational problems can be solved by imposing an intervention targeted at the power/authority domain is a mistake that novice consultants often make. When a surface problem is mistaken for an underlying problem, the intervention that is implemented will often backfire. For example, a clinician-consultant may diagnose a clinic group's practice style as disorganized and unpredictable and then plan an intervention to impose order via the power/authority domain. But, in due time, the group's response to this action may engender an additional set of problems, this time clearly reflective of power/authority issues. Had the consultant accurately diagnosed the underlying problem as one of norms/standards and provided the clinic staff with a structured format for discussing the situation so that constructive norms/standards would emerge, without excusing power/authority dynamics, a quicker and more effective solution could have been reached without the painful side effects.

Blake & Mouton (1983) report a consultation with a retail chain that further illustrates the failure to identify the underlying target problem and the subsequent failure of the intervention. The consultants assisted the organization in changing its structure so that the corporate office could provide its outlet chains with a fuller range of marketing and distribution services. This change involved the norms/standards for operating the organization's structure. In hindsight, the consultants were stunned by their failure to recognize power/authority as the underlying problem. Because power/authority was not the focus of the intervention strategy, the intervention did not produce the expected outcomes. However, had the intervention been initially directed at the power/authority focus, the consultants might then have shifted to a focus on norms/standards as a second phase of the consultation. The point of this discussion is that skill in identifying the basic focal target(s) is one of the important competencies of the effective consultant.

EXECUTIVE PROFILING: A CASE REPORT

This case study illustrates the form and composition of an executive profiling report. It includes dimensions of the four components of the situation (i.e., organizational dynamics, position and family system/social network), style (i.e., personality and leadership styles), skills (i.e., leadership skills and competencies), and synchronism (i.e., the three fits: executive–organization, executive–job, and executive–family–job–organization fit). Finally, I should note that the case is not idealized fiction; rather, it is a composite case study representing executives I have known and consulted with.

Jack Winders is the 45-year-old-vice-president of finance at University Medical Center. He has worked with the medical center's CEO, Wallace Quade (cf. Profile #4 in chapter 1) for 10 years. At the previous hospital he had administered, Quade had recognized Winder's financial talent and Jack was quickly recruited for Quade's top-management team at University Medical Center. Jack has been mentored by the CEO for 8 years, and, though it has never been formally indicated, Jack is being quietly groomed for the position of CEO at University Medical Center or a comparable medical center.

Organizational Dynamics: University Medical Center has a limited affiliation with a medical school in an East Coast metropolitan area. There are residencies in general surgery, urology, and obstetric/gynecology, but no medical student training at the medical center. It is a nonprofit, nonsectarian hospital with 350 beds, an ambulatory day-surgery center, and nearly 2,200 FTE employees. Its core values are compassion, excellence, and collaboration. Its mission is "a premier center for teaching, research and compassionate, state-of-the-art patient care, ever responsive to community need." Because of its medical school affiliation and large professional staff, the medical center has maintained a matrix structure for its 34-year history. Although matrix-structured organizations are chided for engendering byzantine-like reporting relationships, the medical center's matrix design has proved to be quite lean and efficient. For the past 7 years the medical center has been a national model of continuous quality improvement for other large medical centers. The corporate culture is reasonably aligned with the core values of compassion, excellence, and collaboration. There is an almost palpable sense of family and commitment among personnel, and annual turnover is approximately 4%, which contrasts with 18–24% among other hospitals in the region. Surveys repeatedly reflect high job satisfaction and commitment among medical center personnel, as well as moderately high levels of trust for senior management and, in particular, for Mr. Quade. The medical center appears to be at the consolidation stage of development.

Executive Position: Seventeen employees report to the vice president of finance, who oversees an annual budget of $280 million. The VP reports to the CEO and is a member of the top-management team. The job description lists the requirements of a graduate degree in finance and a minimum of 3 years' experience in progressive experience in health care finance. In addition to specific standards on the oversight of financial operations, the job's performance standards require the VP to ensure that the medical center's core values and culture are reinforced in personnel reporting to the VP. The VP has wide decisional authority. The collegial, supportive atmosphere among the top-management team and its staff is a powerful buffer to job-related stressors, the main one being an attempt to maintain balanced budgets amid the complexity of changes in health-care reimbursement.

Family and Social Support Network: Jack has been married for 21 years to Emily, a nurse practitioner who returned to full-time employment when their daughter, Jesse, left for college 3 years ago. Jesse is particularly close to Jack and spends summers with her parents. Jack reports that his marriage is stable and a source of emotional support for him. Because Jack's and Emily's parents, siblings, and extended family members reside in the Midwest, scheduled visits during the Christmas holidays were the extent of the couple's contact with the two respective extended families—except for weekly phone calls. Jack has a best friend, Al, with whom he regularly plays golf and takes part in other social events such as playing couple's bridge—Emily and Cynthia, Al's spouse, are also friends. Members of the top-management team occasionally socialize together. Overall, Jack's family and social system are supportive and healthy.

Personality Style: Jack appears to manifest the conscientious personality style, at the high level of functioning, meaning that he is conscientious, hopeful, and kind and balances integrity with generosity. His staff and peers consider him highly responsible and cooperative and a person of unquestioned honesty. Finally, his personal values are integrity, hard work, excellence, and compassion.

Leadership Style: Jack's leadership style is characterized by a concern for both people and productivity. Yet he is a no-nonsense administrator when it comes to financial resources and insists on holding the medical center's program directors to a very high standard of accountability on fiscal matters. He also holds his staff to mutually agreed upon performance standards, which are formally reviewed monthly.

Leadership Skills: On the "Inventory of Leadership Competencies" (Figure 6.1), it is not surprising that Jack rates high on Financial/Information and Technical/Analytic Skills, and he also rates high on Strategic Skills. He rates in the moderate range on Relational and Personal Development Skills.

Leadership Competencies: On the "Inventory of Leadership Skills" (cf. chapter 3), Jack rates in the highly effective range on Integrity and Balance, Requisite Job Capabilities, and Understanding Corporate Dynamics. He rates in the moderately effective range on Developing a Winning Strategy, Mobilizing Employee Commitment, and Communicates Effectively and Encourages Knowledge Sharing. Noteworthy is that he rates just below moderately effective on Exhibits a High Level of Energy and Health Status. This rating reflects his high caffeine intake, roller-coaster energy level, and chronic insomnia.

Executive–Organization Fit: Jack's values are quite consistent with the core values and culture of the medical center. Furthermore, he is highly regarded by the CEO and has proved his worth to the organization by his financial savvy. In short, he appears to be an excellent fit.

Executive–Job Fit: Jack is a very good fit with his present job in terms of qualifications, skills, competencies, leadership, and personality style and character.

Executive–Family–Job–Organization Fit: Because he enjoys a high level of family and social support and high levels of Executive–Job and Executive–Organization Fit, Jack's overall level of fit is rather high.

Hypothetically, were Jack to seek and assume the medical center's CEO position at the present time, his level of fit would likely be fair to moderate. In many ways, Jack complements the present CEO with regard to personality and leadership style and competencies. The CEO's healthy, self-confident style and his leadership are characterized by a high emphasis on people and creativity. This provides him with the energy to easily engender confidence and commitment from others. Because the CEO's top-management team consists of hand-picked individuals like Jack, who can engender and maintain high levels of productivity, it is no surprise that the medical center is so successful and well-regarded. This is largely because of the CEO's capacity to surround himself with talented management team members. If Jack aspires to a CEO position, he would do well to close some developmental gaps in his skills and competencies and cultivate a leadership style that is more inspiring and people-oriented.

CONCLUDING NOTE

An accurate and comprehensive assessment provides the consultant with a useful basis for formulating targeted interventions to increase functioning and well-being. This chapter has presented executive profiling as a basic assessment strategy for planning targeted interventions with executives. The next five chapters describe and illustrate the use of seven powerful interventions to maximize executive effectiveness—that is, productivity and health—and thereby increase corporate effectiveness.

REFERENCES

Beer, M. (1980). *Organization change and development: A systems view*. Glenview, IL: Scott, Foresman.

Blake, R., & Mouton, J. (1983). *Consultation* (2nd ed.). Reading, MA: Addison-Wesley.

Chandler, A. (1962). *Strategy and structure*. Cambridge, MA: MIT Press.

Cloninger, R., Svrakic, D., & Pryzbeck, T. (1993). A psychobiological model of temperament and character. *Archives of General Psychiatry, 50,* 975–990.

Flambolz, E. (1990). *Growing pains: The transition from an entrepreneurship to a professionally managed firm*. San Francisco: Jossey-Bass.

Flambolz, E. (2000). *Growing pains: The transition from an entrepreneurship to a professionally managed firm* (revised edition). San Francisco: Jossey-Bass.
Giber, D., Carter, L., & Goldsmith, M. (2000). *Linkage, Inc.'s best practices in leadership development handbook*. San Francisco: Jossey-Bass/Pfeiffer.
Goodstein, L. (1978). *Consulting with human service systems*. Reading, MA: Addison-Wesley.
Hogan, R., & Hogan, J. (1995). *Manual for the Hogan Personality Inventory*. Tulsa, OK: Hogan Assessment Systems.
Hogan, R., & Sinclair, R. (1997). For love or money: Character dynamics in consultation. *Consulting Psychology Journal, 49*(4), 256–267.
Leonard, S. (1997). The many faces of character. *Consulting Psychology Journal, 49*(4), 235–245.
McCubbin, H., & Thompson, A. (1989). *Balancing work and family life on Wall Street.* Edina, MN: Burgess International Group.
McCubbin, H., Thompson, A., Kretzshmar, H., et al. (1992). Family system and work environment predictors of employee health risk: A discriminant function analysis. *American Journal of Family Therapy*, *2*(2), 123–144.
Muchinsky, P. (1990). *Psychology applied to work* (3rd ed.). Pacific Grove, CA: Brooks/Cole.
Muchinsky, P. (1993). *Psychology applied to work* (4th ed.). Pacific Grove, CA: Brooks/Cole.
Renshon, S. (1996). *The psychological assessment of presidential candidates*. New York: New York University Press.
Sperry, L. (1996). *Corporate therapy and consulting.* New York: Brunner/Mazel.

7

Intervention Strategies

This and the four remaining chapters describe seven potent strategies for maximizing executive performance. The seven strategies are organizational consultation, leadership development, executive policy advisement, executive coaching, executive consultation, executive counseling, and executive health promotion. The first three of these—organizational consultation, leadership development, and executive policy advisement are described in some detail in this chapter. Executive coaching, executive consultation, executive counseling, and executive health promotion are briefly described here and will be discussed and illustrated in subsequent chapters.

INTERVENTION STRATEGIES: A CAPSULE SUMMARY

Table 7.1 lists and provides a capsule summary of these seven strategies.

ORGANIZATIONAL CONSULTATION

Organizational consultation is a strategy and process in which a consultant provides diagnostic, technical, or facilitative assistance to achieve specific, planned-change goals that impact individuals, work teams, the entire organization, or all of these, including the corporation's strategy, structure, and culture. Whether in the role of an internal or external consultant to an organization, the consultant may function as a diagnostician, expert adviser or process consultant, or in all three role functions, depending on the nature of the consultation. The reader is referred to Sperry (1993) and the chapter entitled "Organizational Consultation" and to Sperry (1996) and

TABLE 7.1
A Capsule Summary of Intervention Strategies

Strategy	Description
Organizational Consultation	The process by which a consultant, acting internally or externally to an organization and functioning in the roles of assessor, expert adviser, process consultant, or any combination of these, provides diagnostic, technical, or facilitative assistance to *achieve specific, planned change goals* that impact individuals, work teams, the entire organization, or all of these, including the organization's strategy, structure, and culture.
Leadership Development	A corporate-wide initiative to identify and develop new potential leaders for an organization, to enhance the skills and competencies of existing executives, or both. Usually linked to the organization's strategic plan, it is often combined with other executive-development strategies.
Executive Policy Advisement	A form of organizational consultation focusing on the development, and implementation of policies specifically involving executive performance, development, and well-being. Can include succession planning, leadership development, executive health and wellness, mental health and substance abuse, career development, work–family balance, disability and return to work, and so on.
Executive Consultation	A form of organizational consultation in which a *consultant,* functioning as a sounding board, expert adviser, evaluator, or any combination of these, forms a collaborative relationship with an individual executive to address a *broad range* of professional and personal issues of concern to the executive.
Executive Coaching	A form of executive consultation in which a *coach* works collaboratively with an executive to improve the executive's skill and effectiveness in communicating corporate vision and goals and facilitating team performance, organizational productivity, and personal development.
Executive Counseling	The process in which a *therapist* and an executive establish a close, collaborative relationship and utilize psychotherapeutic methods to achieve greater *self-understanding and resolution* of work-related problems, symptoms, or both. Usually briefer, less intense, and more focused on work-related issues than traditional counseling or psychotherapy are.
Executive Health Promotion	An approach to promoting and safeguarding executive health and well-being. Emphasizes strategies for preventing and reversing chronic disease processes. Key factors are diet and weight control, exercise, fitness, stamina, and stress management.

the chapter entitled "Organizational Interventions" for a fuller discussion of this topic.

Case Study: Organizational Consultation for Corporate Transformation

The CEO of a 320-bed community hospital was facing some major challenges. He had recently been brought in by the board of directors to turn things around. Yesterday, he finished reviewing the draft report on third-quarter performance. Reading through the report, with its sobering statistics, was painful. The hospital's daily census was low, averaging 48%, whereas last year other hospitals in the area averaged 68%. The fact that patient satisfaction was only 62%, as compared with last year's figure of 84% for nearby hospitals, meant that the hospital had an image problem that needed immediate attention. Equally disturbing was staff turnover, which had been in the range of 22 to 24% the previous 3 years. Furthermore, employee utilization of health benefits had increased nearly 30% in the previous 2 years, and because the hospital's health program was self-insured, it was doubly discouraging. On top of all that, the annual employee survey indicated that morale had dropped even lower than last year. He was surprised that the turnover rate was not higher.

One thing was clear: The board's decision to support a major culture transformation program was justified, and it would be the CEO's job to plan and implement that initiative for the next fiscal year. He had already met with the head of the organizational consultation group about the project. He had previously worked with this group while he was administrator of another hospital. This project would be much more ambitious, with nearly 3 months in which to finalize the plan.

A group was formed and charged with planning and implementing the hospital's transformation. The group consisted of the CEO, the top-management team, directors and representatives of hospital departments, and the four consultants. The consultation began with an assessment that included an organizational analysis, extensive data collection, analysis, form surveys, intensive interviews, and focus groups. Intensive interviews were conducted with some members of the board of directors and with all senior executives and department directors.

The premise upon which this corporate transformation plan was based was that patient satisfaction is a function of patients' perception of the quality of care received, and patients' perception of quality is largely a function of how well they believe that hospital personnel listen to and respond to their needs and concerns. Based on data gathered by the consultants from surveys and focus groups of patients, as well as surveys and focus groups of hospital personnel, it became increasingly obvious that hospital personnel did not adequately listen to and respond to patients' needs and concerns. The planning group agreed that increasing patient satisfaction would require a major change in the way staff recognized and respectfully and conscientiously responded to patients' needs and concerns.

The organizational analysis further revealed that the current corporate strategy, structures, and culture neither expected, supported, nor rewarded staff members who spent time listening and responding to patients. Parenthetically, the planning group dubbed the hospital's culture a "don't bother me, I've got more important things to do" culture, to reflect the lack of concern and caring that patients reported. There was no question that a major change in employee attitudes, thinking, and behavior was essential if the hospital was to break its downward spiral. Furthermore, significant modification in corporate strategy, structures, and culture would also be required.

The group reached consensus on an action plan and envisioned four objectives to guide the transformation strategy for the coming fiscal year. The first objective was to improve patient satisfaction. The second objective was to increase staff commitment, and the third was to decrease employee health costs. The fourth objective was to increase the hospital's market share, which effectively meant to increase its daily census rate.

A 12-month plan was established to accomplish these four objectives. The plan described an initiative that would corporate strategy, structure, and culture. With regard to corporate strategy, significant hospital resources would be refocused to support the transformation effort; specifically, patient satisfaction would be the hospital's number-one priority for the next year. With regard to corporate structure, the initiative established a modification of the hospital's performance management system. Now, a specific performance standard on "scripting" would be required of all hospital personnel, and performance would to be monitored weekly, with formal quarterly evaluations. A performance standard on coaching subordinates in scripting and patient relations was added for every manager, from floor supervisor to the CEO.

Scripting is a standardized method of questioning and responding in one-to-one conversations with customers, clients, or, in this case, patients. Scripts dealing with nearly every conceivable patient issue or concern were developed by the consultants, working with a task force of all department and other hospital personnel who could provide expert input on script development. Scripting was chosen to facilitate two-way communication with patients, for the express purpose of improving recognition and responsiveness of patient needs and concerns. All personnel were expected to learn and use the scripting with each patient they cared for each day. Managers were also expected to talk briefly—using scripting—with each patient on their service every day. Managers were to model scripting behavior, as well as coach each of their reports regarding the implementation of the scripting initiative.

It was expected that as personnel became comfortable and proficient with scripting, they would become more responsive to patient needs and concerns. As the culture began to shift more in the direction of caring and concern for patients, and as the structures rewarded employees' compassionate, caring behavior, personnel would in theory feel increased job satisfaction and commitment. Presumably, these changes would directly and indirectly impact patient satisfaction, the hospital census, and employee health costs.

Because there was support for this transformation initiative at every level of management, buy-in by all department directors and many other personnel, clear expectations, training and coaching, and incentives—including time off, pay raises, front-row parking tied to the exemplary use of scripting, and so on—based on meeting performance standards, it was not too surprising that the scripting initiative was well received. The consultants predicted that utilization or adherence to scripting would be higher in direct patient services, such as inpatient units, clinics, and maintenance, and lower in food service, laundry, and supply services.

Results of the transformation efforts were evaluated at 12 months. The consultants' predictions about adherence were borne out. Several dramatic changes were noted. First, patient satisfaction increased from 62 to 95%. Employee turnover decreased from 22 to 3%. The average daily hospital census increased from 50 to 85%. Finally, employee health costs decreased by 40% in the 1-year period.

In short, as a result of the transformation effort, the hospital did in fact become a more healthy and productive organization. Although this case is a good example of organizational consultation, it should be noted that other strategies for enhancing executive performance also played a part. These included executive consultation, as the consultants met with, advised, and supported the CEO and planning group, particularly the top-management team and department directors. The strategies also included executive coaching of top management in developing competence in the skills of scripting and modeling change, so that these managers could coach the supervisors and staff who reported to them.

LEADERSHIP DEVELOPMENT

What is leadership development and what is its role in maximizing executive performance? Unlike many of the other executive development strategies whose focus is the individual executive, leadership development is a corporate-wide initiative to identify and develop potential leaders for a corporation, to enhance the skills and competencies of existing executives, or all if these. Although, theoretically, leadership development is a separate and independent executive-development strategy, practically speaking, leadership development is often combined with other executive-development strategies.

U.S. corporations have spent approximately 1% of their total revenues to train and develop their executives, amounting to about $40 billion annually (McCall, Lombardo, & Morrison, 1988). Of the 15 major corporations recently surveyed, one half spent more than $1 million in 1999 on their formal leadership development programs (Giber, Carter, & Goldsmith, 2000). Traditionally, leadership development was classroom-based and focused on building and upgrading a set of generic leadership competencies, such as interpersonal skills and financial analysis.

The underlying assumption was that coursework fostered executive performance, as it facilitated the executive's ability to gain technical knowledge, understand leadership models and theories, solve and frame problems, and develop self-confidence and judgment skills. But this assumption has been subject to intense scrutiny, largely because little data exists to cost-justify it. Increasingly, top management has come to believe that the most effective and useful manner of learning about leadership is on the job, rather than in the classroom.

This belief is based on management's experience and mounting research evidence, such as that reported in McCall, Lombardo, & Morrison's *The Lessons of Experience—How Successful Executives Develop on the Job* (1988). Based on their groundbreaking research, the authors concluded that the process of executive development occurs during the course of 10 or 20 years of progressive job experience. They described five sets of lessons that successful executives learned on the job and five developmental events that spawned these lessons. The five lessons are setting and implementing agendas, handling relationships, manifesting basic values, possessing executive temperament, and cultivating personal insight.

The designation of leadership development as a system (Potts & Sykes, 1993) connotes that leadership development is a strategic initiative and not simply classroom instruction. In 1998 a study was launched to answer the question "How are the world's most successful organizations developing their leaders?" This study of 350 corporations found that nearly all respondents recognized the need to develop stronger leaders, but less than 44% had a formal process for developing high-potential leaders. However, those corporations that were successful in producing high-potential leaders utilized structured leadership-development systems (Giber, Carter, & Goldsmith, 2000).

What are the best practices in leadership development today? Looking at 15 of the most successful corporate leadership-development programs provides some clues. In terms of essential components, the best programs emphasized 360-degree feedback, action learning, and exposure to senior executives, which included coaching and mentoring programs. The leadership competencies that most impacted the design of these leadership-development systems were strengthening team building, business understanding, and conceptual thinking. It is interesting to note that despite increasing concern that executives lack the emotional capacity and maturity to lead organizations successfully, emotional intelligence was a low priority in these programs. Three critical factors that most impacted the success of these leadership-development systems were the support and involvement of senior executives, continuous evaluation, and linking leadership development with the corporation's strategic plan (Giber, Carter, & Goldsmith, 2000).

In short, where the consultant's role in leadership development had been to teach or facilitate leadership seminars, now the consultant's role involves the design and implementation of learning experiences that are strategically focused and that often utilize other executive-development strategies, such as executive profiling, executive policy development, and executive coaching or mentoring.

Case Study: Leadership Development

A case study involving the use of executive coaching in a leadership-development program context is illustrated in chapter 8. Please refer to the "Case Study: Coaching in a Leadership Development Program." The case study describes, in some detail, the first 2 years of the leadership-development initiative at MathWorks, an international leader in technical computer software.

EXECUTIVE POLICY ADVISEMENT

In boardrooms and executive suites across the United States, there is increasing awareness of the need for policies that promote executive effectiveness and well-being. Consultants working with boards and top-management executives are being called upon to help develop and implement such policies. In the past, organizational consultants figured prominently in the development of policies for mental health, substance abuse, work–family balance, disability and return to work, employee wellness, and violence prevention. Today, the challenge is to develop similar programs and policies for executives. Space limitations permit only a brief look at one such policy area: mental health and substance abuse.

It may be surprising to note that many corporations have yet to develop and effectively implement a corporate mental health policy for executives. Why is this? Part of the reason is a perceived lack of urgency. Although personal and relational difficulties, substance abuse and dependence, and major psychiatric disorders are endemic within the executive suite, these tend to go undetected for long periods of time. Unlike the corporation's early warning system for detecting distress, substance abuse or dependence, and psychiatric disorders among rank-and-file employees, resulting from a corporate policy on early detection, no comparable early warning system exists for executives. Kiechel (1988) reports that it may take 5 years after the alcoholic executive loses a spouse and family before "bottoming out" on the job. Clinical experience suggests that alcoholic executives are dependent on alcohol for at least 10 years before becoming so dysfunctional that they either die or are too impaired to work. In short, executive distress and impairment can remain hidden for long periods of time.

Because of the nature of their positions, executives—particularly senior executives—lack close day-to-day supervision. Many executives exercise considerable latitude in structuring daily activities and managing their time, particularly because they are expected to travel and may be away from their offices for long periods. Second, out of misplaced loyalties, subordinates often enable the executives' impairment by minimizing or overlooking it. Finally, many executives believe that asking for help is a sign of psychological or moral weakness. They contend that they must maintain an image of toughness to justify their status and position within the organization. Not surprisingly, executives tend to avoid their own in-house professional source of help—such as an EAP—because of fear of a possible break in confidentiality or concern about "reversing" the traditional and clearly defined superior–subordinate roles in the firm (Speller, 1989). Even when a superior becomes aware that an executive is distressed or experiencing signs of impairment, the superior may demand that the impaired executive simply "get his or her act together," without providing appropriate resources or the support to make this possible.

Unfortunately, the longer the executive's impairment goes unrecognized, the greater the likelihood that the problem will result in a full-blown crisis. Such crises often require hospitalization. One of the most valuable features of corporate EAP progress is that problems are detected early and treatment is begun early, which contains costs, usually eliminates hospitalization, and results in minimal disruption to the employee's family and work life. These particular features of early detection programs argue persuasively for the development and implementation of a corporate policy on mental health and impairment for executives.

Essentially, executive policy advisement is a form of organizational consultation on the development and implementation of policies specifically involving executive performance, development, and well-being. It can include succession planning, leadership development, executive health and wellness, mental health and substance abuse, career development, work–family balance, disability and return to work, and so on.

EXECUTIVE CONSULTATION

Executive consultation is an organizational consultation strategy in which a consultant forms a collaborative relationship with an individual executive to address a broad range of professional and personal issues of concern to the executive. Because these discussions can range from complex financial and personnel decisions to delicate personal health issues, this type of consultation is not for beginners. Rather, it requires a seasoned consultant with an encyclopedic knowledge and a broad experience base. The signature characteristic of this form of consultation is that the consultant serves as a sounding board and an expert adviser who can quickly and effective assess the personal and organizational dynamics influencing the executive's concerns. Chapter 10 describes this strategy in more detail.

EXECUTIVE COACHING

Executive coaching is an executive consultation strategy in which a coach-consultant works collaboratively with an executive to improve the executive's skill and effectiveness in communicating corporate vision and goals, as well as in facilitating team performance, organizational productivity, and personal development. Providing executive coaching requires considerably less knowledge and experience than does executive consulting, as described in the previous section. Effective executive coaching requires competency in engaging the executive in a collaborative relationship, assessing and profiling the executive's performance gaps, collaboratively establishing a plan to fill the gap(s), and having the capacity to guide and monitor the executive's progress as the plan is implemented. Chapter 8 illustrates this strategy in more detail.

EXECUTIVE COUNSELING

Executive counseling is a strategy and process in which a therapist and an executive establish a close, collaborative relationship and utilize psychotherapeutic methods to achieve greater self-understanding and resolution of work-related problems, symptoms, or both. It is usually briefer, less intense, and more focused on work-related issues than traditional counseling or psychotherapy are. Chapter 9 describes this strategy in more detail.

EXECUTIVE HEALTH PROMOTION

Executive health promotion is a strategy for promoting and safeguarding executive health and well-being. It emphasizes strategies for preventing and reversing chronic disease processes. Key factors are diet and weight control, exercise, fitness, endurance and stamina, and stress management. Chapter 11 describes this strategy in more detail.

CONCLUDING NOTE

This chapter introduced seven strategies for increasing executive effectiveness. Three of these strategies—organizational consultation, leadership development, and executive policy advisement—were described in some detail in this chapter. A full chapter each will be devoted to the other four strategies. Executive coaching is described in more detail chapter 8. Executive consultation is covered in chapter 9, whereas executive counseling is the focus of chapter 10. Finally, executive health promotion is detailed in chapter 11.

REFERENCES

Giber, D., Carter, L., & Goldsmith, M. (2000). *Linkage, Inc.'s best practices in leadership development handbook.* San Francisco: Jossey-Bass/Pfeiffer.

Kiechel, W. (1988). Looking out for the executive alcoholic. In *Office hours: A guide to the managerial file.* Boston, MA: Little Brown.

McCall, M., Lombardo, M., & Morrison, A. (1988). *The lessons of experience: How successful executives develop on the job.* Lexington, MA: Lexington Books.

Speller, J. (1989). *Executives in crisis: Recognizing and managing the alcoholic, drug addicted or mentally ill executive.* San Francisco, CA: Jossey-Bass.

Sperry, L. (1993). *Psychiatric consultation in the workplace.* Washington, DC: American Psychiatric Press.

Sperry, L. (1996). *Corporate therapy and consulting.* New York: Brunner/Mazel.

8
Executive Coaching Strategies

There is something magical about the term *coaching*. It is nonthreatening, it has little or none of the stigma associated with counseling, and its link with sports coaching gives it instant credibility and status. Perhaps this is why so many executives have little apprehension about becoming involved in coaching, as compared to professional counseling or psychotherapy. Today, executive coaching is being embraced in nearly every sector of the corporate world. It is by far the most common strategy for increasing executive effectiveness. Unlike traditional leadership-training programs, which are expensive and apparently add little value to corporations, executive coaching is viewed by many corporate leaders as a highly promising strategy for increasing profits and competitive advantage, while reducing costs. Not surprisingly, executive coaching has become "the fastest growing 'consulting' practice, with no slowdown in sight. For example, in the United States today the estimated number of executive coaches is in the tens of thousands" (Freas, 2000, p. 27). Why is this?

There are many reasons, but perhaps the most important is the expectation "of attaining quantum improvements in performance, motivation and effectiveness of executives and key people, individually and in teams" (Stephenson, 2000, p. xvii). Another important reason for this rapid growth is its bottom-line benefits, including the fact that executive coaching "is delivered on the job in real time, so it can be tailored to the executive's individual needs" (Freas, 2000, p. 27). So what, exactly, is executive coaching? What are its economic benefits? How is it different from executive consulting and counseling? How is it practiced? These and related queries are addressed in this chapter.

To avoid confusion, it should be noted at the outset that the term *executive coaching* can be used in two ways. First, executives can learn how to become more effective by being coached by a professional; and second, corporations can expect that executives will provide coaching—also called mentoring—to their own subordinates. Executive coaching refers to both of these meanings.

VIEWPOINTS AND DEFINITIONS OF EXECUTIVE COACHING

Two Viewpoints on Executive Coaching

First of all, what is coaching? Simply put, coaching is a process of instructing, directing, or prompting. It involves the acquisition of knowledge or skills for the purpose of improving performance, personal development, or both. There are basically two viewpoints on coaching: one is that the primary purpose of coaching is performance enhancement; the other is that the primary purpose of coaching is personal development *and* secondarily performance enhancement. Those who advocate for the personal development viewpoint stress that the original meaning of the word *coaching*—derived from the word *carriage* in the English language—was "to convey a valued person from where he or she is to where he or she wants to be." Not surprisingly, these advocates insist that the basic purpose of coaching is to bring out the best in individuals, and that focusing primarily on the individual's overall development usually leads to increased professional effectiveness and job performance. Generally speaking, many who ascribe to this viewpoint are more likely to be involved with coaching executives—which frequently focuses on personal and interpersonal development—than with coaching nonexecutives, which more often focuses directly and principally on increasing job performance.

Definitions of Executive Coaching

At the current time, no consensus exists on the scope, format, methods, or duration and frequency of sessions among the various descriptions and definitions of executive coaching. Such a lack of consensus is understandable because this area of professional endeavor is much more recent than executive consultation and counseling. Five representative definitions and descriptions of executive coaching are given in this section; the next section attempts to differentiate executive coaching from executive consultation and counseling.

Witherspoon (2000) insists that coaching is not simply a leadership function, but rather is a growth-oriented personal relationship. Accordingly, he describes executive coaching as "an action-learning process to enhance effective action and learning agility. It involves a professional relationship and a deliberate, personalized process to provide an executive with valid information, free and informed choices based on that information, and internal commitment to those choices" (p. 167). Two expected outcomes of executive coaching should be more effective action and increased ability to learn—that is, asking for feedback and reflecting before and after making a decision or initiating an action. Similarly, Goldsmith, Lyons, and Freas (2000) describe coaching as a strategic process that adds value to those who are coached, as well as to the organization. "Coaching establishes and develops healthy working relationships by surfacing issues (raw data gathering), addressing issues (through feedback), solving problems (action planning), and following through (results)—and so offers a process in which people develop and through which obstacles to obtaining business results are removed" (p. xviii).

Others describe executive coaching from a more performance-based perspective. For instance, O'Neill (2000) defines executive coaching as the process of increasing the leader's skill and effectiveness in three areas: (1) communicating the organization's purpose, vision, and goals to key constituencies; (2) building relationships and facilitating interactions that result in outstanding team performance; and (3) producing results and outcomes (pp. 5–6).

Kilburg (1996) defines executive coaching as "a helping relationship formed between a client with managerial authority and responsibility in an organization and a consultant who uses a wide variety of behavioral techniques and methods to help the client achieve a mutually identified set of goals to improve personal performance and personal satisfaction, and consequently, to improve the effectiveness of the client's organization within a formally defined coaching agreement" (p. 142).

Some believe that coaching is probably a necessary, and perhaps even a sufficient, condition for achieving organizational transformation. Coaching can be transformational, which is to say that "through a behavioral change brought about in individuals, a leader may transform the organization and gain commitment. . . . In coaching, people are offered the chance to align their own behavior with the values and vision of the organization. . . . and then putting these individuals back in alignment, one person at a time—coaching can make real impact and build healthy organizations—top-down, and from the grass roots up" (Goldsmith, Lyons, & Freas, 2000, p. xviii).

Finally, Peterson (1996) mentions three different types of coaching that are offered by consultants at Personnel Decisions International (PDI). These are briefly described in the following paragraphs.

Targeted Coaching is a focused, practical, skills-based approach utilized with individuals motivated to further enhance their skills in one or two key areas. This form of coaching is essentially a form of relatively brief personalized instruction—that is, 4 to 5 half-day sessions over 3 to 4 months, with minimal follow-up.

Intensive Coaching encompasses more complex personal and organizational issues, such as significant changes in role (i.e., moving into a senior position) or major behavior changes (i.e., adopting a more collaborative style). Sessions of 5 to 6 full days are scheduled over a 6 to 9 month period, involve multiple skill areas, and include a 3 to 6 month follow-up to reinforce new behaviors.

Executive Coaching focuses on dealing with complex business decisions, implementing major initiatives, and clarifying options. It is a relationship-based interaction with a seasoned coach who serves as a sounding board and adviser. Less emphasis is placed on skill-building and more on achieving organizational goals and personal development. Sessions are 1 to 2 hours on a weekly or as-needed basis, and the coaching may be ongoing.

Although, Peterson's descriptions of Targeted Coaching and Intensive Coaching are quite consistent with the five previous descriptions and definitions of executive coaching, his description of Executive Coaching is rather similar to what some (Levinson, 1981; Sperry, 1996) describe as Executive Consultation. The next sections further articulate these and other distinctions.

EXECUTIVE COACHING, CONSULTATION, AND COUNSELING

Although similarities exist among executive coaching, consultation, and counseling, there are also differences. This section describes how executive coaching differs from executive consultation and executive counseling.

Coaching and Consultation

What is the relationship between coaching and consultation? Schein (2000) contends that coaching is a subset of consultation. According to Schein, an advocate of process consultation, the consultant has three roles: diagnostic, expert, and process. The focus of the process role is on helping clients help themselves. The consultant must move freely among these three roles, but, of necessity, must begin in the process role in order to accurately determine the type of help the client really needs. The overarching goal of the consultant is to be helpful to the client, as well as be mindful of the impact of interventions on the larger client system and the community. Schein suggests that coaches are often ineffective in their efforts because they fail to recognize the importance of the process role. "If coaching is to be successful, the coach must be able, like the consultant, to create a helping relationship with his or her client. To create such a helping relationship it is necessary to start in the process mode, which involves the learner/client, identifies the real problems, and builds a team in which both the coach and the client take responsibility for the outcomes" (Schein, 2000, p. 72).

Coaching and Counseling

What is the relationship between coaching and counseling? Barwick (2000) indicates that coaching involves telling employees specifically what they are doing well or poorly in areas limited to their work. Once the manager has communicated that a problem exists and what improvement is necessary, both employee and manager form an expectation of the future. "Counseling, on the other hand, engages people with issues that are deeply important to them and about which they hold strong feelings. These issues may go beyond the work situation and are often large and difficult to define" (Barwick, 2000, p. 286).

Counseling and coaching overlap in many ways. However, Stephenson (2000) points out that counseling is the modality more suited for "personal problems or organizational changes affecting job performance or motivation," whereas coaching is more appropriate "when there is a lack of skill or knowledge about job responsibilities, or about desirable leadership, in-team or interpersonal behavior" (Stephenson, 2000, pp. 48–49).

Salters (1997) puts it even more succinctly: Counseling is primarily for "won't do" issues (i.e., issues reflecting character, motivation, or emotionality), whereas coaching is for "can't do" issues (i.e., issues reflecting lack of skill, capability, or knowledge). Another difference is that unlike executive counseling, where the executive engages in deep disclosure, the need for a close personal bond and confidentiality is not as great in coaching.

Table 8.1 summarizes these distinctions.

ECONOMIC BENEFITS OF EXECUTIVE COACHING

This chapter began with a quote stating that an important bottom-line benefit of executive coaching was that it was delivered on the job, in real time, and tailored to the executive's needs. Although these aspects are im-

TABLE 8.1
Executive Coaching, Executive Counseling, and Consultation

Strategy	Distinctive Features
Executive Coaching	A form of executive consultation in which a *coach* works collaboratively with an executive to improve the executive's skill and effectiveness in communicating corporate vision and goals and facilitating team performance, organizational productivity, and personal development. Usually of short duration.
Executive Consultation	A form of organizational consultation in which a *consultant,* functioning as a sounding board, expert adviser, evaluator, or all of these forms a collaborative relationship with an individual executive to address a *broad range* of professional and personal issues of concern to the executive. Often of longer duration, an ongoing process.
Executive Counseling	The process in which a *therapist* and an executive establish a close, collaborative relationship and utilize psychotherapeutic methods to achieve greater *self-understanding and resolution* of work-related problems, symptoms, or both. Usually briefer, less intense, and more focused on work-related issues than traditional counseling or psychotherapy are. Often, weekly meetings. Short to medium duration.

portant, there are other, even more compelling, economic benefits to advocate executive coaching. In terms of return on investment (ROI), Stephenson (2000) insists that the basic reason corporations have embraced executive coaching is that it saves significant amounts of time and money. He points to three significant savings. First, coaching typically reduces the amount of time it takes for a newly appointed executive to "get up to speed" (i.e., assimilation time), and become "profitable" in the job by approximately 50%. Invariably, this "can in effect, save 20 percent of their first year's cost of employment" (Stephenson, 2000, p. 42). Second, coaching can improve executives' "personal leverage on their team and staff, and the budgets for which they are responsible by one-third in the first 12 months" (p. 42). Third, coaching increases the retention of motivated talent and reduces derailment and dismissals significantly. Stephenson notes that these savings run into the hundreds of thousands of dollars for a senior executive, including the cost of a search to hire and assimilate a replacement. Essentially, "the bottom line regarding economic benefits is that executive coaching, as we have defined it, invariably yields more than a 20-fold return in the investment in it, within an 18-month period" (p. 47). Possibly no other corporate endeavor yields such a high ROI.

THE PRACTICE OF COACHING

What is the profile of a highly effective executive coach? How do effective coaches practice the art of coaching? This section briefly address both questions.

Qualities and Values of Effective Executive Coaches

The first question is easy to answer: There is no answer—or, more correctly, no consensus on what constitutes excellence in executive coaching. At the present, little or no research addresses this question. There is not even consensus, at this time, on the basic requirements to be a coach; no accepted certification or licensure exists, nor do people agree on what constitutes ethical behavior in coaching.

The most effective executive coaches whom I know have organizational consulting or corporate leadership experience, in addition to experience in psychotherapy and human development. They may have received formal training and certification or licensure in a counseling or psychotherapy field, or they have had firsthand experience in counseling themselves. Whatever the case, they seem to effortlessly shift between asking pointed questions about business issues, leadership, and organizational dynamics and considerations and being ever cognizant and respectful of underlying psychological dynamics.

Unlike the specialties of executive coaching and consulting, little consensus exists, at the present time, on a number of pressing ethical and professional value issues. One ethical issue is whether strict confidentiality should characterize coach–coachee relationships. One professional issue involves the "professional performance–personal development" split. I believe that the latter may be the most basic professional issue facing coaching at the current time. Some view it as both a professional and an ethical issue. Elizabeth and Gilford Pinchot (2000) frame the basic issue this way: The more corporations demand superhuman efforts from their senior executives, the more these executives will experience distress, disaffection, and burnout. Is it not counterproductive to sacrifice the health and well-being of executives in the long term for short-term productivity gains? The Pinchots' answer is no. In their coaching and consulting practice, they have found that corporations with the best performance and productivity invariably support the executive's personal development. "Boosting the individual's personal development by coaching employees toward congruence and creativity, can accrue to the bottom line health of the company as a whole" (p. 45). Nevertheless, a number of coaches believe that maximizing professional performance is the necessary and sufficient condition for effective coaching.

The Practice of Executive Coaching

The second question about the effective practice of the art of coaching is challenging because there are nearly as many answers as there are coaches. In some ways, executive coaching shares a number of commonalities with the California gold rush of 1848. The gold rush attracted a diverse group of individuals, it fostered a pioneer spirit, it involved staking a claim, and it promised those who participated the chance to strike it rich. Similarly, executive coaching attracts a diverse group because it doesn't require credentials, it permits coaches to practice however they choose, those who do it can easily establish a practice and a reputation, and fees of $250–$1,500 an hour rival those of attorneys or other consultants.

That being said, I will describe four models or patterns of practice. In the first model, the executive coach meets face-to-face with the coachee in a one-on-one format for a limited time frame. The coaching format is intensive, usually involving a few to several hours over the course of a day or two until the goal of coaching is reasonably achieved. Benton (1999) describes this approach.

In the second model the executive coach meets face-to-face with the coachee for scheduled sessions of 1–1½ hours, usually weekly, and usually for 3 to 6 months or so. The coaching sessions are scheduled in the executive's worksite, but in a neutral office or meeting room. Stephenson (2000) typifies this pattern.

In the third model the executive coach meets face-to-face with the coachee in various formats: one-on-one, with a work team, with the coachee and the work team, or in a one-on-one session with the executive and the employee the executive is coaching. Formal sessions are scheduled, but the duration and frequency of the sessions are a function of the format and goal(s) to be achieved. O'Neill (2000) describes this approach.

In the fourth model the executive coach meets primarily by telephone with the coachee. Although the first meeting may involve a 1-hour face-to-face session, the first session can also be by phone. A specific number of half hour, weekly telephone sessions are scheduled—usually four to six such sessions—as is a final session, which may or may not be face-to-face, wherein progress is reviewed and a determination is made to extend the coaching contract. This model seems to be less attractive to senior executives.

These models of coaching practice are quite diverse and do not appear to reflect any specific theory or research, but rather seem to have evolved based on the coaches' or the executive clients' preferences or circumstances. At the present time, no comparative outcomes research suggests that one model is more effective than another. Nevertheless, most approaches share at least one commonality. They specify at least four phases of the coaching process.

Phase one involves establishing a viable relationship and some agreement about the nature of the coaching. Establishing a collaborative relationship is considered by many as a necessary condition for the success of the undertaking. A collaborative relationship presumes that both coach and coachee are ready and motivated to participate in the coaching process. The coach cannot blindly assume readiness and motivation, because if it is lacking, the coaching effort will surely fail. The agreement or contract for coaching usually specifies the goal, methods, frequency, and duration of the meetings, as well as remuneration.

Phase two includes some sort of assessment of the executive. This may be quite broad or narrow. It might include an evaluation of the job description, functions, and performance standards, skills, talents and competencies, reporting relationships, and so on. An increasing number of executive coaches incorporate some form of 360-degree evaluation that serves as a baseline to monitor and evaluation progress. Sophisticated coaches also assess the executive's motivation and level of readiness for coaching.

Phase three includes some sort of action planning that specifies the goal to be achieved and articulates the methods and techniques for achieving it. The goal usually is learning a new skill, improving performance, developmental or career planning, and so on.

Phase four involves implementation of the action plan. It can include skills training, modeling, roleplaying, the use of executive resources, and so on. Monitoring and evaluation of outcomes against the agreed upon goal or objective(s) is an essential component of the coaching process.

Coaching Effectiveness and Readiness for Change

We have noted that effective coaching is usually a collaborative venture. What does this really mean? It means that both coach and coachee must be ready and willing to become fully involved in the coaching process. Irrespective of the extent of an executive coach's experience and expertise, unless the executive or coachee is really invested in the coaching process, the expected outcomes will not be achieved. This readiness and willingness to engage in the coaching process—that is, to change—cannot be taken for granted. In fact, lack of readiness for change probably accounts for most failures in coaching. This is also true for other organizational change efforts, whether these concern quality, continuous product improvement, or work teams.

Readiness for change and the dynamics of the stages of change were developed by Prochaska, Norcross, and Diclemente (1994). They have identified six stages of change. Those practicing executive counseling, consulting, and coaching would do well to have a working knowledge of these stages and of the underlying construct of readiness for change. As individuals being coached cycle through these stages, the executive coach needs not only to understand the stage of readiness, but to know how to respond appropriately to facilitate the individual moving to a higher stage of readiness.

The first stage is *precontemplation,* in which there is a denial or lack of awareness of the need for change. In terms of coaching, this means that the individual refuses to even talk about coaching. It represents the lowest level of readiness for change. At this stage, the coach's best strategy is to provide information, establish trust, and create doubt. A key question to pose at this stage is "What's wrong with the way things are right now?"

The second stage is *contemplation;* although an individual may be aware that a problem exists, that person perceives no need to do something about it. As with the first stage, for anyone to insist that an individual in need of coaching begin a coaching process or to appoint a coach to work with that individual is not only premature, it is counterproductive. It would be much better to actively listen to the individual and perhaps identify the positives and negatives about making a change. A reasonable question at this stage is "Will making a change be worth it?"

The third stage is decision or *determination,* in which the individual not only recognizes the problem and the need to do something about it, but decides to change and begins to make plans to change. Although a higher level of readiness exists than in the first two stages, there is no guarantee that the individual will actually engage in the coaching process. Nevertheless, helping individuals consider the "what" and "how" of coaching, providing them with information on the types and process of coaching, or offering to introduce them to potential coaches can facilitate movement to the next stage of change.

The fourth stage is *action,* in which the individual actually engages in the change process. In terms of coaching, this stage represents the optimal level of readiness for change. Only at this stage can the coachee work collaboratively with the coach to assess, plan, and implement a coaching plan. Among other things, the coach's primary responsibilities are to support the change efforts and affirm the coachee's commitment and involvement. A basic question here is "What will you do?"

The fifth stage is *maintenance,* in which the plan for change is still in process, but the expected outcome has not yet been achieved or the change does not feel "natural" to the individual. It is important for coaches to recognize coachees' uncomfortableness at this stage and support them, possibly even help them with the so-called soft skills—such as assertive communication, problem solving, or other relational skills—that provide them with new ways of viewing their jobs and the necessary skills to increase their sense of empowerment during this uncomfortable stage. A basic question to ask at this stage is "What could help?"

The sixth stage is *recycling*, or relapse, which means that the coaching outcome was not sustained because of lack of support from top management, the coaching ended prematurely, or the individual has relapsed and slips back to a lower stage, usually contemplation. At this stage, individuals are decidedly ambivalent about trying again and are usually full of excuses to explain their failure. They need help in resolving this ambivalence and in evaluating their commitment to change—and, often, assistance in identifying and eliminating obstacles to successful change. A basic question to ask at this stage is "What's your intention to change today?"

THREE BASIC TYPES OF EXECUTIVE COACHING

As I have pointed out, executive coaching is a strategy or method for improving the executive's personal and professional effectiveness. Depending on the specific goal or focus of coaching, three different types or approaches to executive coaching can be specified. When the focus is on the individual's current task or project, skill-based coaching is the appropriate type. If, however, the focus is on the individual's effectiveness or competence, performance-based coaching is appropriate. Finally, when the focus is on the individual's future job responsibilities or career, developmental coaching is called for (Witherspoon, 2000).

Each of these three types are described and illustrated with case studies in this section. Table 8.2 summarizes these types.

Skill-Based Coaching

Skill-based coaching is typically what most people associate with the term *coaching*. Distinct from teaching, which relies on one-way instruction, coaching relies on "observation, inquiry, dialogue, and discovery. The essence of coaching executives is helping them learn, rather than training or tutoring them. To coach in this sense is less to instruct than to facilitate" (Witherspoon, 2000, p. 168). Skill-based coaching addresses deficits in the core leadership skill sets: technical—analytic, relational, strategic, financial—informational, and self-management skills.

TABLE 8.2
Three Basic Types of Executive Coaching

Type of Coaching	Purpose of the Coaching	Setting and Time Frame	Coaching Strategy and Tactic
Skill-Based Coaching	Focuses on enhancing leadership skills: analytic, relational, strategic, information/financial, or self-management skills	Sometimes informal; other times formal and scheduled; one or more sessions	Assess, model, or facilitate and monitor skill acquisition
Performance-Based Coaching	Increases overall performance and job effectiveness regarding leadership competencies	Usually formal and regularly scheduled; several sessions over months	Assess and intervene to remedy derailment or other risk factors and to enhance performance
Developmental Coaching	Focuses on future job responsibilities, a career move, or both	Mostly in "coachable moments" and brief; sometimes formal sessions over an extended period	Assess and facilitate career development

It is interesting to note that some executive coaches "specialize" in certain skill sets. Coaching executives to develop relational skills is an area of focus for many coaches. Many coaches share Harry Levinson's view that of all the strategies for enhancing executive performance, executive coaching is the most useful means of teaching human relations skills to senior managers (Levinson, 1981). For example, D. A. Benton (1999), in *Secrets of a CEO Coach*, describes eight coaching cases in which she coached senior executives to increase their capacity for relating to subordinates, peers, and customers more effectively.

The primary purpose of skill-based coaching is to sharpen skills in one or more areas that will facilitate the executive's efforts with a current project or task. Typically, an executive will work collaboratively with a coach to achieve the following objectives: First, they assess the executive's current level of skills. Second, they clarify expectations: the executive's expectations and stated performance standards, as well as priorities for current projects or tasks. Third, they develop a plan for skill-building. Fourth, through the use of modeling and other methods, the executive learns and practices the new skill or skills. Fifth, results of skill-building are evaluated. Coaching for skill acquisition typically occurs in a relatively short period of time, usually over a matter of weeks, but sometimes a little longer. It may be as short as a session or two.

Case Study: Skill-Based Coaching

Cynthia Walker is the 35-year-old manager of the product division of a recently merged financial institution. Her last performance review noted morale problems in her division. Fearful that she would be terminated, Ms. Walker sought the advice of an executive coach, who was also a member of her country club. He reviewed her concerns and concluded that the primary source of disharmony in the division was an older secretary, Janice Davis, who was disgruntled with the recent merger and was generally difficult to work with and for, because of her almost incessant demands for special privileges. Ms. Walker felt intimidated by Mrs. Davis. Walker believed that her problem managing the division and the difficult employee stemmed from her passive nature and her domineering mother and thought that she might need formal psychotherapy. The executive coach suggested framing the problem as one of skill deficits in assertive communication and negotiation and offered to provide some time-limited coaching. If the coaching was not sufficiently helpful, the matter of psychotherapy would be revisited.

In a one-on-one context, the coach utilized role-playing to assess Walker's communication and negotiation skills. The coach modeled both skills in the context of role-playing and role reversal; the coach first took the role of manager and then that of the difficult employee. During the remainder of the first 2-hour session, the two worked on preparing the manager for a forthcoming 6-month performance review with the difficult employee. Roles were practiced and reversed until the manager was confident that she could reasonably handle the performance review. When she and the coach met the second time, Walker reported that the review had gone reasonably well, as compared to previous reviews. Specific expectations for the employee's "attitude" and productivity had been mutually negotiated. Nevertheless, Walker was still somewhat intimidated by the employee. Skill building continued, with role-playing that focused on typical encounters between both women. The coaching was also directed at replacing the manager's denigratory self-talk with more positive self-talk when she anticipated dealing with the secretary.

By the time of the third coaching session, morale in the division was better and Walker felt more confidence as a manager. In this example, coaching, rather than psychotherapy, appeared to be the initial intervention of choice and was effective. Had an adequate course of coaching been only partially successful, formal psychotherapy might then have been offered.

Performance-Based Coaching

"Performance" refers to an individual's competencies and personal styles as they impact, positively or negatively, work outcomes. As noted in chapter 3, a competency is an amalgam of skills, talent, and experience. Requisite competencies may or may not be specified in an executive's job description, functions, and performance standards. Whatever the case, high-level executive performance requires these basic competencies. Because a skill component is present in competencies, some measure of overlap occurs between skill-based coaching and performance-based coaching. Sometimes, personal styles interfere with and negatively impact an executive's effectiveness.

So what exactly is performance-based coaching? It is a strategy for increasing, correcting, or recalibrating the executive's overall performance and job effectiveness as a function of leadership competencies and personal style. "As a rule, coaching to correct performance involves interventions to remedy problems that interfere with an executive's job performance or that risk derailing a career" (Witherspoon, 2000, p. 169). In short, the primary purpose of this type of coaching is to reduce or eliminate impediments to higher-level executive performance.

Typically, an executive will work collaboratively with a coach to achieve the following objectives: First, they assess the executive's overall competencies for that individual's current position. Second, they clarify expectations—both the executive's and those of the executive's superior—for current job performance. Third, they prioritize the executive's needs as these relate to current job performance. Fourth, they establish a plan for continuing improvement. And, finally, they implement that plan and periodically evaluate outcomes. Coaching for performance improvement tends to be an ongoing process that typically spans several months or quarters.

Fournies (2000) provides a detailed description of the process of performance- based approach to coaching, which emphasizes behavioral analysis. Detailed transcripts of actual coaching sessions are included, which make his approach appear quite tangible and practical.

Case Study: Performance-Based Coaching

Four months ago, Jennifer Lopez had been promoted to vice president of customer services for a large retailer. Previously, she had held an executive staff position for 4 years and prior to that was the manager of customer relations at one of the corporation's largest stores. She was enthusiastic, easy to get along with, and well liked and regarded by those with whom she worked. One of her responsibilities was to lead team meetings. Because of her dissatisfaction with a number of recent team meetings, she sought out coaching to improve her performance as team leader. She had previous experience in leading meetings, and though she wasn't the most assertive person in the corporation, she had always managed to get the job done. But now she wasn't getting the results she expected from her new team.

The executive coach suggested that it would helpful for her to sit in on one or two upcoming meetings and observe the process. Ms. Lopez agreed.

After the next team meeting, the two met and the coach described her assessment. Both agreed that although a considerable amount of lively, somewhat tangential interaction, had occurred, only four of the seven team members verbally participated. Furthermore, there seemed to be a lack of clarity in group problem solving and decision making. Lopez and the coach contracted to work together on achieving three objectives: increasing input from all team members, increasing the focus of discussion, and improving team problem solving and decision making. They also agreed that the coach would be involved in the next few meetings, but this time in the role of performance coach, as well as observer.

At the start of the next meeting, the VP laid out the meeting's agenda and then mentioned the three objectives she wanted to accomplish, indicating that the coach was there to help her achieve them. As was agreed beforehand, the VP also said that she expected the team members to give her feedback whenever they noticed she was straying from the two objectives. The purpose of this statement was to activate the team to take responsibility for the process and outcome of the meeting.

Not surprisingly, in the next 30 minutes Lopez and the team lost track of the discussion. Only some were participating, and there was considerable imprecision and lack of clarity about the decision they attempted to make. Ms. Lopez also seemed to have lost track of her role and her three objectives. The coach then intervened and, looking at and speaking directly to the VP, indicated that the discussion seemed to be disjointed and asked her what she wanted to focus on at that point. Lopez gracefully took the cue and focused the discussion. Fifteen minutes later in the conversation, the coach intervened again. This time she asked if Lopez was ready to move to the next point of the agenda, or did she want to hear from some of those who hadn't spoken. Lopez took the cue and specifically asked two of those who hadn't spoken for their comments. About 10 minutes before the meeting was scheduled to end, the coach said that even though a decision had just been made, the team didn't appear to be clear about it. She suggested that Lopez check out what the team members thought they were committing themselves to do.

At the end of that and the next two meetings, the VP asked the team for feedback about her effectiveness in leading the meeting and to what extent she had achieved her three objectives. Each time the coach intervened, the VP seemed to take the input and decide what she would do about it. Lopez's performance as meeting leader continued to improve in subsequent meetings. After the fourth meeting, with the active involvement of the coach, the VP indicated that she felt she had met her objectives and both agreed that the coach's in-meeting involvement was no longer needed.

This case study illustrates the application of performance-based coaching in reducing the VP's impediment to achieving her expected competency to effectively lead her team.

Developmental Coaching

Developmental coaching is an effective method for dealing with an employee's future job responsibilities or a career change. Although managers readily agree that employees are their most important resource, some managers insist that career issues are the responsibility of the human resources specialist. Managers may believe that they have insufficient skills, or they are wary about raising expectations they cannot meet, particularly involving promotions or raises. Other managers who agree that an employee's developmental needs are part of their job responsibility are likely to postpone dealing with the developmental needs and career issues of their employees in favor of more pressing matters. They might like to sit down and discuss the employee's future in the corporation or that person's overall career for an hour or two, but they point to having too many employees and too little time for it. The result is that average employees may receive very little developmental coaching and even less career counseling over the course of their lifetime.

Is developmental coaching very different from career and developmental counseling? Yes. Career counseling is an area of professional expertise that requires formal training and experience. It is a process that typically involves scheduled sessions; a formal assessment of vocational interests, abilities, and personality needs; and focused discussion and inquiry for the purpose of maximizing person–career fit. Chapter 8 further describes career counseling. Interestingly, though retirement counseling is a popular form of career counseling that is increasingly offered in corporations today, relatively little career and development counseling is being offered to early- and mid-career employees. On the other hand, developmental coaching requires only limited training and can easily be done by most managers any time they have contact with an employee. Kaye (2000) contends that managers need only take advantage of "coachable moments"—those short, informal, spontaneous opportunities for career development—that occur throughout the course of a typical work day.

This approach to development coaching has three steps: recognize, verbalize, and mobilize (Kaye, 2000). The manager first recognizes a coachable moment by picking up cues from an employee whose actions or words suggest an openness to developmental feedback. Next, the manager verbalizes or talks to an employee in a way that helps the employee focus on developmental options. Finally, the manager needs to mobilize or suggest—on the spot—some immediate, specific career-development steps the employee can take.

This approach to developmental coaching is a skill that is easily learned and utilized. Developing a sensitivity to coachable moments is more likely to occur in organizations that actually embody the corporate value that employees are their major human resource and where coaching is formally specified as one of the executive's job standards. Whether this coaching skill becomes second nature to an executive is a function of both the desire to develop personnel and the effort to practice the skill. The following example illustrates this straightforward method.

Case Study: Developmental Coaching

Joseph Stillman, VP of sales and marketing, whose job standards include developmental coaching, had two occasions the other day to do developmental coaching. Early that morning he learned that one of his regional managers, Jorge Ybarra, was under fire from several account managers because of late postings and recording errors done by some of Ybarra's administrative staff members. Following a meeting of regional managers, Stillman pulled Ybarra aside to discuss those concerns. Ybarra responded: "Yeah, I can understand their complaints. There have been some errors. The only way to avoid them is to monitor my staff very closely. But it's not my job, and I don't really want to do it." Stillman recalled that when he talked to Ybarra about taking the regional manager position a year earlier, Ybarra had reluctantly agreed, saying that his strengths were more in research than in line management. At the time Stillman needed someone to take that region and Ybarra was a loyal, steady player. But it was becoming clear that this regional manager was experiencing a poor job fit. The VP said: "Jorge, you've really helped me out this past year. I know you have some valuable modeling and forecasting skills, but this job is not allowing you to use those skills and your interests as much as you probably could. Maybe there's a way to apply those skills more directly to our marketing efforts. Would you be willing to draft up a proposal along those lines?"

When Stillman returned from lunch, Jackie Sims, one of the word-processing personnel, handed him a set of visuals that she had produced on her computer. They were as slick as anything the corporate graphic design department could produce. She said: "I was getting this mock ready to send to graphics, but I thought I'd try out what I learned in the computer imaging course I'm taking at the university. That new color laser printer we just got does everything." Stillman recognized and acknowledged Ms. Sim's new skill and interest. Then he added: "You might want to ask Raymond in graphic design if they have some new computer imaging programs that you could to learn."

When a manager picks up cues that an otherwise conscientious employee is not performing adequately or consistently, it may reflect poor job fit, as with Jorge Ybarra. Similarly, if managers pick up cues about employees' new skills or interests, it means that employees may be engaged in self-assessment about their career. Although these interests may not result in a different job or new career, they reflects employees' self-directedness, a broadening of skills, and increased job satisfaction, as in the example of Jackie Sims. In either instance, a coachable moment is at hand.

Coaching as a Core Component in Leadership Development

Research indicates that approximately 80% of leadership-development training occurs on the job, often through interactions with coaches or mentors (Morgan, 1992, cited by Thach & Heinselman, 2000, p. 222). Formal leadership-development programs have been around for years, but only in the past decade have progressive corporations placed a high priority on leadership development. Interestingly, as these corporations have increased their investment in formal programs, some have emphasized coaching as a core component. Thach and Heinselman (2000) noted that organizations espousing the philosophy of continuous improvement can easily incorporate a coaching model as the basis for leadership development. They describe a four-phase model for a corporate leadership-development program. The phases are assessment, developmental plan, public announcement, and implementation.

The first is the assessment phase, and its goal is to evaluate current leadership skills. Using a variety of assessment devices, such as interviews and 360-degree feedback data, a benchmark of current leadership competency is established. The next phase is the creation of a developmental plan or contracts. Each leader selects one or two high-impact areas on which to focus and then specifies a plan for achieving the goals in these areas.

The third phase is public announcement, in which others are informed of the leader's developmental goal. This action purportedly raises the leader's own commitment to the announced course of action, as well as laying the foundation for periodic follow-up conversations with observers in assessing progress toward the goal. The implementation phase is perhaps the most tangible and important. It involves both formal developmental activities and informal follow-up with feedback participants. The leader meets with the coach, typically in regularly scheduled monthly meetings, as well as in follow-ups by e-mail and phone. Follow-up with feedback participants occurs every 60 days. This process does not stop when the leader's goal is reached, but rather the leader begins the cycle again with an updated development plan.

Several major corporations have established leadership-development programs that are either based on executive coaching or incorporate it as a component of the program. Ford Motor Company and Alabama Power Company are corporations whose leadership programs are based on an executive coaching model. Both of these corporations went through downsizing and re-engineering programs in the 1970s and 1980s. As a result, both faced a potential shortage of senior managers. Executive coaching was instituted in both corporations to increase the leadership pool, as well as to transform the culture. With Ford, another objective of the leadership program was for executives to be coached into becoming coaches to their managers and staff (Freas, 2000). Bose Corporation and Securities Industry Automation Corporation (SIAC) exemplify corporations that have incorporated executive coaching as a key component of their leadership development programs.

Case Study: Coaching in a Leadership Development Program

MathWorks is a global leader in developing and supplying technical computer software to universities, government research labs, financial institutions, and the technology sector. Privately held and profitable every year since its inception in 1994, MathWorks employs 500 employees. Despite its innovative software products and profitability, the corporation had some major concerns, particularly with one unit.

Top management's concerns were shared by employees as well. In an employee survey, in which one item asked employees to identify the corporation's biggest internal hassle, they overwhelming named the operations division. This division had the reputation of being consistently behind in fulfilling orders, which resulted in increased and increasing customer complaints. Because of low productivity, poor customer satisfaction, and a culture that accepted poor performance as a norm, the VP of operations' proposal to institute a leadership-development program was approved by the president. The VP, aided by outside consultants, took the lead in planning and implementing the program.

At the outset of the program, a detailed analysis of the division's work flow and process was undertaken. It indicated that the work process was so fragmented and circuitous that any hope for inspiring employees' sense of ownership and pride in workmanship was unlikely. Lack of leadership ability within work teams further compounded matters. What was needed was a new work structure and effective leadership that would transform the division's culture to one of teamwork, ownership, and pride. The program was to be a 2-year experiment in transformation, in which coaching was one of three critical components. Team development and training team leaders were the other two components. The hope was to establish cross-functional teamwork that would "force a more mature level of interaction and empowerment. The newly formed culture—now filled with leaders—would be the key to better business results. Each person would see themselves as part of this interconnected business unit, responsible for its success or failure" (Slobodnik, Slobodnik, & Haight, 2000, p. 283). The coaching component was to be the keystone to accomplishing this transformation. Only the coaching component is described here.

Because of turnover and other factors, many employees in this division were inexperienced and were overly dependent on their managers for direction. At the same time these employees resented being told what to do. Thus, the new leadership style would have to provide employees with the experience and support they would need to grow and mature in their work patterns. It was to be a collaborative form of leadership. Performance-based coaching is, of course, an excellent approach to redirecting employee work patterns. "Using managers as a triage team proved to be an excellent mechanism for providing that support initially and was probably the most important reinforcement of the new way of working. . . . Managers were able to observe the old patterns as they happened and redirect the behavior" (p. 283).

Because senior executives had framed the transformation as a systemic change for the division, rather than as a leadership problem, there was minimal resistance and maximal ownership of the process by the division managers. Senior management also gave its full support, as well as the expectation that division managers would function as coaches and role models of the collaboration. Thus, managers were not simply talking about teamwork and collaboration, they were actually doing it. Not surprisingly, these managers began to communicate and interact differently than before, and employees responded by becoming more participative and proactive.

Managers spent considerable time coaching and teaching employees how to manage their emotions, to foster effective two-way communication, and to resolve conflict. "Managers benefitted from the parallel process of coaching each other, the team leaders and anyone who came knocking. They read a lot of current management thinking and attended conferences. . . . They learned from daily experiences about the competencies they needed in this new weblike system. . . . They started to view themselves not as managers, but as change agents, coaches and internal consultants" (p. 286). Interesting, the managers developed a 360-degree review process for evaluating themselves.

An early success of the coaching initiation was "open-door Friday," which provided employees with a weekly opportunity to "contribute new ideas or vent their emotions in a safe, receptive forum. Managers also used it to introduce some basic tools and analytical problem-solving skills to get team members through some difficult roadblocks early in the process"

(p. 286). As the new culture stabilized, it became clearer that managers who were resistant or incapable of functioning as coaches were eventually counseled to move on.

The 2-year leadership-development experiment at MathWorks succeeded. The culture of the operations division was permanently transformed and remains in place. Productivity, quality, and customer satisfaction have continually exceeded expectations, and turnover has been minimal.

CONCLUDING NOTE

It is anticipated that executives will increasingly seek out executive coaching. Even though the number of psychologically minded and trained professionals who are attuned to the inner world and the process of executive coaching is increasing, it is likely that the demand for such coaches will also increase. However, coaching is currently an unregulated professional endeavor, with no minimal educational or experiential qualifications, no certification or licensure requirements, and not even ethical guidelines. Thus, it is incumbent on individuals who practice executive coaching or aspire to its practice to act with a sense of professional responsibility, integrity, and good judgment.

REFERENCES

Barwick, J. (2000). Interpersonal techniques for leaders. In M. Goldsmith, L. Lyons, & A. Freas (Eds.), *Coaching for leadership: How the world's greatest coaches help leaders learn* (pp. 285–297). San Francisco: Jossey-Bass/Pfeiffer.

Benton, D. (1999). *Secrets of a CEO coach.* New York: McGraw-Hill.

Freas, A. (2000). Coaching executives for business results. In M. Goldsmith, L. Lyons, & A. Freas (Eds.), *Coaching for leadership: How the world's greatest coaches help leaders learn* (pp. 27–41). San Francisco: Jossey-Bass/Pfeiffer.

Goldsmith, M., Lyons, L., & Freas, A. (2000). Preface. In M. Goldsmith, L. Lyons, & A. Freas (Eds.), *Coaching for leadership: How the world's greatest coaches help leaders learn* (pp. xv–xx). San Francisco: Jossey-Bass/Pfeiffer.

Kaye, B. (2000). Career development: Anywhere, anyplace. In M. Goldsmith, L. Lyons, & A. Freas (Eds.), *Coaching for leadership: How the world's greatest coaches help leaders learn* (pp. 235–243). San Francisco: Jossey-Bass/Pfeiffer.

Kilburg, R. (1996). Toward a conceptual understanding and definition of executive coaching. *Counseling Psychology Journal, 48*(2), 134–144.

Levinson, H. (1981). *Executive.* Cambridge, MA: Harvard University Press.

O'Neill, M. (2000). *Executive coaching with backbone and heart: A systems approach to engaging leaders with their challenges.* San Francisco: Jossey-Bass.

Peterson, D. (1996). Executive coaching at work: The art of one-on-one change. *Counseling Psychology Journal, 48*(2), 78–86.

Pinchot, E. & Pinchot, G. (2000). Roots and boundaries of executive coaching. In M. Goldsmith, L. Lyons, & A. Freas (Eds.), *Coaching for leadership: How the world's greatest coaches help leaders learn* (pp. 43–64). San Francisco: Jossey-Bass/Pfeiffer.

Prochaska, J., Norcross, J., & Diclemente, C. (1994). *Changing for good*. New York: William Morrow.

Salters, L. (1997, October–December). Coaching and counseling for peak performance. *Business and Economic Review*, 26–28.

Schein, E. (2000). Coaching and consulting: Are they the same? In M. Goldsmith, L. Lyons, & A. Freas (Eds.), *Coaching for leadership: How the world's greatest coaches help leaders learn* (pp. 65–73). San Francisco: Jossey-Bass/Pfeiffer.

Slobodnik, D., Slobodnik, A., & Haight, E. (2000). MathWorks. In D. Giber, L. Carter, & M. Goldsmith (Eds.), *Linkages Inc.'s best practices in leadership development handbook* (pp. 277–297). San Francisco: Jossey-Bass.

Sperry, L. (1996). *Corporate therapy and consulting*. New York: Brunner/Mazel.

Stephenson, P. (2000). *Executive coaching: Lead, develop, retain motivated talented people*. French's Forest, NSW: Pearson Education Australia.

Thach, L., & Heinselman, T. (2000). Continuous improvement in place of training. In M. Goldsmith, L. Lyons, & A. Freas (Eds.), *Coaching for leadership: How the world's greatest coaches help leaders learn* (pp. 219–230). San Francisco: Jossey-Bass/Pfeiffer.

Witherspoon, R. (2000). Starting smart: Clarifying coaching goals and roles. In M. Goldsmith, L. Lyons, & A. Freas (Eds.), *Coaching for leadership: How the world's greatest coaches help leaders learn* (pp. 165–185). San Francisco: Jossey-Bass/Pfeiffer.

9

Executive Counseling Strategies

In the "Case Study on Skill-Based Coaching" in chapter 8, you may recall that Cynthia Walker, fearful that she would be terminated from her managerial position, sought executive coaching, despite the nagging sense that she might need psychotherapy. She believed that her problems with managing the division and its difficult employees stemmed from her passive nature and her domineering mother. The executive coach suggested framing the problem as one of skill deficits in assertive communication and negotiation, and if the coaching effort proved not to be sufficiently helpful, psychotherapy might be indicated. In this case, developing more effective assertiveness and negotiation skills were sufficient for Ms. Walker. However, conceivably the skill focus, though necessary, might not have been sufficient.

It should not be surprising that many executives would prefer to work on difficult issues and personal concerns in the context of executive coaching, given the stigma still associated with professional counseling and psychotherapy. However, the indications for, and the methods of, executive counseling and psychotherapy are different than those for coaching. When indicated, executive counseling and psychotherapy are the executive development strategies of choice.

So what are some of the indications for executive counseling? Executive counseling is an executive-development strategy that is particularly well-suited for dealing with personal problems or organizational changes that impact the executive's motivation, job performance, or personal well-being. Concerns such as fear of failure, relationship issues, career dilemmas, symptoms or impairment related to depression and anxiety, substance abuse, or work addiction can be addressed in this form of counseling. Unlike in other executive-development strategies, the provider of executive counseling is expected to have formal training and certification—and perhaps licensure—to practice counseling or psychotherapy. Unlike "employee counseling," wherein a supervisor or manager deals with "correcting" job-related problems, solving a workplace conflict, or confronting an employee about a substance-abuse issue, executive counseling is a professional undertaking that is usually provided outside the workplace and involves a much higher degree of confidentiality than do either executive consultation and executive coaching.

This chapter describes and illustrates executive counseling as an effective strategy for maximizing the executive's professional and personal performance and well-being. The chapter begins by situating executive counseling amid two somewhat related strategies, executive consultation and executive coaching. Then I describe two forms of executive counseling that I utilize regularly in my clinical practice. The first type is dual-career couples counseling, and the second is what I have come to call "work-focused psychotherapy." Each of these types of executive counseling is described in considerable detail, and case studies illustrate their application.

EXECUTIVE COUNSELING, AS DISTINCT FROM CONSULTATION AND COACHING

Although similarities exist among executive counseling, consultation, and coaching, there are also differences. This section provides a capsule summary of the distinctive features of executive counseling, executive consultation, and executive coaching. See chapter 7 for a more detailed description of these differences. Table 9.1 highlights some of these basic distinctions.

EXECUTIVE COUNSELING WITH DUAL-CAREER COUPLES

The number of dual-career couples is increasing dramatically. When both spouses hold jobs outside the home, the marital relationship is called "dual earner." But when both spouses hold professional or executive-level positions, their relationship is referred to as "dual-career." The workplace implications of conflict among dual-career couples are profound, and clinicians-consultants who can effectively engage these couples therapeutically can greatly impact the lives of these individuals. This intervention is different enough from individual psychotherapy and traditional marital therapy to be considered an area of subspecialization.

Stoltz-Loike (1992) notes six underlying themes related to effective dual-

TABLE 9.1
Executive Coaching, Executive Counseling, Consultation

Strategy	Distinctive Features
Executive Coaching	A form of executive consultation in which a *coach* works collaboratively with an executive to improve the executive's skill and effectiveness in communicating corporate vision and goals and facilitating team performance, organizational productivity, and personal development. Usually of short duration.
Executive Consultation	A form of organizational consultation in which a *consultant,* functioning as a sounding board, expert adviser, evaluator, or any combination of these forms a collaborative relationship with an individual executive to address a *broad range* of professional and personal issues of concern to the executive. Often of longer duration; an ongoing process.
Executive Counseling	The process in which a *therapist* and an executive establish a close, collaborative relationship and utilize psychotherapeutic methods to achieve greater *self-understanding and resolution* of work-related problems, symptoms, or both. Usually briefer, less intense, and more focused on work-related issues than traditional counseling or psychotherapy are. Often, weekly meetings. Short to medium duration.

career couple functioning. The first is that couples must establish boundaries between themselves and others. Second, spouses must be able to express supportiveness—both emotional and physical—to each other. Third, effective couple relations depend on mastering and using basic communication skills. Fourth, effective couple relations depend on mastering and using conflict-resolution skills. Fifth, dysfunctional couple patterns can be framed as problems in need of solutions. And sixth, effective couple relations involve the process of change, which couples tend to fear and resist. The obvious implication is that the clinical consultant can greatly enhance the functioning of dual-career couples.

Depending on the level and severity of conflict, treatment can range from simply psychoeducational interventions, to focused systemic interventions or more in-depth psychodynamic interventions. Although psychoeducational and systemic strategies aim to teach relational and coping skills or to achieve adaptive solutions, these approaches tend to be of limited use in helping dual-career couples work through resistance to change or the developmental blocks that lead to relational and therapeutic impasses. Therapeutically confronting these resistances and impasses may require exploring issues from early childhood in each spouse's development.

Confronting and resolving such unfinished developmental business in one or both spouses is often part of the process of becoming a mature, dual-career couple. Developmental issues underlie the six common conflict areas for dual-career couples (Glickhauf-Hughes, Hughes, & Wells,

1986). Three of these—power conflicts, competition, and commitment—will be briefly described.

Power conflicts often reflect the spouses' childhood experience that others cannot be counted on to meet their needs; as adults, they are likely to develop a look-out-for-number-one attitude. In addition, when parents are insensitive to their children's needs and frustration level, these children will likely become adults who have difficulty tolerating the frustration of unmet needs. Thus, compromise with a spouse may be both difficult and painful because it is associated with loss rather than with mutual gain. Equity is often proposed as the corrective solution for resolving power conflicts or struggles. But this solution requires several things. First, each spouse must keep the other's needs in mind; second, both individuals must be able to tolerate the frustration of not getting their own needs met immediately; and third, each person must cultivate the ability to view a spouse's requests as legitimate and not as attempts at control or to dominate. In terms of Erikson's stages of psychosocial development, the resolution of power conflicts by equity is difficult if either or both spouses have insufficiently mastered the developmental tasks of trust and autonomy.

Another common conflict of dual-career couples is competition. The opposite of competition is cooperation or collaboration. Collaboration requires the capacity to separate one's own feelings from one's spouse's feelings and behavior, the ability to sustain and augment self-esteem via encouragement, and an acceptance of competitive feelings, both within oneself and in one's spouse. The developmental obstacle that can impede a couple's resolving conflicts about competition results from insufficient mastery of the tasks of autonomy and initiative by one or both spouses.

A third common conflict involves commitment. Because many dual-career spouses value success, achievement, and independence and respond more to external than to internal validation, these individuals find it easy to "hedge their bet" about relationships and thus place a higher priority on personal attainment and satisfaction. To commit oneself to another requires the ability to be intimate, to develop an internal reward system, and to make the spousal relationship a priority. The developmental tasks that must be mastered involve industry and intimacy.

Essentially, psychodynamic intervention strategies are necessary when problem solving and communication training are not working or are only partially effective because of resistances and impasses secondary to more basic developmental issues (Rice, 1979).

Case Study: Counseling Dual-Career Couples

Daniel and Marie Epstein have been married 6 years and have a 3-year-old son. They appeared for therapy after a particularly hostile argument, during which Daniel slapped Marie in the face. Although this was the first such incident, both were sufficiently shaken to seek professional help.

Daniel, 41, is chief financial officer for a manufacturing corporation. Marie is 43 and a partner in a major law firm. She had worked full-time for 6 years in her firm before her son was born. She then took a 3-month maternity leave and returned to her job on a 20-hour a week basis. She hoped to be made a full partner in the firm 6 months ago, but was told she would not even be considered until she returned to full-time status. This greatly distressed her, as she felt strongly about spending "enough" time with her son, at least until he began the first grade. She felt some guilt about working at all during her son's "most formative years," as her mother continued to remind her.

Both Marie and Daniel come from traditional families, in which their mothers were full-time homemakers and fathers were the sole breadwinners. Marie and Daniel were also the first generation of their respective families to attend college. Both began careers immediately and were quite successful. They met about 2 years before their marriage and discussed their desire to balance having a family with continuing their careers. Things never quite worked out that way after the baby was born. Marie ended up assuming nearly total responsibility for child care. When the child was 2½, the couple decided that the child would change from having half-time to full-time day care so that Marie could return to her career full time. But Daniel never seemed to be free to drop off or pick up the child from the day-care site and was always too tired to help with household chores or spend time alone with Marie. For 3 weeks she attempted to juggle her work and home responsibilities before dropping back to 20 hours a week, much to the consternation of the senior partners and Daniel, but to the delight of her mother. Daniel insisted that they needed her full-time income to meet their increasing expenses because they had recently purchased a ski lodge condo.

These events served to fuel an already chronically incendiary relationship, marked by periods of sharp verbal exchange followed by the same "cold shoulder" treatment or "stonewalling" (Gottman, 1995) that they noted in their parents' relationships. Although they have never seriously considered separation or divorce—"our religion doesn't permit it"—they noted a decline in sexual relations since the baby was born, to a point in the previous year when Daniel complained that he had "lost all interest, because I'm too tired and stressed out."

Daniel's corporation was recently involved in a hostile takeover and he spent a considerable amount of time and effort making the merger work. It was very stressful for him because of the increased travel demands and the fact that he had much less time to play golf and ski with his buddies.

Because Marie had moved with him when Daniel was transferred, right after they were married, she left behind the support network she had been a part of since college. Except for one unmarried woman in the firm, Marie has not had or taken the time to develop other friendships.

After two sessions of comprehensive assessment were completed, issues of inequality of power, gender stereotyping, and inhibited sexual desire were prominent. Results of a formal evaluation confirmed the therapist's impression of low marital cohesion and adaptability, with unclear boundaries. The negative impact of Marie's mother was obvious to the couple. Psychological testing suggested narcissistic and obsessive-compulsive personality traits in Daniel and prominent histrionic personality traits in Marie. Both were quite successful in their careers, but skills of communication, negotiation, encouragement, and conflict resolution were not evident in their relationship, although the time management skills seemed adequate. Daniel's support network was adequate, but Marie's was not. Marie felt considerable couple and career asynchronism that she experienced as a moderate stressor. Because of the chronic nature of their presenting concerns, the couple met criteria for Level 3 marital discord. Blaming and projection were common and reflected both their hostility and increasing hopelessness. Their different personality styles, lack of relational skills, and power, boundary, and intimacy issues led to their ongoing conflict and inability to resolve their differences. Given their relatively strong motivation to make changes and commitment to stay together, their prognosis appeared favorable. Relevant goals were mutually negotiated to increase the likelihood that the couple would assume ownership and be more motivated and adherent to the treatment process. The treatment goals were: (1) reduce the present level of conflict and distress; (2) establish clearer boundaries regarding their careers and their families of origin; (3) establish a more equitable relationship and gender-sensitivity; (4) develop more effective relationship skills of communication, conflict resolution, negotiation, empathy, encouragement, and time management; (5) increase their understanding of individual and couple dynamics; and (6) assist Marie in better understanding and resolving her career and family asynchronism.

These six goals were stated in the developmental order in which they would be addressed therapeutically. That is, symptom relief and boundary restructuring would be a prerequisite for working on equity and gender-sensitivity, along with skill building, which would be followed by insight and awareness. Based on the assessment dimensions of situation/severity, systems, skills, and support network, three therapeutic strategies were matched. The interpersonal-systems strategy would be employed to achieve the first three goals. A psychoeducational strategy was planned for the fourth goal, whereas a psychodynamic strategy was envisioned for the fifth and sixth goals. Because the couple had a sufficient level of readiness for change, commitment to the marriage, and motivation for treatment, it was anticipated that a collaborative therapeutic relationship could be achieved and that an active, albeit supportive, therapist style would be well tolerated.

Considerable in-session modeling of effective communication, conflict resolution, and negotiation skills was needed, given the couple's incendiary style, family history, and limited success in this area. For this reason, the use of a co-therapist would be indicated in this case. Both therapists modeled and enacted potentially conflictual situations for the couple to observe, discuss, and then role-play. Similarly, because both spouses reflect cultural gender stereotyping, in which histrionic behavior in females was considered feminine, whereas obsessive-compulsive behavior in males tended to be rewarded professionally, more androgynous co-therapist interaction could greatly enhance efforts to increase gender-sensitivity.

Because of Daniel's empathic deficits, reflective of his narcissistic personality style, the therapist utilized mirroring, as well as empathy training. However, the therapist's use of encouragement through reframing and stroking was necessary for both spouses, given their narcissistic and histrionic styles.

As anticipated, the treatment process eventually became a collaborative endeavor, but not until they were able to reduce their hurtful, incendiary communications and establish reasonable boundaries involving their job and family demands. Surprisingly, they responded quickly to skill-building tasks and other psychoeducational interventions. By the eighth session, they had met the first four treatment goals and had stabilized their relational system. The next 12 sessions were primarily focused on individual and family-of-origin dynamics that Marie and Daniel brought to their marriage. During this time, relapse-prevention strategies were introduced. The last session reviewed their progress and current level of functioning. Both agreed that they were less stressed and much happier about their relationship and careers. Daniel recognized the need for additional work on issues of entitlement and blame. Subsequently, he continued for six additional individual sessions with the couples therapist.

WORK-FOCUSED PSYCHOTHERAPY

Psychotherapy can be directed toward general treatment goals or toward more focused goals. Today, because of both economic and clinical advances, psychotherapists place an increasing emphasis on focused treatment. Well-known examples include Klerman and Weissman's *Interpersonal Psychotherapy of Depression* (1984) and Beck and Freeman's *Cognitive Therapy of Personality Disorders* (1990). Furthermore, because executives have a strong bias toward problem solving and the pragmatic, they tend to find long-term dynamically oriented psychotherapy foreign and tedious. Production of fantasy material and disclosure of affects may be initially resisted. Similarly, the slow pace of progress and change in long-term therapy may be a significant source of frustration for them. Not surprisingly, executives tend to prefer time-limited and focused approaches, in line with an executive's natural inclination toward action and outcomes. Accordingly, work-focused psychotherapy was developed to meet these expectations (Sperry, 1996).

Lowman (1993) noted the need for psychotherapy to specifically address work and work dysfunction. He defines work dysfunction as any persistent difficulty or failure in the work site associated with psychological characteristics of the individual. These dysfunctions can be independent or interactive with the nature of the worker's job or the organizational context in which the work takes place. He proposes a classification of work dysfunction and differentiates psychopathology and work dysfunctions, with the understanding that the two types of problems can coexist. The clinician's first task is to assess the presence of psychopathology and its relation, if any, to work functioning, while also assessing the presence of work dysfunction and its impact on psychopathology.

As therapeutic goals of treatment have become more delimited, work problems have emerged as one area where clinicians can make important contributions to individual well-being. Furthermore, such therapeutic goals can often be accomplished without a major restructuring of personality and in a relatively time-efficient manner. Lowman (1993) contends that for most individuals, issues involving work and the workplace are resolved in a relatively nonconflictual manner. Individuals typically find a career or job that is to some degree satisfying and fulfilling, and they are able to function reasonably well in a work setting. It is the failure to find, implement, or sustain a satisfactory work role or a change in the person or the work situation that creates psychological difficulties called "work dysfunctions." Clinicians are consulted by executives or corporate officials regarding those employees for whom the usual development process has proved in some way dysfunctional. The clinician's role would be to assist such individuals in understanding and changing what is dysfunctional about their personality, work, or work environment.

Lowman (1993) has developed a classification or taxonomy of work-related dysfunctions that I have found quite useful in both clinical and organizational consultation situations. The taxonomy describes patterns of undercommitment (i.e., underachievement; procrastination; organizational misfit, occupational misfit, or both; fear of success; and fear of failure); patterns of overcommitment (i.e., workacholism, Type-A behavior pattern, and job and occupational burnout); work-related anxiety and depression (i.e., performance anxiety, generalized anxiety, and work-related depression); personality dysfunctional patterns (i.e., problems with authority and personality-disordered work behavior); life role conflicts (including work–family conflicts); transiently situational stress; and perceptual inaccuracies. A final category of the taxonomy is dysfunctional working conditions (i.e., defective job design, defective supervision, and dysfunctional interpersonal relationships).

A central theme of Lowman's approach is that characteristics of individuals that combine to create work difficulties do not exist separately from those of organizations and occupations. In providing psychotherapy to executives who present with work-related concerns, the clinician must evaluate the executive's workplace, even if evaluation must occur outside the actual work context. In treating work-related issues, the clinician must caution against allowing a psychological view to mask from consideration other factors that may be germane. Ignoring features of the work itself or of the work context that may be the primary source of the executive's difficulties is a common error of clinicians who begin to treat work-related issues.

Determining whether work difficulties exist independently of, in combination with, or secondarily to psychopathology is an important diagnostic consideration. The clinician, if not the executive, needs to be clear on the plan for addressing work-related difficulties and, when appropriate, psychological difficulties unrelated to work. In cases in which both psychopathology and work difficulties are present, it is useful to have some sense of which is primary and how the one relates to the other. For instance, an executive who is recently divorced, clinically depressed, and about to be laid off may need help in determining which is the most pressing issue and which will be the initial focus of the therapy. On the other hand, executives whose work difficulties are much broader and involve overarching conflictual life themes, such as procrastination or fear of success, may benefit from working on the central theme or focal issue, addressing both work and nonwork concerns. Among executives, common themes and focal issues are particularly noted in seven areas. They are over- or undercommitment, loss, interpersonal conflict, developmental dysynchrony, characterological issues, life–role conflicts, and symptoms. Table 9.2 further specifies these issues.

The clinician does well to keep these central dynamics firmly in mind and then interpret or reframe behavior—whether work-related or not—in light of the central theme. However, in manifesting resistance, the executive may attempt to shift the treatment focus among significant life concerns or may undermine genuine progress made in one area by lamenting lack of progress in another.

In work-focused psychotherapy (Sperry, 1996) the quality of the therapeutic relationship depends to some extent on executives perceiving the clinician to be on their side, and in many treatment approaches, self-discovery is the goal. Thus, assuming the validity—or, at least, perceived va-

TABLE 9.2
Focal Issues in Psychotherapy with Executives

1. Over- Undercommitment:	Burnout, fear of success or failure, work addiction, procrastination
2. Loss:	Job; death; failed expectations; anticipation of loss, as in succession and retirement
3. Interpersonal Conflict:	With an employee, peers, board of directors, family, spouse
4. Developmental Dysynchrony:	Relational, children, career, or any combination of these
5. Characterological Issues:	Narcissism, compulsivity, paranoia, authority issues, stonewalling, and so on
6. Life–Role Conflicts	Work–family issues
7. Symptoms:	Performance anxiety, depression, psychosomatic issues, bipolar disorder, substance dependence, and so on

lidity—of the executive's understanding of the work situation may be a better stance than unnecessarily or prematurely bringing in outside parties. However, clinicians can still raise questions or interpretations, particularly when they have reason to doubt the reality of the executive's presentation of a work concern, but they can do so in the context of a private relationship between two parties attempting to understand and work through issues at hand. Besides, if the executive's lifestyle dynamics are the source of the work-related problems, it is very likely that these will present themselves in the therapeutic relationship or in a pattern of reactions that will become apparent with time.

Furthermore, the clinician needs to guard against overanalyzing and overinterpreting work issues, except when clear and compelling evidence indicates that such factors are the driving force. For example, an executive presenting with depression and complaints of job burnout may be manifesting clinical depression or may simply be exhibiting common symptoms of burnout. Accordingly, the clinician could intervene with various strategies. Suggesting a job or career change, at least on a temporary basis, is one practical, perhaps well-founded, way to proceed. Recommending physical exercise and vigorous nonwork activities as antidotes to the emotional exhaustion associated with the job might also be appropriate. Or, the clinician might assist the executive in exploring reasons for the career choice or the tendency to become overly involved with high-flown goals, which result in depression when personal efforts are ineffective. These strategies might be pursued over the course of therapy, particularly when issues are related to family-of-origin or family-constellation dynamics.

Short-term, behaviorally focused interventions seem to be particularly effective in treating many work dysfunctions, provided that more complicated psychopathology or severe personality disorders are not present or, at the least, that the broader, contextual issues are kept in mind (Sperry, 1995). Lowman (1993) suggests that metaphorical approaches encapsulating the person's central dynamic through the presenting work concerns are also effective. Kopp (1995) describes various strategies for utilizing metaphor in the psychotherapeutic context that are particularly valuable in working with executives in short-term psychotherapy.

The clinician may need to "work around" lifelong characterological issues with individuals experiencing both personality disorders and work dysfunctions. Whether in executive consultation or in work-focused psychotherapy, it is quite useful to distinguish between "working through" and "working around." The process of "working through" usually involves extensive and repeated utilization of interpretation, confrontation, or cognitive restructuring to effect changes in personality structure. In contrast, the process of "working around" is not directed at the arduous task of changing or modifying personality structure, but rather at psychologically sidestepping the facet of the individual's personality structure that is operative in a given situation. Accordingly, the specified intervention strategies use reframing, redirection, distraction, minimization, and paradox (Sperry, 1995). For example, the clinician or consultant working with an executive who reports experiencing a narcissistic injury could say: "I know you're upset. But when you look at the bigger picture, you really have a lot going for you, so why sweat the small stuff" (minimization); or, "Letting him get to you like this is really giving him a lot of power over you. Do you want that?" (redirection).

Practical career counseling and career management can also be useful with some executives, particularly those with relatively pervasive personality disorders. For instance, stern warnings about the real-life work consequences of continued aberrant work behavior may be as instructive and influential in working with certain personality disorders as long-term psychotherapy may be. Such executives might be more compliant if they faced job loss or restriction.

Finally, marital and family issues are common among hardworking, hard-driving executives who travel frequently and spend long hours away from home. Not surprisingly, communication difficulties, role conflicts, and sexual problems are common. Family therapy can promote more functional interaction and improved conflict resolution and communication. Similarly, couples therapy can be quite useful for relational and sexual issues, particularly when the executive is involved in a dual-career marriage. In short, adjunctive family or couples therapy might complement work-focused individual psychotherapy with the executive.

Case Example #1: Work-Focused Psychotherapy with a Male Executive

James Nealy, III, the vice president of corporate accounts, caught the attention of the corporation's outside psychological consultant after a top-management meeting. Nealy mentioned that he was having some difficulty with concentration and asked if the psychologist could see him "for a few sessions." The consultant indicated that he could not because of double agentry and offered a referral. The vice president agreed that this was a delicate matter and accepted the outside referral with a psychologist who specialized in work-focused psychotherapy. In the course of the first meeting, the psychologist learned that the executive had been with this corporation for nearly 15 years and had held his current position for the last 2 years. Nealy oversaw a sales force of over 135 insurance agents and 4 regional sales managers and reported directly to the executive vice president of administration. He presented with insomnia, depressed mood, low energy, and increased worry, and these symptoms had been present for nearly 4 months. Furthermore, he had little response to the antidepressant prescribed by his family physician.

To remain competitive the corporation had undergone a series of downsizings over the previous year. One of the most difficult parts of Nealy's job was laying off or discharging regional managers and insurance agents whom he had befriended over the years. He found this task increasingly difficult and painful and didn't believe he could continue doing it. Nealy described lying awake nights, ruminating about his laid-off friends: Had they found jobs yet? Were they angry with him? And could he face the prospects of discharging any more of the people who reported to him? He even imagined himself as "a 'hatchet man,' doing the senior VP's dirty work, and scorned by everyone who knows me." He reported that his personal life had never been better: He was happily married and had just returned from a family reunion that he attended with his wife and three grown children. Furthermore, he could not identify any precipitants other than his job.

The psychologist decided that a brief, work-focused psychotherapeutic approach would be more appropriate than a traditional, insight-oriented focus on the early life determinants of the executive's current problem and symptoms. Such an approach might require between 20 and 50 sessions, rather than the 4 sessions that the work-focused treatment utilized. The psychologist's goal was considerably more focused: achieving symptom reduction and assisting the executive in moving forward with his life, particularly on the job. To that end, he worked together with the executive to come up with a detailed list of factors and circumstances that were and were not under the executive's immediate control. Not surprisingly, the list of work factors was relatively short. The psychologist utilized reframing so that the executive could begin to visualize other options. One of these was that the executive could exercise the option of acting more proactively, rather than to continue acting reactively and passively as he had during the last several months. The psychologist framed the executive's stance of waiting for his boss, the executive vice president of administration, to announce the next round of layoffs, as a portion of no control. Rather, Nealy was helped to explore more proactive alternatives that were within his control. A four-fold plan of proactive action was devised: He could engage in various cost-cutting measures in his office and in some "fatter" regions; revise sales territories; update the marketing plan; and consult with his regional managers about prospective layoffs. The executive was able to make progress in all of these areas. Perhaps the most heartening for him was to share responsibility for layoffs with his regional managers. This not only reduced his stress and guilt, but also provided him with considerable emotional support from his colleagues. In addition to reframing, the psychologist utilized the metaphors of controlling both the tempo of the game and the strokes used while playing tennis—the executive's favorite activity—and his job activities, in an interchangeable fashion such that the executive could feel more empowered and in control. By the fourth session, the vice president was considerably less stressed, was sleeping better, and no longer viewed himself as the corporation's "hatchet man."

Case Example # 2: Work-Focused Psychotherapy with a Female Executive

Christine Webster was a 35-year-old single white female, who was the manager of MIS services for an up-and-coming biotech firm that developed cutting-edge pharmaceutical products. She was referred by the vice president of human resources because of anxiety and "memory" problems. The initial evaluation involved an assessment of Christine's current and past levels of functioning, her strengths, her personality style, her capacity to develop a therapeutic relationship, her readiness for treatment, and her presenting concern: memory lapses and anxiety.

Although she indicated that "memory problems" had been constant throughout her life, they had worsened in the last 2 months. She also reported engaging in considerable fantasizing and daydreaming, particularly when authority figures, like her boss, gave her a task with a deadline. These fantasies were largely about men and sex. She indicated a single incident of fondling by her older brother when she was 10 years old, after which she was frightened and confused. Reportedly, she had only recently recalled this incident. However, Christine remembered instances of "memory lapse" that occurred much earlier in her life, and these usually involved her mother and father. Furthermore, she had experienced considerable difficulty in establishing and maintaining intimate relationships with eligible men over the last 5 years. Prior to that, she indicated that she had seldom dated, even though she was quite attractive, interesting, and available. The four men she had become intensely attracted to turned out to be "womanizers," who would flaunt other women with whom they were involved in front of Christine. Her response was to become "insanely jealous" of these women and "promise to do anything" to hold onto these men. She also reported indulging in occasional binge drinking—particularly on weekends.

She denied prior psychotherapy or psychiatric treatment. Her family consisted of both parents, who were alive and well and still resided in the home where Christine had been reared. Christine is the youngest of five siblings, the four others being male. Her mother was described as emotionally distant, demanding, and "unconcerned" with Christine's feminine needs. Thus, Christine seldom wore dresses, used make-up, or adopted "feminine manners" until she started college. The mother had a "breakdown" when Christine left home for college, presumably a depressive episode. The father was described as caring and concerned, but he made little effort to shield Christine from her mother's demands. He apparently was grieved over his wife's expectation that Christine "dress and act like a boy," but did not voice his concern, at least publicly. The four brothers were described as "jocks" who were extremely competitive. Christine describes herself as a "tomboy" in grade school, but she was "boycrazy with hormones" throughout high school.

An investigation of her current life functioning showed that she had a stable network of female friends, had some difficulty relating to her parents, and was in an unsatisfying and distressing relationship with her current boyfriend. However, she described moderate impairment at work, particularly a confusing and distressing relationship with her female boss. She had received high evaluations for her job performance from her subordinates and from her superior's boss, but not from her immediate superior. The mental status exam was unremarkable. Based on these findings, her *DSM-IV* diagnosis was V 62.2 Occupational Problem, Anxiety Disorder NOS, with Histrionic, Passive-Aggressive, and Self-Defeating traits.

Although quite anxious at the beginning of the initial session, she was easily calmed and showed other indications that she could and probably would be able to form an effective collaborative therapeutic relationship. Because she had been quite successful in meeting personal goals she had set for herself (i.e., losing about 18 pounds and maintaining the weight loss for 3 years; giving up smoking years before that), she seemed to have sufficient capacity and readiness for change in therapy. A contract for five sessions was agreed upon with Christine and was subsequently authorized by her insurance. The focus of the sessions was to be in reduction of both anxiety and "memory loss." Accordingly, five weekly sessions were scheduled.

Session 2

At the beginning of a second meeting, Christine mentioned that she had not binged on the weekend or consumed any alcohol since our last session. Furthermore, she reported that she had refrained from hair pulling when she was anxious, even though she was quite anxious at work after meeting with her boss. It seemed that drinking and hair pulling served as anxiety reducers for her. This disclosure was interesting because I had not suggested that she reduce or stop either behavior. Furthermore, it confirmed my prediction that she was indeed ready and motivated for therapeutic change.

I then suggested a tentative interpretation of her symptoms and sought her feedback. She was initially surprised at the psychological meaning of her "memory loss," but agreed that the formulation was accurate. Specific treatment objectives were mutually negotiated. The work of the remaining three sessions was to explore the ways in which "memory lapses" served to safeguard Christine from expressing her anger and subsequent anxiety at her parents, especially her mother, as well as at her female boss. An additional objective was to experiment with more effective ways of dealing with her anxiety and anger.

Sessions 3 to 6

The discussion of "memory lapses" as a safeguard proved painful, but freeing, for Christine. She shared her feelings of hopelessness and rejection regarding her difficult relationship with her mother, her current and past boyfriends, and her inability to emancipate herself from abusive relationships. By the fifth session, it became clear that systemic issues involving authority and power at home and in the workplace were very deeply intertwined with Christine's personal dynamics and that additional sessions would be necessary. Although Christine was relieved that she did not have a dissociative disorder and experienced some symptomatic relief (i.e., reductions in anxiety and binge drinking, and no further hair pulling), she was hesitant "to be psychoanalyzed for life." This concern led to a discussion about differences between psychoanalysis and other long-term psychotherapies and work-focused psychotherapy. I explained that framing therapy around work-related issues both reduced therapeutic regression and complex transferences and required fewer sessions than when more global interpersonal and intrapsychic issues were the focus. I assured Christine that subsequent sessions would focus primarily on job functioning and career development and secondarily on her enmeshed relationship with her mother and the abusive nature of her relationships with male friends and lovers. She indicated that she was "not out of the woods yet" and agreed to continue in work-focused treatment.

Sessions 7 to 11

These sessions focused largely on examining Christine's relationship with her female boss. Christine viewed the woman as essentially incompetent at the newly created position to which she had been promoted 6 months prior to Christine being hired. Because the position was new and her boss frequently traveled for the company, this woman had little oversight or accountability. She refused to meet regularly with Christine to review Christine's performance. Instead, she would delegate much of her work to Christine and provided only vague feedback to Christine: "Don't worry about things, I'll let you know when you screw up." Some rather obvious similarities existed between this woman and Christine's mother, which we discussed in detail. With both women, Christine was non-assertive and essentially backed away from any conflict. Because she could not directly express her concern or anger, Christine utilized indecision, underachievement, and "memory lapses." As a result, Christine was frustrated, dissatisfied, and anxious, which she dealt with by drinking, hair pulling, and becoming increasingly attracted to and jealous about the abusive men she dated. Assertive communication training accompanied this insight work, as did cognitive restructuring.

Sessions 12 to 15

In the 12th session Christine reported that despite her increasing assertiveness with her boss, she was unwilling to continue "in such a sick relationship with that woman." As a result, she resigned from her position. Her plan was to begin an MBA program and look for a part-time position in a broader area of management than accounting. She also indicated that she would no longer allow her boyfriend to continue his emotional abusiveness by his unfaithfulness. She would now require that the relationship be exclusive, or she would leave. In the 14th session she reported ending her current relationship and said she would now look for men who treated her with respect and caring.

In the 13th session she felt more confident that she could control her anger and anxiety without drinking. Career issues dominated the next two sessions. She had planned to be a literature major and become a teacher, probably at the college level, but had been "talked out of it" by her family during her second semester of undergraduate studies. Although her adviser had judged her to be the most capable student in the accounting program, Christine did not apply herself and underachieved, completing her degree with a C+ average, She now believed that she could make her own decisions about how she would spend her life.

Session 16

This session reviewed the progress of the previous 10 sessions. This review showed no "memory lapses," with her short-term memory intact. She had not pulled out any more hair and had recently started dating a fellow student who so far was quite loving, respectful, and supportive. As she became more assertive, Christine did note increased discord with her mother. As a result, Christine stopped her daily telephone calls home. Although she was proud of herself, this act was painful and anxiety-provoking.

Sessions 17 to 19

These sessions focused largely on reorienting Christine's self-view and worldview, specifically as they related to job and career. A focus on strengths and interests was the basis for modifying and restructuring her view of self and others. Christine was able to accept that she possessed a number of talents and capabilities. She was also able to accept that choosing to recognize and develop her strengths and interests was not only possible, but necessary for her to grow and individuate from her family. Doing so would not result in disastrous consequences for her parents. She had feared that becoming successful would dishonor and somehow annihilate her mother. Furthermore, she came to acknowledge and accept that being successful would not emasculate her father or brothers.

Sessions 20 to 23

In the 20th session Christine reported that she was doing well in her MBA courses, particularly in organizational behavior. Her professor was impressed with her ability and had urged her to consider pursuing a PhD in organizational behavior, predicting that she would find teaching at the university level very rewarding.

In the next session Christine announced what she had decided about her job and career: She had left an abusive relationship with a female boss in a profession she was ambivalent about for a job and career track that was of her own choice and was based on her needs and strengths, rather than on family expectations. Interpersonally, she began choosing less abusive or nonabusive friends and intimates, and she individuated from her family—particularly from her brother—to a considerable degree. Her presenting symptoms of memory loss, hair pulling, nail biting, and occasional binge drinking were significantly altered or eliminated. Although additional sessions could be helpful in working through and reorienting the client's interpersonal relationship with family members and further modification of lifestyle convictions, she had considerable facility with the therapeutic process and could now become her own therapist. Her HMO authorized one further session; however, the client was comfortable with the plan for brief followup sessions by phone at 4- and 12-month intervals.

The client did in fact follow up by phone at the 4th and 12th months and indicated that her symptoms remained in regression and that she and Chris, her boyfriend, were considering marriage. Family relationships were cordial, yet Christine still maintained a healthy distance, suggesting that individuation had occurred. After a lot of inner turmoil, she realized that she had to make a career decision based on her needs and strengths, rather than on family expectations. In the 22nd session she reported finding a part-time job that was not only challenging and well-paid, but that involved working for a older male who not only respected, but encouraged and supported her career plans. By now, she had dated Jerry for nearly 6 weeks and found it rewarding, but somewhat frightening, to share deeply of her dreams and fears with another person. Jerry quite easily shared feelings and represented a significant change from previous boyfriends. Further reorientation utilizing the ER themes of talent and competence was the focus of these sessions.

Session 24

This was the last of our planned formal sessions. At this point, therapeutic progress was reviewed and plans for follow-up sessions, should they be needed, were discussed. My progress note for this session stated: "This is the last of 24 planned sessions. While the original referral was to evaluate and treat a dissociative disorder, an atypical anxiety disorder was diagnosed and individual psychotherapeutic treatment involving systemic, psychodynamic, and cognitive-behavioral strategies was employed. The client collaborated fully and effectively in the treatment process and several positive changes were noted. While she occasionally drank, she denied binging or intoxication."

Eighteen Months Later

Approximately 18 months after our last formal session, Christine called, indicating that she and Jerry were engaged to be married 4 months hence. She requested some premarital counseling, saying, "I don't want to repeat my parents' experience." Subsequently, we scheduled three conjoint sessions. These sessions focused on helping Christine and Jerry understand their families-of-origin and relational expectations and patterns. It was heartening to note that Christine had maintained all the therapeutic gains of our formal therapy, and it appeared that Jerry would show her the respect, caring, and companionship she sought in a partner.

CONCLUDING NOTE

I hope that these three case studies, particularly the extended case example of Christine Webster, delineate the manner in which the professional counselor or psychotherapist might proceed in executive counseling in the context of brief and focused therapy. Whether in an individual or a couples context, executive counseling that focuses on work-related themes, associated with individual psychodynamics, relational and systemic dynamics, or both of these is often shorter in duration. This is largely because work is a relatively adaptive and less primitive focus for therapy. Consequently, complex transferences and regression are less likely to occur, as they might in less-focused treatment. As indicated earlier, executives generally prefer this focused approach to more exploratory, longer-term therapy .

The chapter began by noting executives' wishful thinking and preference for working on difficult issues and personal concerns in the context of executive coaching, given the stigma still associated with professional counseling and psychotherapy. As mentioned previously, the indications for, and the methods of, executive coaching and psychotherapy are different from those of executive coaching. A related concern—actually, the opposite side of this issue—is that some who practice executive counseling or even traditional psychotherapy offer to work with executives under the guise of providing "executive coaching," but actually provide psychotherapy instead. It is not uncommon for me to hear of psychotherapists who admit to having no formal training or experience in executive coaching take pride in saying that they started doing psychotherapy with another executive who approached them about executive coaching. This seems to be misrepresentation. It also appears to have ethical ramifications.

REFERENCES

Beck, A., Freeman, A., & Associates. (1990). *Cognitive therapy of personality disorders*. New York: Guilford.

Glickhauf-Hughes, C., Hughes, G., & Wells, M. (1986). A developmental approach to treating dual-career couples. *American Journal of Family Therapy, 14*(3), 254–263.

Klerman, G., Weissman, M., Rounsaville, B., et al. (1984). *Interpersonal psychotherapy of depression*. New York: Basic Books.

Gottman, J. (1995). *Why marriages succeed or fail.* New York: Fireside.

Kopp., R. (1995). *Metaphor therapy: Using client-generated metaphors in psychotherapy*. New York: Brunner/Mazel.
Lowman, R. (1993). *Counseling and psychotherapy of work dysfunctions*. Washington, DC: American Psychological Association.
Rice, D. (1979) *Dual-career marriage: Conflict and treatment*. New York: Free Press.
Sperry, L. (1995). *Handbook of diagnosis and treatment of the DSM-IV personality disorders*. New York: Brunner/Mazel.
Sperry, L. (1996). Work-focused psychotherapy with executives. *Individual Psychology, 52*(1), 48–57.
Stoltz-Loike, M. (1992) *Dual-career couples: New perspectives in counseling.* Alexandria, VA: American Counseling Association Books.

10

Executive Consultation Strategies

Executive consultation can be one of the most gratifying activities for psychologically trained consultants. This form of consultation is broad, ranging from evaluating executives and candidates, to advising executives, to advising on policy. Unlike organizational consultation, where the focus is the team or the entire organization, executive consultation focuses primarily on the individual executive. In my experience, executive consultation requires considerably more knowledge, skills, and experience than do executive coaching and counseling. Accordingly, those who consult with executives "must have detailed knowledge about the executive's work as well as of the organizational setting. Above all, they have to know how people stay well at least as much as how they get sick" (Greiff & Munter, 1980, p. 195). Mindful of this admonition, this chapter and chapter 11 emphasize health, as well as illness and impairment, in executives.

The chapter begins by describing executive consultation, as distinct from executive coaching and counseling. It then distinguishes the two main types of executive consultation. The first type is executive evaluation, which involves both executive selection and the evaluation of executive impairment. The second type is personal advisement, which covers consultation in regard to leadership and corporate decisions and issues, as well as career and family issues and concerns. Five case studies illustrate these different types of executive consultation.

EXECUTIVE CONSULTATION AS DISTINCT FROM COACHING AND COUNSELING

Although similarities exist among executive counseling, consultation, and coaching, there are also differences. This section provides a capsule summary of the distinctive features of executive counseling, executive consultation, and executive coaching. See chapter 7 for a more detailed description of these differences. Table 10.1 highlights some basic distinctions.

TYPES OF EXECUTIVE CONSULTATION

There are at least two main types of executive consultation: evaluation and advisement. The evaluation role usual entails a diagnostic or clinical assessment of executive functioning, whereas the advising role is much broader and involves corporate, personal, or policy advisement. The first type of executive consultation is evaluation. The next section provides an extended discussion of executive evaluation. It includes a profile of healthy, distressed, and impaired executives and approaches to executive selection and evaluation of executive impairment. The second type is advisement. A subsequent section of this chapter covers three types of advisement: advisement

TABLE 10.1.
Executive Consultation Distinguished from Executive Coaching and Counseling

Strategy	Distinctive Features
Executive Coaching	A form of executive consultation in which a *coach* works collaboratively with an executive to improve the executive's skill and effectiveness in communicating corporate vision and goals and facilitating team performance, organizational productivity, and personal development. Usually of short duration.
Executive Consultation	A form of organizational consultation in which a *consultant,* functioning as a sounding board, expert adviser, evaluator, or all of these forms a collaborative relationship with an individual executive to address a *broad range* of professional and personal issues of concern to the executive. Often of longer duration, an ongoing process.
Executive Counseling	The process in which a *therapist* and an executive establish a close, collaborative relationship and utilize psychotherapeutic methods to achieve greater *self-understanding and resolution* of work-related problems, symptoms, or both. Usually briefer, less intense, and more focused on work-related issues than traditional counseling and psychotherapy are. Often, weekly meetings. Short to medium duration.

TABLE 10.2
Types of Executive Consultation

Types	Examples of Executive Consultation
Evaluation	1. Executive selection 2. Evaluation of executive impairment
Personal Advisement	1. Leadership and corporate decisions and issues 2. Career and family issues and concerns

on corporate leadership issues, advisement on career and family issues, and advisement on personal and health issues.

Although an executive consultant could conceivably function in a therapeutic role with executives, this role is typically avoided because of the potential conflict of interest and complex confidentiality issues that it poses. Table 10.2 indicates the two types of executive consultation and examples of each type.

EVALUATION IN EXECUTIVE CONSULTATION

The evaluation function requires executive consultants to be competent in assessment and diagnostic skills, as well as knowledgeable about corporate life and job issues, and to effectively evaluate distress and impairment in executives. At the beginning of this chapter I quoted Greiff and Munter (1980), to the effect that consultants working with executives need to know how executives "stay well at least as much as how they get sick" (p. 195). This section describes executive health, as well as executive distress and impairment and executive selection.

The Healthy Executive

What characterizes the healthy executive who has achieved sustained professional success and personal well-being? According to a well-regarded group of researchers on executive health and well-being, executive health is defined as physical, psychological, spiritual, and ethical well-being (Quick, Gavin, Cooper, & Quick, 2000). This definition recognizes the importance of the spiritual and ethical dimensions. These researchers contend that "when each of these four dimensions is strong, executives can be most effective as individuals, as manager, as peers and colleagues, and as leaders within their organizations" (p. 37).

Four Dimensions of Executive Health

The four dimensions will be briefly described. The first dimension is *physical well-being*. Physical well-being is a function of biological inheritance and physical fitness. Total physical well-being includes cardiovascular fitness, musculoskeletal strength, and muscular flexibility. These aspects of physical health form the foundation on which psychological, spiritual, and ethical well-being develop. Furthermore, physical well-being reduces the executive's exposure to heart attacks and other fatal and nonfatal medical conditions that place the executive's health at risk.

The second dimension is *psychological well-being*. Psychological well-being is the "ability to deal constructively with reality, the capacity to adapt to change, the capacity to love, and the ability to direct one's emotional energy in creative and constructive outlets" (Quick et al., 2000, p. 37). Psychological health is crucial because it impacts the quality of the executive's decision making. Furthermore, executives with high levels of psychological well-being "enable the organization and its members to be well adjusted. Alternatively, diminished psychological health, such as through defensiveness and a poor reality orientation, may weaken if not destroy an organization" (p. 37).

The third dimension is *spiritual well-being*. Spiritual well-being is the capacity to transcend the immediate situation and view situations and life more globally. "Spiritually whole executives can move beyond themselves to embrace the needs and desires of others. They can recognize their ability to go beyond the basic functions of the organization, using their positions and power to enhance the love of the organization's members and community as well" (p. 38).

The fourth dimension is *ethical well-being*. Ethical well-being reflects character which is "who you are when no one is watching, the personal code that provides the strength and insight to make the ethical and right decisions, especially in difficult situations" (p. 38). As with psychological well-being, ethical well-being is essential for effective decision making. Ethical well-being "allows executives to make difficult decisions in the short-run in order to ensure the best for all in the long run" (p. 38).

Markers of Executive Health

The research literature provides a number of markers of executive health. James Rippe, MD, a cardiologist and exercise physiologist, surveyed 1,139 successful chief executives and found that stamina and energy characterized them. Rippe (1989) found that 67% of these chief executives—average age 50 years—exercised regularly; 90% watched their diets and believed there was a clear connection between a healthy lifestyle of diet and exercise and executive performance. These CEOs were significantly healthier than male and female executives who didn't make it to the top. As noted earlier, a high need for power and control is basic to the executive role. Although executives regularly experience high degrees of stress with their work, their high level of control over their job negates much of the harmful effect of their stress. Furthermore, risk taking is a key feature of executive life. Rather than avoiding risk, effective executives "attempt to control the risks by placing their best bet and then changing the odds even more in their favor" (Quick, Nelson, & Quick, 1990, p. 19). Stressors are both external and internal. One internal source of stress for executives is the ego ideal that activates their personality and impels them to positions of leadership, wherein they exercise their need for power and influence. This ego ideal actively shapes the organization's ideal, which energizes the organization. Also, healthy executives tend to be relatively stress-resistant, owing in large part to their being self-reliant while embedded in a rich network of professional and personal relationships that sustain and nurture. In short, the healthy executive is interdependent: able to be autonomous, while investing in relationships in a healthy manner. More recently, Quick et al. (2000) revised their view of executives and now indicate that three key markers of executive health are present: individual vitality, low morbidity and mortality, and organizational health.

The Distressed Executive

The discussion now shifts from healthy to distressed executives. Who are distressed executives, how are they different from impaired executives, and what is the consultant's role with them? Basically, distressed executives are active, functioning members of their corporation, their family, and their community. Yet they are not able to consistently function well on the job, at home, or in the community because of varying stressors in their lives. Despite their distress and occasional crises, though, they are able to bounce back from setbacks, unlike impaired executives, who cannot. Epidemiological data are difficult to find on distress in executive populations. Nevertheless, Smith and Siwolop (1988) estimate that approximately 15% of executives would be considered distressed. Unrealistic deadlines, overly heavy workloads, and poor communications are cited by these authors as job-induced stressors, not to mention a host of competing personal, family, and social stressors.

Leonard Moss, MD, an organizational consultant, notes the most frequent reasons why distressed executives seek consultation: marital problems, personality clashes with peers and supervisors, suppressed emotional reactions to peers and superiors, problems with controling hostility, difficulty asserting or responding to authority, hidden conflicts over dependency and disappointed ambition, and unconscious fear of success, with an associated tendency toward self-defeat that is often triggered by problems related to career choices or relations with superiors (Moss, 1981, p. 233).

In *DSM-IV* terms, these would constitute V-codes or adjustment reactions. Kiechel (1990) reports another common form of distress for executives: insomnia. Insomnia in executives appears to be a function of stress, evening socializing, heavy travel across time zones, and general workaholism. Aggressive Type-A personalities experience anxiety in disproportionate numbers, which further exacerbates their insomnia.

Suffice it to say, the primary prevention strategies for managing stress in executives are a balanced work/family perspective; effective use of leisure time; time management, planning, and goal setting; and an effective social support system. Secondary prevention strategies include exercise, relaxation, prayer, and faith (Quick, Nelson, & Quick, 1990). Prepackaged stress-management programs and seminars do not appear to be as effective as individual and group therapy that includes some coping-skills training (Pelletier & Lutz, 1991).

So, what is the executive consultant's role with reference to the distressed executive? First of all, the consultant should assess levels of distress, evaluate the need for primary and secondary prevention-oriented stress programs for the executives, and advocate for such programs. Referrals of overly distressed executives for focused individual or group therapy would be a second task. A third task would involve developing and advocating a policy regarding the distressed executive. This policy would become part of an overall corporate mental health policy for executives, as discussed in greater detail later in this chapter.

The Impaired Executive

How does impairment present itself in the executive suite? Let's begin with the term *impairment*. Nearly 30 years ago, the American Medical Association offered a definition of impairment with regard to physicians. The impaired physician is "one who is unable to practice medicine with reasonable skill and safety to patients because of physical or mental illness, including deterioration through the aging process, or loss of motor skills, or excessive use of drugs including alcohol." Typically, the media portrays both the impaired physician and the impaired executive as a substance-abusing, middle-aged male. However, among physicians who have been sanctioned by state licensure boards, the six most common presentations of impairment are personality disordered, substance abusing, suicidal, major mental disordered, elderly with dementia, and sexually acting out (Logan, 1989).

In short, the range of physicians' impairment is much broader than media stereotypes would indicate.

There are very little reported epidemiological data on impairment among executives. The Human Resources Group study of impairment among eight major U.S. corporations specified the following disorders: drug and substance abuse disorders, stress-related disorders, and marital problems (Kiechel, 1988). Perhaps the most detailed epidemiological study of impairment in executives was reported by Bromet, Parkinson, Curtis, et al. (1990). They studied 1,870 executives from one major U.S. corporation and reported on *DSM-IV* major depression and alcohol abuse/dependence. Among men, the lifetime and 1-year prevalence rates for depression were 23% and 9%, respectively, whereas the rates were 36% and 17% for women. Lifetime and 1-year prevalence rates of alcohol abuse/dependence were 16% and 4% for men and 9% and 4% for women.

In *Executives in Crisis*, Speller (1989) offers no incidence or prevalence data, but lists alcoholism, drug abuse, depression, bipolar disorder, and schizophrenia as the commonest forms of impairment among executives. There was no indication that sex differences were observed in this study. Pasick (1990) likewise notes that male executives entering therapy most commonly present with depression, anxiety, and substance abuse or dependence disorders. However, he finds that further exploration of these presenting problems reveals underlying work-related issues, such as workaholism; stress-related disorders; success addiction—similar to workaholism, except that the craving is specifically for success, rather than for increased work time; work dissatisfaction; and underemployment. Unlike Logan's (1989) data on physicians, there is little indication that severe personality disorder or dementia are considered forms of impairment among executives.

It may be helpful to operationally define executive impairment as a dysfunctional pattern of behavior that reflects a lack of "fit" or a negative interaction between predisposed executives and their corporations that has clear precipitants and perpetuants and meets criteria for one or more *DSM-IV* Axis I, II, or both diagnoses.

The dysfunctional pattern will be observed as decompensated behavior, in which impaired executives lose touch with their surroundings and behave strangely, unpredictably, or inappropriately. They may become apathetic and pessimistic, indecisive and confused, or forgetful. Their insight, judgment, or both may deteriorate, or they may lose their business sense and savvy. They might get violent or overreact to relatively insignificant matters. Or they may become overwhelmed in the face of intense and painful affects. Unlike the distressed executive, who is able to recover from unexpected setbacks and master challenges, the impaired executive is not. Predisposition refers to various biopsychosocial vulnerabilities in the executive. It might include some biological loading for an affective or addictive disorder. It might involve any number of intrapsychic representations, conflicts, or dysfunctional cognitions, such as a belief that self-worth is totally dependent on achievement. It could reflect deficiencies in coping skills such as assertiveness or decision making or represent reenactments of early parental/authority issues with a CEO or a member of the board of directors. It could even reflect the absence of a caring social support system.

Corporations can also be thought of as having vulnerabilities. In this regard, each of the neurotic organizational styles described by Kets de Vries and Miller (1984) predisposes such organizations to characteristic corporate culture reward systems, leadership styles, and so on. For example, a paranoid organization would be more vulnerable to rumors about a takeover bid than a depressive organization would be.

Precipitants can include an event of obvious importance, such as a spouse unexpectedly demanding separation or divorce, the death of a parent or sibling, job loss or unexpected reassignment, or a major investment that soured. Precipitants may also be less obvious, but nevertheless may represent a loss or unfulfilled expectation such as a minor traffic accident, the school suspension of a teenage daughter, and so on.

Perpetuants refer to any number of personal, family, or corporate reinforcements for the impaired pattern. Co-workers "covering" for the increasing absences, forgotten appointments, tempter tantrums, and the like, of a troubled executive are exceedingly commonplace. Such enabling behaviors only delay treatment for the impaired executive and are indicative of the need to establish a corporate mental health policy for executives.

A few words on "lack of fit" are in order. A basic premise in this book is that pathology and impairment do not reside solely in the executive or the employee. An executive's vulnerabilities might well be expressed in symptomatic or even impaired behavior in one corporate setting, but not in another, or at one point in time, but not at another. Whereas the clinician is trained to search for the patient's vulnerabilities and predisposition, the executive consultant must search for patterns, precipitants, perpetuants, and vulnerabilities within the corporation, as well as within the executive. The competent executive consultant will be able to articulate the protective, as well as the distressing and impairment-provoking, features of the corporate environment. Finally, the *DSM-IV* criteria are included in the operational definition of impairment for two reasons. First, although severe depression, acute psychosis, and many manic episodes are considered bona fide types of executive impairment by organizational researchers, other Axis I and most Axis II disorders apparently are not. The personality-disordered executive is probably as prevalent as the personality-disordered physician, who is considered the most common type of impaired physician (Logan, 1989). Kets de Vries (1989) provides several case examples where personality-disordered executives wreaked corporate havoc. Second, the status of epidemiology of executive distress and impairment will not improve until data collection efforts are systematically undertaken and consistent criteria—for example, *DSM-IV* diagnosing criteria—are utilized.

Case Study: Evaluation of Executive Impairment

The president of a major investment corporation hired an executive consultant about the firm's vice president of international services, George Berenson. The president, William Bartos, had received the consultant's name from a trusted colleague who was the CEO of a commercial insurance corporation that regularly retained the consultant's service. In the past 4 months, three female employees in Berenson's division had complained to the vice president of human resources, Jillian Fairweather, that Berenson was "coming on to them" and they wanted it stopped. Ms. Fairweather immediately brought the matter to the president, requesting that he deal directly with "this delicate matter." Initially, Mr. Bartos had not acted on the complaint because he considered Berenson a valuable performer and the most loyal of his senior vice presidents. Although Mr. Berenson was not particularly close to anyone in the firm, he had been generally well respected during the 6 years with the corporation. He was a low-key individual who had tripled the firm's international accounts and had kept the firm relatively unscathed following the October 1987 market crash. Because no corporate policy existed on distressed and impaired executives, Ms. Fairweather usually handled concerns on a case-by-case basis, occasionally involving the president. When one woman threatened legal action, Mr. Bartos contacted the consultant for advice on dealing with Mr. Berenson. The consultant questioned the president about Berenson's job performance, which had notably deteriorated over the past few months. The consultant proposed that Mr. Bartos confront Berenson about his job performance and inappropriate behavior. Furthermore, the president was to recommend an evaluation by the consultant. When confronted by the president, Berenson denied that his performance had slipped, defended his behavior toward the women, and refused the psychiatric evaluation. When Mr. Bartos indicated that he might be forced to take disciplinary action, Berenson reluctantly agreed to the evaluation. At the onset of their meeting, the consultant informed Mr. Berenson that he was being evaluated for the firm and that a release-of-information form was necessary. Berenson signed the form and went on to describe the situation as "I see it." Berenson was a rather thin, handsome, 47-year-old male with a slight right hand tremor who appeared somewhat older than his stated age. He flatly denied any use of alcohol or drugs. The consultant requested a meeting with Mrs. Berenson, to which Berenson reluctantly agreed. Mrs. Berenson admitted that she had initiated divorce proceedings "for all his philandering and drinking." Apparently, Berenson was a weekend binge drinker and cocaine user and had been all during their 4 years of marriage. The consultant met with Mr. Berenson again and confronted him about his alcohol and cocaine problem. With great reluctance, Berenson admitted that his drinking was out of control and that he was concerned about his blackouts, the recent appearance of the hand tremor, and tarry stools. A 7-day inpatient detox program for impaired professionals, with follow-up outpatient treatment, was recommended. Predictably, Mr. Berenson refused. The consultant then spoke with Mr. Bartos and reported that Berenson had a significant substance-dependence problem that needed immediate treatment. Bartos met with Berenson and threatened disciplinary action if the treatment recommendation wasn't followed. As it worked out, Berenson entered the detox program and followed up with outpatient treatment, which included daily AA and NA attendance—at meetings specifically geared to executives—for 90 days, weekly substance-abuse counseling, and biweekly couples therapy sessions. Two weeks later Mr. Berenson returned to a partial work schedule, and within one month returned to full capacity. Twelve months after the initial intervention he remained abstinent, his productivity returned to baseline, and he and his wife continued in their marriage, with the aid of occasional couples therapy sessions.

Evaluation Involving Executive Selection

The executive assessment is to a normal population what the clinical assessment is to an abnormal population. The executive assessment emphasizes health, rather than pathology, and has dramatically more wide-ranging potential. It is an in-depth, comprehensive assessment of a person's overall functioning. It assesses people's capacities, style, level of emotional maturity, and the degree to which they capitalize on basic potentials. It is the consultant's way of gathering a maximum amount of data, usefully integrating that data, and predicting future functioning.

The executive assessment serves many purposes: as a descriptor and predictor of performance, as a developmental manual for the individual's manager, as an inventory of organizational talent and, as the beginning of a trusting relationship with the consultant.

The Seven Dimensions of Executive Assessment

Tobias (1990) describes a useful outline for organizing the report of the executive assessment in terms of six dimensions. To these, others would add a seventh dimension.

1. *Intellectual Dimension*: indicating the degree and kind of intelligence, cognitive styles, and the extent to which the individual works up to capacity
2. *Emotional Dimension*: indicating emotional stability, maturity, modes of adjustment, ego strength, core values, degree of integration, stamina, and so on
3. *Motivational Dimension*: indicating level of drive, psychological needs, and so on
4. *Insight Dimension*: indicating the capacity for insight into self and others, particularly in terms of flexibility, objectivity, self-scrutiny, defensiveness, receptivity, sensitivity, perceptiveness, psychological-mindedness, empathy, and so on
5. *Interpersonal Dimension*: indicating adaptability, dominance, friendliness, cooperativeness, tact, and poise
6. *Vocational Dimension*: indicating technical skills; leadership skills; ability to organize, coordinate, direct, plan, and take charge; managerial style; organizational strengths and shortcomings; and it highlights the implications the foregoing material has for on-the-job performance.
7. *"Fit" Dimension*: indicating the degree to which the candidate's values, talents, skills, knowledge, prior experience, and attitudes match the job description and functions—that is, person–job fit, as well as the degree of fit with corporate, unit, and work team cultures

This outline has the advantage of starting with deeper personality characteristics, moving through the bridge of insight, and ending with the social and occupational manifestations of personality in behavior.

Executive assessment reports of prospective candidates include a recommendation section that reflects the consultant's judgment of the psychological fit between the applicant and the job in question. In reaching this judgment, the consultant needs to consider the promotability of the candidate; the nature of the organizational culture; the characteristics of the applicant's prospective manager, co-workers, and subordinates; and barriers or special circumstances that could affect the applicant's performance, as well as the nature of the job itself (Special Issue, 1994). In addition, the consultant should endeavor to take into account the inevitability of change and of adversity in all of these areas, as well as in the applicant's personal life and in the corporation's fortunes. Finally, a prediction of how the individual will likely respond under conditions of crisis, stress, pressure, uncertainty, disappointment, rejection, loss, failure, and lack of control are critical considerations.

Executive assessments are typically reported in both oral and written form. The oral presentation has the virtue of immediacy, informality, give-and-take between psychologist and evaluee, and the ease of shifting focus from broad to narrow, from abstract to concrete, and from the descriptive to the experiential. The written report allows for comprehensiveness, subtle differentiation, and a consistent message and tone for anyone who reads it. An oral report without a written one is apt to lack comprehensiveness and to be imprecise. However, a written report without oral feedback does not have the advantage of further clarification and reader input, and it tends to be perceived as impersonal.

Character: An Eighth Dimension of Executive Assessment

Lately, corporations are increasingly questioning the efficacy and predictive value of psychological assessment methods in screening candidates for executive positions. Besides knowing whether a specific candidate will be a good "fit" with the corporation, corporate officers need to know if the candidate's work performance will be *consistent* over time, and if the candidate will demonstrate *sound judgment when threatened, tempted, or when doing the right thing may not be in that individual's best interest*. Consistency and good judgment in difficult situations are two very useful markers of character. They are related to the three essential markers of character: self-determination, cooperation, and self-transcendence, as described in chapter 4. In other words, corporations need to know about basic character dynamics of executives. Needless to say, the second and third considerations, as well as other dimensions of character, are seldom addressed in traditional personality assessment. Accordingly, I insist that a comprehensive executive evaluation must include an eighth dimension of assessment: the character dimension.

The following case illustrates that failure to complete a comprehensive evaluation—that is, one that includes an assessment of all eight dimension—can prove disastrous. In this case, a candidate who appeared to be a good "fit" for both the job and the culture during the evaluation and selection process turned out to lack both consistency and good judgment.

Case Study: Executive Selection

Jason Fredricks had only recently come on board as senior vice president of group insurance. He was handsome, self-assured, articulate, and winsome in manner, and his ideas about expanding market share were novel and provocative. The chairman of the board, president, and top-management team were deeply impressed by him during the interview process. His letters of recommendations were glowing, as was the psychological consultant's report. He seemed to be an all-around "fit" for the corporation, even sharing the corporation's family-friendly culture and values. Two days after he started, Jason took off for a 3-day trip to visit the East Coast regional office. Although the president had expected to spend most of that first week orienting Jason, he wasn't going to restrain Jason's take-charge enthusiasm in getting out in the field. At least, that was his first thought. When Jason returned, he immediately took on three important projects, but in each instance he delegated the projects to a key subordinate. Later, when asked to report on the progress of these projects to the management team, Jason would defer to that subordinate, who would accompany him and give the report. Jason seemed to talk about his family constantly: the soccer and tennis activities his kids were involved in and the seemingly endless number of games and tournaments that he implied occupied nearly all of his free time when he was in town. His office was described as a "shrine" to his family, with pictures of family members filling every available space. He would drop in to see the president and inevitably would steer the conversation to his family-involvement activities. Because the corporation was family-friendly, the president was initially quite pleased by this. In hindsight, however, the president concluded that this family talk usually was Jason's method of excusing a missed deadline or absolving himself for canceling or rescheduling a meeting or an appointment. Within 6 months, it became increasingly evident that Jason wasn't pulling his weight. When he was at the corporate office, Jason would defer to subordinates on nearly all of his projects and duties, would cancel meetings at the last minute, or would leave early to deal with family issues or emergencies. The last straw was his failure to deliver the annual marketing plan for the board's approval on schedule. The board was furious, and within a week Jason was terminated.

PERSONAL ADVISEMENT IN EXECUTIVE CONSULTATION

Personal advisement is much less formalized and structured than executive evaluation. Although some executive consultants specialize in executive evaluation, most consultants prefer the personal advisement–type of executive consultation. Personal advisement typically involves an ongoing relationship between a consultant and an executive. This relationship may extend for years, continuing even when the executive changes corporate affiliations.

Unlike the kind of trusting relationship that develops in psychotherapy and that limits behavior both inside and outside the therapeutic setting, the trusting relationship in executive consultation has fewer limits and boundaries. For example, consultants and executives might get together for lunch or dinner, play golf or tennis together, or speak by telephone whenever necessary. They can establish a close, personal friendship, exchange gifts, and attend events such as a family wedding, bar mitzvah, funeral, and so on. Not surprisingly, executives who deal regularly with high stress and a myriad of top-level decisions view personal advisement as a key factor in achieving and maintaining high-level executive performance.

Personal advisement of leaders is far from being a recent development. In olden times, a monarch often had a grand vizier, who served not only as an executive of the realm but as a confidant. Rulers could trust this grand vizier in a way that they couldn't rely on lesser ministers, friends, or even family members. The vizier was totally loyal to the ruler in a personal way that others were not. In today's business society, senior executives hold positions much like the rulers of ancient realms. The position is a lonely one. Executives must often make crucial decisions on the basis of inadequate information and without the knowledge of the people most affected. At times, these difficult decisions threaten to raise the ire of those who are most closely associated with the executive. To ease this stress-filled existence, executives need a modern-day version of the grand vizier, a truly knowledgeable outsider who is objective, trusted, and intelligent, with a wide range of corporate experience.

Executive consultants are typically external consultants, meaning that they have no position within the organization. As outsiders, they are not encumbered by loyalty to any member of the organization, which affords them the capacity to be objective. Above all, such a consultant can provide an executive with support during the lonely and worrisome times. Previously, the executive may have discussed corporate matters with a significant other, trusted staff member, colleague, or friend. However, close personal relationships can sour, and the executive faces the possibility that the former listener will be indiscreet with the privileged information that has been shared. On the other hand, executive consultants uphold strict confidentiality. The consultant also provides insulation from flatterers and opportunists. And the consultant is free to question and confront the executive on major decisions, a path not open to those on staff without fear of repercussions. The chances of an executive making a gross error are minimal when backed by this kind of relationship.

As the executive–consultant relationship develops, the consultant may become involved in the executive's social life and activities. The consultant may be asked to play tennis or golf, to have dinner at a club, or to spend a weekend at the family summer home. Consultants may find themselves in situations where it would seem very natural to disclose personal information such as would be expected with a close friend. However, there is a difference between a friendly client and a close friend. Furthermore, issues of transference can easily arise, to which the consultant must be sensitive (Tobias,

1990). This can be new territory for consultants who do not have formal clinical training, and they may need some time to become acclimated.

The Format for Personal Advisement

Executive consultation usually involves directed discussions initiated by the executive, who sets the agenda. Talks may focus on immediate people problems, such as staff conflict, an employee grievance, or a hiring or firing decision. Talks could cover nagging concerns, such as office relocation, morale in a subsidiary, personal health or fitness, or a family problem. Extremely sensitive considerations, such as a possible merger, executive–board relations, succession, or retirement concerns could also be dealt with. Whatever the issue, this type of executive consultation typically occurs in the executive's office and may last a short time or a whole day.

Executive consultation involves both a sounding board role and an expert advising role. In the sounding-board role, the consultant actively listens to the executive's ideas or concerns and objectively poses pertinent questions to assist the executive in developing perspective on the issue. This process can greatly clarify executives' impressions and validate the reasonableness of their conclusions. While listening, the consultant monitors for mistakes and is especially alert to patterns of errors that the executive might not recognize. In the expert role, the executive consultant provides specific suggestions bearing on the decision, whether regarding a personnel matter or a personal concern.

Executive consultants often deal with executives whose characterological style may preclude sensitivity and empathy to others. However, unlike psychotherapy, the consultant needs to work obliquely around characterological issues, so that the adaptive effort of the executive and the client organization may be supported (Levinson, 1991). Also unlike the 50-minute psychotherapy hour, the consultation may last 10 minutes or 10 hours straight. Extended consultations allow the consultant to directly observe a variety of encounters between the executive and others, which provide firsthand data, as well as the opportunity to give feedback to the executive.

Advisement on Leadership and Corporate Issues

Typically, discussions of leadership and corporate issues are initiated by executives and are most likely to take place in their offices. The agenda is set by the executive and typically consists of here-and-now issues.

Executives tend to hold certain expectations of the executive consultant. First, they believe that the consultant will be able to increase their effectiveness as both leaders and individuals. A second expectation is that the consultant will help them integrate information, providing not only perspective and objectivity, but also a keen insight into problems with people. Although senior executives expect that their staff members will give them briefings and financial reports, feasibility studies, and projections in advance of major decisions, they can't expect that these insiders—who tend to be close to these decisions—to provide objectivity and perspective. This is why the consultant's skills as a sounding board and an expert are so appreciated by executives. Third, executives expect that it will be safe to share their deepest concerns and even immature thoughts, believing that the consultant will help them grow personally and become more effective in meeting the scrutiny of more critical audiences.

During the course of their meetings, the consultant guides the executive to think through the presenting concern by asking key questions and helping the executive formulate the problem, generate and consider various courses of action, as well as anticipate the consequences of these options. Accordingly, helping an executive formulate the right questions and make informed judgments is a critical task for the executive consultant.

Finally, the consultant must also be available to advise the executive, because the executive may not be able to act wisely without specific information that provides a reasonable rationale for appropriate action. In all this, relationships that develop with executives must remain professional and friendly, rather than friendships, nor should they be the type of therapeutic relationships that would develop in executive counseling.

Case Study: Advising on Leadership and Corporate Concerns

Stephanie Castleman is the CEO of a health-information technology business that she began 2 years ago. The corporation has nearly 160 employees in two East Coast metropolitan areas. She had previously worked her way up through the ranks to become vice president of information technology at a major banking corporation. During those 4 years as VP, she was the corporation's top performer. However, when she realized that she was unlikely to crack the "glass ceiling," she moved on and began her own firm. Last year, Ms. Castleman was recognized as Woman of the Year by a regional business council. She is bright, entrepreneurial, and well-regarded by her employees and competitors.

She had previously worked with an executive consultant while at the corporate headquarters of the banking corporation and had found the advisement and mentoring relationship with this female consultant to be extremely useful and supportive. Stephanie was the first woman to occupy a VP position and found her male peers to be competitive and distrustful of her. When she left to begin her own corporation, she didn't believe that her corporate budget would permit her to continue the consultation, so it was terminated. During the beginning of the second year of her corporation's meteoric growth, she felt that she needed to resume the consulting relationship. It was an exhilarating time to be in on the ground floor of health-information technology, yet she was becoming overwhelmed with the number and gravity of decisions facing her. A year ago she had started with 5 employees, including herself; now she had 30. A recent market analysis indicated that if she expanded she would need to add another 60 within 6 months, at a minimum. One option was to stay with the original software-development mission, and the other was to expand the mission to include product distribution and service to software development. Although the financials made it seem like a no-brainer and her board of directors would approve the expanded mission, her intuition told her that the expansion was fraught with danger. She was also concerned about her vice president of product development, who, though brilliant and incredibly productive, was eccentric and moody and engendered turmoil in her unit. In addition, corporate turnover seemed awfully high, about 24% the first year. Her board was not worried, believing that such turnover rates were the norm for a high-tech company. The board also reminded her that this was a start-up and not a mature organization. But neither explanation was comforting to her. While at the insurance corporation, she had carefully chosen her staff, and once they joined her team, she nurtured their career development. Not surprisingly, they were grateful, committed, and extraordinarily productive, just as her executive consultant had predicted. "Yes, she did keep me on target and gave me great advice," Stephanie thought to herself.

Meeting again with her consultant was most heartening. Before the consultant turned to the matter of mission and squeaky wheel concerns, such as the VP of product development, she suggested that Stephanie review her own job function and responsibilities. It didn't take long before Stephanie realized that she was focusing too much of her time and efforts on operations to the neglect of key CEO functions. Her executive VP had the title of chief operating officer, but he was not meeting his standards. Rather than coach him, Stephanie felt too stretched and stressed and eventually took on some of his responsibilities herself. It became evident rather quickly that Stephanie had relinquished many of her cherished leadership principles and practices in the past 2 years. Specifically, she had not taken sufficient time to hire the best "fit" people for her top-management team, and she hadn't spent sufficient time developing them. Stephanie met with the consultant for a full day a week, and by the end of the third meeting she was more confident that her intuition was correct. It would be a mistake to expand the mission and double the number of employees. Yes, she would probably capture a bigger share of the market, but would it be worth it? Would she be satisfied with the quality of her product and the culture of her corporation? Would she be true to her values? The answer was no to all three. She knew what she needed to do and was again confident that executive consultation had made a difference.

Advisement on Career and Family Issues

Executives may have some concerns about their own careers, a particular job issue, or even a family matter. Like many Americans, executives have difficulty balancing job, family, and personal needs and demands (Zedeck, 1992). This section focus on issues of career–family balance.

At least seven issues or stressors confound an easy solution to achieving balance and harmony among job, family, and personality. These issues are job-related travel, executive pressures, a dual-career marriage, relocation, job loss or promotion, retirement, and the female executive. Related issues include the effects of work, divorce, and single parenting on children, self, and job. The first three will be briefly discussed in this section.

Job-Related Travel

Greiff and Munter (1980) note that executives travel for a variety of reasons beyond job demands. These personal reasons include restlessness, status, intimacy, self-esteem, release from pressure, excitement, and freedom. They also describe the psychodynamics of such travel in terms of anticipation, separation, and regeneration. Boss, McCubbin, and Lester (1979) studied the effects of the traveling absent husband-father from the family-systems perspective and concluded that such travel is stressful for families, in that exits and returns require constant change in the family-system boundaries and role assignment. Their research found that corporate wives who coped best with their spouses' travel focused on self-development, interpersonal relationships, independence, and self-sufficiency and easily "fit" into the corporate scene.

More recently, researchers have formalized the study of the stress of job-related travel and call it "travel stress." They indicate that travel stress can cause emotional upset, physical illness, decreased job performance, and other problems for the executive in achieving corporate objectives (DeFrank, Konopaske, & Ivancevich, 2000). These researchers offer several interventions for preventing and reducing travel stress for the executive.

Executive Pressures

Greiff and Munter (1980) report that the most common personal pressures impacting job and family are time, money, health, value conflicts, age, and self-appraisal. They note that divorce and dual-career marriage are the most important family pressures on the executive, whereas performance appraisals, public speaking, the inner circle, and authoritarian and opaque bosses are the organizational pressures that most stress the executive. Cooper (1981) reports research findings that confirm most of Greiff and Munter's observations. However, whereas Greiff and Munter's list relates primarily to male executives, Cooper also reports on the unique pressures of female executives at home and on the job. These include threats of sexual involvement, threatened male colleagues, a patronizing male or a "queen bee" female boss, being "superwoman" at home and at work, blocked promotions and the "glass ceiling" phenomenon, and overly high expectations of others and self to succeed in a male-dominated workforce.

The Glass Ceiling Phenomenon

The so-called glass ceiling remains a very real career issue for female executives. Women comprise about 12% of corporate offices of *Fortune 500* corporations and about 8% of CEOs in corporate America. Granted, these figures have increased considerably over the past decade, yet women represent half of the total workforce but are not equally represented in upper-level positions. It should be noted that 9.1 million women-owned businesses are in the United States, which translates to women owning and directing approximately one third of the business population (National Foundations for Women Business Owners, 2000). Some have suggested that instead of trying to shatter the glass ceiling in major corporations, women should redirect their leadership efforts to starting new businesses. Although this remains a viable option, many female executives want to continue to rise to the top in major corporations. Mary Kay Haben, executive vice president of Kraft Foods and president of the Kraft Cheese Division of Kraft Foods, observes that women who are most likely to shatter the glass ceiling share two commonalities. First, they have been exposed to female "role models in high places who model appropriate behavior and show you that you really can have a high-powered career and life" (Haben, 2001, p. 10). Second, they are, or seek to be, involved in a major corporation that has made a commitment to gender equality and has a culture, policies, and procedures that support it.

Dual-Career Marriages

It was estimated that approximately 58 million people were in dual-career marriages in 1985, and in 2000 about 64% of all married couples with children were in dual-career marriages (quoted in Adkins, 2000). As women continue to seek self-identity and fulfillment in careers, as well as in the housewife/mother role, the number of such marriages is expected to continue increasing. Morse and Furst (1982) note that specific problems are related to the dual-career marriage. Among them are overload, role reversal, mixed priorities, money, jealousy, conflict over accepting job offers, and deciding to start or postpone raising a family and happiness. Stringer (1985) lists some ingredients for the success of dual-career couples. The research she cites is based on couples who define themselves as successful and have been married for at least 10 years. First, couples who have a high level of commitment to their careers report a greater degree of marital satisfaction than traditional couples do. Second, these couples tend to be flexible and make decisions that provide mutually satisfying decisions: for example, they are willing to relocate, commute, and make adjustments to fit each other's career; they are interdependent; they have common interests, sharing mutual leisure-time activities and being physically active with each other; and they encourage the self-actualization of their spouse. Third, they spend more time together than other couples. And, fourth, they are realistic about their limitations and don't expect to have it all.

Achieving Balance of Self, Family, and Career

Work–family issues are increasingly problematic in the corporate world (Hill, Hawkins, Ferris, & Weitzman, 2001) and serve as a major source of stress to complicate the lives of executives. Not surprisingly, female executives experience work–family issues as being more stressful than do male executives (Nelson & Burke, 2000).

What do the research findings in the previous sections mean for the consultant who is advising an executive to achieve better life balance? First of all, the consultant would do well to assume that this threefold balance must be a joint responsibility of organizations, as well as of executives and their families. On the organization's side, Cooper (1981) suggests a number of policy changes, including flexible work schedule, sabbaticals, changes in relocation policies to minimize the stress of job transfers, paternity and maternity leave, on-site child care, creating informal support networks for female executives, helping male executives come to terms with female executives, providing senior management sponsorship, job awareness seminars, and programs to improve executive health and well-being. On the executive's and family's side, Cooper (1981) suggests seminars and counseling on stress management, assertiveness, communication, and priority-setting skills.

McCubbin and Thompson (1989) systematically studied the effects of the October 1987 stock market crash on investment executives and their families, as well as on their organizations. They offer a profile of the resilient, hardy executive who apparently was successful in the threefold balance, even while under severe stress. These researchers studied variables such as the vulnerability of the individual executive; family and workplace environment; and resilience resources, such as family type, personal lifestyle, community support, degree of job autonomy, and supervision support. They also studied levels of adaptation, in terms of work–family balance, spousal functioning, family-system functioning, and worker–workplace balance. Finally, they developed prediction equations regarding the extent and type of adaptation of investment executives and their families to this economic crisis.

Specifically, individual adaptation was measured by indices of emotional distress and job satisfaction and, at the family level, was measured by indices of family well-being and disruption interacting with the factors of hardship, vulnerability, family typology, resistance and adaptive resources, appraisal, social support, and problem-solving patterns. Essentially, the hardy and resilient investment executives were those who had their superiors' support on the job; had affirming communication, social support, and family hardiness at home; and exhibited a personal lifestyle of health promotion and a strong sense of coherence or meaning in life.

Flextime

Another source of stress is long hours, with work weeks averaging between 60 and 70 hours for most executives. Although job flexibility, called "flextime," is usually associated with hourly workers and professional staff personnel, it has not been considered a realistic option for senior managers. The reason given was that senior executives needed to be available on site to effectively discharge their duties. However, increasing numbers of female executives have experimented with arranging their work schedules so that they might have an extra day a week to deal with family matters. Some recent studies have reported that perceived job flexibility is related to improved work–family balance and appears to be beneficial for both the individual and the corporation (Hill, Hawkins, Ferris, & Weitzman, 2001).

Family Leave Policy

Provisions of the Family Leave and Medical Act enacted in 1993 provide employees with up to12 weeks of unpaid leave per year to attend to specified family and health matters. It is reportedly one of the most common measures used by public and private organizations to help families reduce conflicts between work and family obligations. Because the leave would be unpaid, framers of this legislation anticipated that only a small number would use the benefit. Nevertheless, it was deemed to be a humane and helpful benefit. Current data indicate that only about 4% of employees in the private sector utilize this benefit in a given year, and the average amount of leave taken is 10 days. Research is now being conducted on the actual impact of this work–family benefit. Recently reported research indicates that family leave appears to benefit both the employee and the corporation. Specifically, the study found that family leave positively impacts the employee's organizational commitment, work satisfaction, and productivity. Equally important, it also reduces work stress (Kim, 2001). Executives and professional friends whom I know who have taken advantage of this benefit would confirm these findings.

Establishing Work–Family Boundaries

Although information technology and the electronic revolution have immense benefits for globalization and business, they also have the potential to increase work–family conflicts and stress. The widespread availability of notebook computers, cell phones, pagers, and instant Internet access means that executives are virtually on the job 24 hours a day, 7 days a week, wherever they may be. Until just 5 years ago, leaving the office meant that an executive was, for all practical purposes, away from the job. A physical boundary separated work and family and private life. "Flexplace" is another recent development that permits and even encourages employees to spend a given number of hours working at home. Psychologically speaking, the work–family boundary could be breached any time an executive was at home and mentally considered upcoming business decisions or played out past or future work scenarios. It was up to the executive to decide on the permeability of that psychological boundary. Today, basically only a psychological boundary exists because the physical boundary has been effectively removed by the information revolution.

Now, more than ever, executives must proactively plan and choose to establish clear psychological boundaries between family and work. Actually taking vacations and other planned time off to spend with family is an important and tangible way to establish appropriate work–family boundaries. It is surprising how many executives never or seldom use their vacation time, believing that they will fall behind or be seen as uncommitted or because of the fear that when they return, they might find that their position was eliminated. Linda Whitman, president of Ceridian Performance Partners, a $1.4-billion information services corporation, believes that it is good business for executives to take vacations because it is a proven method of self-care. She insists that they take the vacation time coming to them. "It can be a matter of arrogance or poor planning if one doesn't. It's not a badge of courage to fail to take care of oneself. I always take my vacations. I find that when I'm not as effective with employees as I want to be, it is usually because I haven't done a good job taking care of myself" (Adkins, 2000, p. 30).

Case Example: Advising on Career and Family Concerns

Jerod Willens is the 43-year-old married chief financial officer of a third-generation family-owned corporation. The corporation has 75 employees and garnered $11 million in sales each of the past 4 years. Willens sought executive consultation because of increasing job dissatisfaction, concern about his future with the corporation, and guilt feelings when he considered leaving it. Willens's grandfather had started the company 75 years ago at a time when there was little competition. Now competition in this market was intense. Leadership was passed to Willens's father, who served as CEO until his unexpected death in 1980. Succession went to Willens's older brother. Loyalty and family pride were basic values. When Willens graduated from college in 1974, he had refused his father's offer to join the family business as head of accounting, saying that he wanted to be free to travel throughout Europe and the United States and "find himself." Besides, he was more excited over the prospect of meeting people than of peering over spreadsheets, and he wondered how he had ended up an accounting and finance major when he really liked sales and marketing. His father was quite saddened by this decision, but in time was able to accept his son's decision. The young CFO believed that his guilt feelings were related to his father's expectation that the company would always be run by his loyal sons and their sons. Willens's fascination with travel continued unabated over the years. He was happy and energized in his off hours planning long, elaborate trips to remote spots in South America and Asia for himself and his wife. Yet he felt uncomfortable and even guilty when he was away from the office on scheduled vacations. Often, he wondered what it would be like to own and manage a corporation geared to international business travel.

The consultation consisted of two half-day meetings and took place in the executive's office. The meetings focused on Willens's career issues, as well as on his guilt feelings. At the outset of the consultation, the consultant primarily listened to Willen's story about the family business and his own hopes and dreams. Eventually, Willen was able to admit that the company could survive, and even prosper, if he was not in his office every day of the year. The consultant reframed the CFO's job dissatisfaction and ambivalence as markers of his ambition to "find himself," rather than simply as family and corporate disloyalty. Willens then began to wonder if the company might do well to develop business in Eastern Europe and the former

Soviet Union. If so, he could combine the interests of the family business with his personal interest in travel. Willens decided that he would develop such a business plan and present it to the executive committee and the board. He proposed that he would spend up to 3 months, twice a year, selling and marketing the company's machine products overseas. Needless to say, the plan was approved. As a result of the consultation, Willens had discovered how he could be loyal to the family business and to his own interests and ideals.

CONCLUDING NOTE

Executive consultation is a professionally gratifying and broad-ranging strategy for enhancing executive development. This chapter has described and illustrated the two most common, and traditional, types of executive consultation: evaluation in executive selection and executive impairment; and advisement on corporate, family, and career issues. Currently, executive consultants are becoming more involved with executive health and are being asked to advise their executive clients on health issues. The next chapter—chapter 11—is entirely devoted to the topic of maximizing executive health.

REFERENCES

Adkins, J. (2000). Ceridian Performance Partner's president Linda Hall Whitman on navigating work and life. *Academy of Management Executive, 14*(2), 28–33.

Boss, P., McCubbin, H., & Lester, G. (1979). The corporate executive wife's coping patterns in response to routine husband-father absence. *Family Process, 18,* 79–86.

Bromet, E., Parkinson, D., Curtis, C., et al. (1990). Epidemiology of depression and alcohol abuse/dependence in a managerial and professional work force. *Journal of Occupational Medicine, 32*(10), 980–995.

Cooper, C. (1981). *Executive families under stress.* Englewood Cliffs, NJ: Prentice-Hall.

DeFrank, R., Konopaske, R., & Ivancevich, J. (2000). Executive travel stress: Perils of the road warrior. *Academy of Management Executive, 14*(2), 58–71.

Greiff, B., & Munter, P. (1980). *Tradeoffs: Executive, family and organizational life.* New York: New American Library.

Haben, M. (2001, April/May). Shattering the glass ceiling. *Executive Speeches,* 4–10.

Hill, E., Hawkins, A., Ferris, M., & Weitzman, M. (2001). Finding an extra day a week: The positive influence of perceived job flexibility on work and family life balance. *Family Relations, 50,* 49–58.

Kets de Vries, M. (1989). *Prisoners of leadership.* New York, Wiley.

Kets de Vries, M., & Miller, D. (1984). *The neurotic organization: Diagnosing and changing counterproductive styles of management.* San Francisco, CA: Jossey-Bass.

Kiechel, W. (1988). Looking out for the executive alcoholic. In *Office hours: A guide to the managerial life* (pp. 216–233). Boston, MA: Little, Brown.
Kiechel, W. (1990). The executive insomniac. *Fortune, 122*(9), 183–184.
Kim, S. (2001). Perceived impacts of family leave policy: Do organizational factors matter? *Public Personnel Management, 30*(2), 221–239.
Levinson, H. (1991) Counseling with top management. *Consulting Psychology Bulletin, 43*(1), 10–15.
Logan, W. (1989). The evaluation of the impaired physician. In R. Miller (Ed.), *Legal implications of hospital policies and practices* (New Directions for Mental Health Services, No. 44, pp. 33–53). San Francisco, CA, Jossey-Bass.
McCubbin, H., & Thompson, A. (1989). *Balancing work and family life.* Wall Street Edina, MN: Burgess International Group.
Morse, D., & Furst, M. (1982). *Women under stress.* New York: Van Nostrand Reinhold.
Moss, L. (1981). *Management stress.* Reading, MA: Addison-Wesley.
National Foundations for Women Business Owners. (2000). *Key facts about women-owned businesses.* Silver Spring, MD: National Foundations for Women Business Owners.
Nelson, D., & Burke, R. (2000). Women executives: Health, stress, and success. *Academy of Management Executives, 14*(2), 107–121.
Pasick, R. (1990). Raised to work. In R. Meth & R. Pasick (Eds.), *Men in therapy: The challenge of change* (pp. 35–53). New York: Guilford.
Pelletier, K., & Lutz, R. (1991). Healthy people—healthy business: A critical review of stress management programs in the workplace. In S. Weiss, J. Fielding, & A. Baum (Eds.), *Health at work* (pp. 189–204). Hillsdale, NJ: Lawrence Erlbaum.
Quick, J., Gavin, J., Cooper, C., & Quick, J. (2000). Executive health: Building strengths, managing risks. *Academy of Management Executive, 14*(2), 34–44.
Quick, J, Nelson, D., & Quick, J. (1990). *Stress and challenge at the top: The paradox of the successful executive.* Chichester: Wiley.
Rippe, J. (1989). *Fit for success: Proven strategies for executive health.* New York: Prentice-Hall.
Smith, E., & Siwolop, S. (1988). Stress: The test Americans are failing. *Business Week, 30*(47), 74–78.
Special Issue: Issues in the assessment of managerial and executive leadership. (1994). *Consulting Psychology Journal, 46*(1).
Speller, J. (1989). *Executives in crisis: Recognizing and managing the alcoholic, drug addicted or mentally ill executive.* San Francisco, CA: Jossey-Bass.
Stringer, D. (1985). Counseling dual-career couples. In D. Myers (Ed.), *Employee problem prevention and counseling* (pp. 191–206). Westport, CT: Quorum Books.
Tobias, L. (1990). *Psychological consulting to management: A clinician's perspective.* New York: Brunner/Mazel.
Zedeck, S. (Ed.). (1992). *Work, families and organization.* San Francisco: Jossey-Bass.

11

Maximizing Executive Health

The subtitle of this book is "Strategies for Maximizing Executive Productivity and Health." Although much of the focus of previous chapters has been on productivity, this chapter emphasizes the executive's health and well-being. As a group, executives tend to be somewhat healthier and more energetic than the general population. They are likely to value their health and well-being because of their recognition, at some level, that productivity is related to health. Effective executives recognize that high levels of energy, endurance, and stamina are essential to high performance and productivity. As a result, many endeavor to maximize their energy, endurance, and stamina. Interestingly, although executives have recognized the link between physical health and leadership effectiveness for years, only recently have leadership theorists and researchers begun to make this connection.

For decades, physical health was dismissed by leadership theorists and researchers as an extraneous variable. Now it appears to be an essential factor influencing executive performance and effectiveness. Models of executive health have expanded from being essentially psychologically based models to more comprehensive and holistic models of executive health. This, I believe, represents a major shift in the study of leadership.

This chapter begins with a discussion of the financial impact of executive health. Then it overviews some of the unique health issues and stressors of women executives, before detailing a useful model of executive health. The largest section of this chapter describes a practical and results-oriented approach to consulting with executives on health issues and concerns. In particular, the approach maximizes executive health and performance and is tailored to the executive's unique nutritional, exercise, and stress-management needs. An extended case study describes the application of this approach.

THE IMPACT OF EXECUTIVE HEALTH ON CORPORATIONS

Why be concerned about executive health? Researchers now point out that healthy executives, particularly CEOs, can and do enhance employee health, as well as corporate profits, whereas unhealthy executives can and do negatively impact employee well-being and corporate profits (Quick, Gavin, Cooper, & Quick, 2000). For instance, when Jack Welch, the fit and vibrant CEO of General Electric, underwent scheduled cardiac bypass surgery in 1995, a routine surgical procedure, GE stock was not much affected. In fact, it has reportedly doubled twice since 1995. However, the effects of Robert Goizueta's health problems were not as favorable for Coca-Cola. Goizueta, the CEO, was known to do little to safeguard his health. He was a chain smoker, indulging in a known health risk that ultimately resulted in his death from cancer in 1997. Reportedly, Coca Cola's stock suffered a 15–20% decline afterward. Similarly, when Jerry Junkins, CEO of Texas Instruments (TI), suffered a fatal heart attack, TI's stock fell by 25% in the following weeks (Quick, Gavin, Cooper, & Quick, 2000). Furthermore, in 1955 when then president Dwight Eisenhower suffered a massive heart attack, the Dow Jones Index showed its worst decline since the stock market crash of 1929 (Gilbert, 2000).

HEALTH ISSUES OF EXECUTIVE WOMEN

Compared to other female workers, CEOs and other executive women "reported greater overall job satisfaction, fewer psychosomatic symptoms, fewer work days missed because of illness, and greater life happiness. . . . The higher the woman's level in the organization, the more she is likely to experience healthy, as opposed to unhealthy work" (Nelson & Burke, 2000, p. 110). What accounts for these health differences? Although executive positions may place higher demands on executive women than on women in entry-level positions, executive positions permit a very high degree of decision-making authority. This explanation is consistent with job strain theory (Karasek & Theorell, 1990) and supported by considerable research indicating that holders of high-demand, high decisional–control jobs, such as senior executive positions, experience less health-debilitating stress than do holders of low decisional–control jobs.

Executive women share common stressors with executive men. These include time pressures, conflicting demands, role conflict, role ambiguity, and responsibility for employees. Nevertheless, female executives experience a unique set of task-related, role, and interpersonal stressors in the workplace. Task-related stressors include "barriers to achievement, tokenism, overload, and downsizing," whereas role and interpersonal stressors include "organizational politics, social-sexual behavior, work–home conflict, and workacholism" (Nelson & Burke, 2000, p. 111). Certain unique health consequences of work stress are also gender related. Work stress has been associated with increased rates of spontaneous abortions and preeclampsia and possibly higher rates of breast, ovary, and uterine cancer.

A MODEL OF EXECUTIVE HEALTH

How is executive health defined? What are the markers or key characteristics of executive health? Some major changes have occurred in the way these questions were answered during the past decade. For instance, a prominent research group based its definition and characteristics of executive health on a large-scale study of male and female chief executives. Essentially, executive health was psychological well-being, characterized by active leadership, high need for power and control, and high levels of stress and risk-oriented behavior. This contrasts with unhealthy executives, who were characterized as passive followers, with a low need for power, and who experienced little stress and avoided risk. These researchers defined executive health exclusively in terms of psychological well-being (Quick, Nelson, & Quick, 1990). A decade later, their definition of executive health expanded considerably to include physical health and well-being, among other dimensions (Quick, Gavin, Cooper, & Quick, 2000).

Quick, Gavin, Cooper, & Quick (2000) have proposed a useful model for conceptualizing executive health. They "define executive health as physical, psychological, spiritual and ethical well-being. Each of these four dimensions of executives' health must be developed if they are to stand on solid foundations. When each of these dimensions of health is strong, executives can be most effective as individuals, as managers, as peers and colleagues, and as leaders within their organizations" (p. 37).

This model of executive health includes four specific "health risk factors" and four "strength factors" that influence executive health, as well as the "personal and organizational outcomes" of executive health. The four risk factors are (1) the "Achilles heel," or inherited or acquired vulnerabilities to certain health conditions; (2) the loneliness of command, which refers to the social isolation inherent in top-management positions, and the resulting need for social support, contact, and reassurance; (3) work demands and overload, which refers to the stressfulness of extensive travel, political pressures, and performance pressures; and (4) crises and failures that range from business disruptions to industrial accidents or bankruptcy, to physical attacks or personal threats.

The four strength factors are: (1) physical fitness; (2) networks of professional and personal relationships; (3) balance across the domains of life; and (4) stress-management skills. Researchers indicate that healthy executives must possess the following stress-management skills: "planning, time management, relaxation, spiritual disciplines, and cognitive/behavioral skills" (p. 41). Presumably, an executive would utilize cognitive/behavioral skills to challenge any unhealthy beliefs and assumptions that are stress-provoking.

With regard to the outcomes or consequences of executive health, these researchers describe three "personal and organizational outcomes." The first is individual vitality, which is the capacity to live with mental and physical vigor. The second is low levels of disease and death, and the third is organizational health. "High levels of executive health along all four dimensions contribute to individual vitality, low morbidity and mortality rates at the individual level. In addition, we contend that high levels of executive health within an organization contribute to organizational health, as defined in terms of high performance, adaptability, and flexibility of the firm" (Quick, Gavin, Cooper, & Quick, p. 37). It should be noted that these researchers admit that currently, little research supports the hypothesized link between executive health and the three personal and organizational outcomes.

For these researchers, enhancing executive health is a process of managing risks and building strengths. "Executives can manage health risks by identifying threats to their health, then taking appropriate steps to guard against the threats having an adverse impact. Executives can build strengths by identifying inherited abilities that are complemented with acquired skills and activities" (pp. 38–39).

POSITIVE PSYCHOLOGY AND EXECUTIVE HEALTH

A noteworthy trend is occurring in the field of psychology that appears to have significant implications for executive leadership. Recently, major figures in the psychology research community have begun retrieving part of psychology's early interest in character and health. This retrieval effort is being called "positive psychology." Positive psychology emphasizes strengths, health, and well-being. It is based on the developmental or growth model, rather than on the pathology model, with its human foibles, deviance, and disease. Unfortunately, much of contemporary psychology and psychotherapy has become preoccupied with healing and concentrates on repairing damage within a disease model of human functioning. Ironically, psychology and the other social sciences have come to view human strengths and virtues, such as altruism, courage, honesty, duty, and responsibility, as essentially defensive patterns, while weakness and negative motivations such as anxiety, lust, selfishness, paranoia, anger, and sadness are viewed as "authentic" traits (Seligman, 1999). The aim of the field of positive psychology "is to begin to catalyze a change in the focus of psychology not only with repairing the worst things in life to also building positive qualities" (Seligman & Czsikszentmihaly, 2000, p. 5).

Three pillars have been proposed for positive psychology: subjective well-being, positive character, and positive community. Subjective well-being includes contentment, satisfaction, hope, and optimism, whereas positive character includes "the capacity for love and vocation, courage, interpersonal skill, aesthetic sensibility, perseverance, forgiveness, originality, future-mindedness, spirituality, high talent and wisdom" (Seligman & Czsikszentmihaly, 2000, p. 5). Finally, positive community includes "the civic virtues and the institutions that move individuals toward better citizenship: responsibility, nurturance, altruism, civility, moderation, tolerance, and work ethic. Though some humanistic psychologies have also championed human strengths and self-actualization over the past 4 decades, only positive psychology has endeavored to achieve a scientific understanding and effective interventions to achieve virtue and human flourishing.

Consultation experience, as well as some preliminary research, suggests that positive characteristics such as optimism, tolerance, and interpersonal skills can be increased with focused training and coaching. Not surprisingly, the positive psychology perspective seems to resonate well with both executives and consultants, because both are concerned with self-development, health, and personal well-being.

CONSULTING ON EXECUTIVE HEALTH CONCERNS

Sooner or later, the matter of health comes up in the consultation setting. Executives briefly mention that their insomnia is worsening, or that they have been diagnosed with insulin-resistance, or they wonder if you think they should try Viagra. These and other health concerns are not uncommonly posed to the psychologically trained consultant. Although senior executives tend to be among the healthiest of all Americans, they nevertheless contend with a number of common concerns, such as weight, sleep problems, and symptoms of chronic degenerative disease (e.g., heart arrhythmias, insulin-resistance, and Type II diabetes), as well as balancing job and family responsibilities, substance use and abuse, and sexual performance. Perhaps the most common concern of executives over the age of 40 involves energy level, endurance, and stamina. Until their middle or late 30s, many executives were able to eat almost any food and drink nearly every day of the week; they never seemed to be sick, and they could get by on only a few hours of sleep and still have unlimited energy and stamina on the job. Now they notice that certain foods don't agree with them, that they don't recover quickly from alcohol or jet lag, or that they can't maintain their high-paced life as before. They want advice, usually a quick fix. So how might a consultant deal with these matters? The options range from referral to a physician or other health provider to dealing with these matters directly. This section provides a framework for conceptualizing these consultation issues.

Tailoring Health Promotion Prescriptions to Executives

It is my firm conviction that health promotion prescriptions need to be tailored to the unique needs of executives. I also believe that optimal health is a function of more than simply physical fitness and nutrition. I would also contend that other key factors in optimal health include psychological and spiritual well-being and the capacity to effectively manage stress.

Interestingly, in the last few years, awareness has been growing among consultants and researchers that individual differences exist not only in energy patterns (i.e., nutrition and exercise patterns), but in stress response patterns. Just as there is no uniform energy pattern, there is no single stress-response pattern. This means that "one-size-fits-all" nutritional and exercise programs, as well as "one-size-fits-all" stress-management programs, are probably suspect.

Kenneth Cooper, MD, founder and medical director of the famed Cooper Aerobic Center in Dallas, Texas, is also convinced that executives who maintain optimal health exhibit optimal job performance. He considers optimal health to be a function of optimal fitness and nutrition. This conviction is based on several research studies, including research completed at the Cooper Aerobic Center on over 100,000 adults, including several thousand executives. Essentially, executives with optimal health "possess higher levels of energy and enjoy enhanced feelings of well-being" (Neck & Cooper, 2000, p. 73).

Based on this research, Cooper has developed a detailed set of exercise and diet guidelines for enhancing executive performance (pp. 75–80). To his credit, Cooper describes guidelines, at least for exercise, that are specific for men and women. Nevertheless, they are basically one-size-fits-all guidelines, because they do not recognize the unique individual differences between male and female executives.

This section offers some guidelines for tailoring advice to executives with regard to health issues and concerns. I have found these guidelines particularly effectively in assessing and advising executives about optimizing energy and endurance, as well as on reducing stress. These guidelines have been modified from an approach developed by Elliot Abravanel, MD (1983, 1987, 1999). This approach recognizes four different nutrition, exercise, and stress types.

Four Strategies for Tailoring Diet, Exercise, and Stress Management

Although a number of strategies for optimizing leader effectiveness were described in previous chapters, these strategies focused primarily on the technical, strategic, and relational issues and challenges that executives face. They did not involve health issues and concerns facing executives. How does a consultant deal with these? The multidimensional typology described in this section shows how nutrition, exercise, and stress-reduction strategies can be utilized to optimize executive functioning. This typology and related strategies can be useful in consultation with the full spectrum of executives, ranging from derailment-prone to highly productive leaders.

Over the past years, I have found this typology and its assessment and intervention strategies to be quite useful and effective in my consultation with senior executives. It has been clinically useful in assessing those "other" individual differences in executives—not usually assessed or monitored by common psychological instruments and categories—particularly the subtle biological dimensions of executive functioning. Furthermore, it has been absolutely invaluable in tailoring the advice and counsel I provide executives. I hope that the detailed case example at the end of this section demonstrates how this approach can be utilized in executive consultation.

In the following pages each of these four types is described in terms of its characteristic energy pattern, body shape, personality pattern, and stress response. Then a custom-tailored nutritional strategy, exercise strategy, and stress-reduction strategy to optimize energy are presented. Clinical research suggests that one of these four types accurately characterizes about 75% of adults, whereas the remaining 25% are a combination of two types. These types are designated as A-Type, T-Type, P-Type, and G-Type.

A-Type/Strategy 1

Individuals characterized by the A-Type are hard-working, steady individuals with tremendous perseverance. Not surprisingly, their energy level remains high throughout the day, while decreasing somewhat in the evenings.

In terms of disposition, they tend to be friendly, open, and practical. Others enjoy being around them. They characteristically value stable relationships, particularly with their families and significant others, although they have difficulty with intimacy. Nevertheless, they tend to have a number of social friends. At work, they are likely to cultivate friendly, but competitive, relationships. They typically are not easily angered, but when they do get angry they often remain upset for quite a while. Talking about it can help them resolve it. They seem to have cast-iron stomachs, in that they can eat and drink just about anything, and they seem to need less sleep than the other types. Balanced male A-Types appear to be strong and sturdy, with a muscular appearance. Balanced females also appear strong and sturdy, but their strength derives from strong bones more than from muscles. Their personalities reflect this power and warmth in their personal liveliness and strength. Balanced A-Types can and do learn to relax and enjoy. Both males and females, when unbalanced, typically put on weight, so they appear sturdy and heavy-looking, particularly in the front of the body, in what is commonly referred to as a pot belly. Their main food craving is for greasy, salty food such as cheeseburgers.

These individuals prefer situations that are relatively predictable, controllable, and nonemotional. Accordingly, they tend to be single-minded in their efforts and capable of dealing with detail and repetition. They typically experience stress in situations and circumstances that involve change in their daily routines. To the extent that circumstances are unpredictable and not under their control, they are likely to become distressed. Because their children and adolescents tend to act unpredictably, these executives typically favor their jobs over home situations because of their difficulty relating to this source of unpredictability. Similarly, because the expression of emotions can be unexpected and uncontrollable, these individuals will avoid situations where emotionality is likely. Not surprisingly, they are often workaholics, with a commitment to their job lives that seems stronger and safer than their commitment to their families. Even vacations, where circumstances and events cannot be adequately anticipated and controlled, tend be a source of considerable stress. Alcohol and drugs may be used to dull the edges of unpredictability in their social lives.

Optimal Nutrition Strategy: The optimal nutritional strategy for A-Types to achieve balance includes plentiful amounts of low-fat or nonfat dairy foods such as yogurt, cottage cheese, string cheese, and skim milk; fruits, vegetables, whole grains, and legumes; moderate amounts of fish, poultry, eggs, coffee or tea, vegetable oils, and light desserts; and rare use of salty foods, aged cheeses, red meat, shellfish, butter, and alcohol. In short, the strategy is to eliminate craved foods—that is, spicy and salty ones—and emphasize poultry, fruits, vegetables, and light dairy foods.

Optimal Exercise Strategy: Because of their unique metabolism, these individuals are already strong and muscular; they have considerable stamina and endurance. However, they need to improve cardiovascular conditioning, flexibility, and eye–hand coordination. Accordingly, the primary focus of this exercise strategy is on cardiovascular conditioning, with only a limited focus on strength training. Exercises that increase both conditioning and eye–hand coordination include squash, handball, and tennis. Regular jogging, walking, or swimming will increase cardiovascular conditioning. Yoga or a simple stretching routine will increase flexibility. Dr. Abravanel notes that some A-Types engage in compulsive weight lifting on a daily basis because they crave the spaced-out feeling associated with pumping iron. Not surprisingly, this can become quite addicting and further unbalances the A-Type's metabolism. Thus, strength training once a week, using light weights, has its place in this exercise strategy, but regular heavy weight lifting and Nautilus workouts should be avoided.

Optimal Stress-Reduction Strategy: Following the A-Type nutrition and exercise strategies should considerably improve the individual's capacity for flexibility and creativity in stressful situations. In addition, it is essential that these individuals set aside some time every day to just "be," to "smell the roses," or just plain relax. Spending just 15 to 20 minutes a day, in which they shift their thoughts away from productivity—tasks, problems, and deadlines—and just mentally vegetate can trigger the relaxation response. If applicable, these individuals need to be counseled to reduce their alcohol and nicotine usage. Often, these individuals use alcohol, nicotine, and other drugs as stress reducers. But given their unique metabolism and the continuous high stress load they live with, alcohol not only jeopardizes their general health but increases their vulnerability to substance addiction. Because positive social support—particularly close interpersonal relationships—is an important stress buffer, A-Types need to focus more on listening and on being available to those who could provide this buffering in stressful, difficult times. Unfortunately, A-Types tend to discount the importance of their significant other, family, co-workers, and subordinates, viewing these people as uninteresting and unimportant to their high priority goals. And so they spend little quality time in these relationships. Enhancing these relationships is beneficial to all.

T-Type/Strategy 2

Individuals characterized by the T-Type usually experience bursts of energy, but they seldom maintain a high level of energy for long. Rather, their energy pattern noticeably varies from high to low throughout the day. In an attempt to keep it high, they are likely to resort to easily available stimulants such as caffeine, sugar, and nicotine in an almost addictive fashion when their energy starts fading. In terms of disposition, they are lively and changeable, even temperamental. They easily experience impatience and angry feelings and become depressed when their efforts are thwarted. Resting is a good antidote for resolving these feelings. They value variety and stimulation in relationships and so tend to have a number of friends. On the job, they can be quite comfortable working alone at times, but at other times they prefer to work with others. Balanced T-Types have the uncanny ability to eat almost endlessly without gaining weight. They are energetic, with little apparent need for rest. Likewise, they tend to be slender and streamlined in appearance, with a good balance of weight and strength above and below the waist. When unbalanced, they can quickly gain weight, noticeably a roll or tire around the midsection, usually referred to as "love handles." Their main food craving is for sweets and starches such as a candy bars, cookies, or a sweet roll.

These individuals prefer situations that are novel and challenging and experience as stressful situations that involve repetition, detail, lack of change or stimulation, and continuing demands. Unpredictability, far from being stress-producing, is perceived as a stimulant. They become energized and creative when beginning projects, but find it difficult to focus and experience considerable stress when they must deal with deadlines, minutiae, and pressure to complete projects. However, they are likely to experience pain, even relatively minor pain, such as a cut or an injection, as stressful. In interpersonal relationships these individuals are overly sensitive to rejection. Interestingly, of all the stress types, hypochondriacal concerns and complaints (i.e., unrealistic fears of illness), are a common stress response for them.

Optimal Nutrition Strategy: The optimal nutritional strategy for T-types for achieving balance includes plentiful amounts of eggs, poultry, fish and shellfish, and fresh vegetables; moderate use of red meats, legumes and whole grains, butter, and fruit; and rare use of refined grains, caffeine, and sugar. In short, the strategy is to eliminate craved foods (i.e., sweets, starches, and caffeine) and emphasize eggs, poultry, fish, and vegetables.

Optimal Exercise Strategy: Because T-Types cannot naturally sustain high energy levels for long periods of time, their primary exercise need is to develop stamina and endurance. Thus, the primary focus is on strength training, with a secondary focus on cardiovascular conditioning. A complete set of strength exercises, such as Nautilus or free weights, three times a week, along with a light cardiovascular work out up to four times a week is recommended. These individuals do well with a personal trainer who can tailor and monitor a specific strength-training program to increase muscle mass. Walking may be sufficient for maintaining cardiovascular fitness. However, exercises such as tennis that require intermittent, rather than sustained, effort are not particularly useful for these individuals.

Optimal Stress Reduction Strategy: Following the T-Type nutrition and exercise strategies should considerably improve these individuals' capacity for endurance, steadiness, and personal power. It is important to look carefully at their job because it may be a source of considerable stress for them. A good-fit job for these individuals is one that allows them to conceptualize, develop support for, and initiate projects. Jobs that primarily involve these functions tend to energize T-Types. On the other hand, jobs that demand attention to detail, follow-through, deadlines, and tedium are poor fits because they devitalize and enervate these individuals. If these poor-fit job functions can be modified to better accommodate the T-Type individual's style, changing to a better-fit job may considerably reduce stress. T-Types often find themselves in overstimulating environments—that is, ones with constantly ringing phones, lots of foot traffic, buzzing office machines, or with the ongoing pressure of deadlines. Modifying such an overstimulating environment to one that is more relaxing can significantly reduce stress.

Irrespective of their jobs, these individuals tend to ignore their need for rest and sleep. They must be counseled to take periodic rest breaks throughout the day and get a minimum of 7 to 8 hours of sleep a night. Finally, another major source of stress is that these individuals want to do everything at once, rather than pace themselves. Taking one day at a time, doing one thing at a time, and alternating activity with periods of rest can be powerful stress reducers.

P-Type/Strategy 3

Individuals characterized by the P-Type exhibit an energy pattern that is noticeably high in the mornings, compared to the rest of the day, and they are likely to think of themselves as morning persons. In terms of disposition, they are often considered detached, idealistic, and intellectual. When frustrated, they are likely to feel hurt, but have a difficult time communicating their concerns and feelings. They are typically slow to anger and quick to get over it, after they have had a chance to think about it. They value companionship, and although they may have only a few close personal friends, these relationships are intense and meaningful. At work, they can be pleasant, but do not easily share personal information with others, as they often keep their professional and personal lives separate. Balanced P-Types are likely to maintain a youthful appearance far longer than other types. Because they are naturally comfortable in their heads, ideal development for them involves an integration of mind and body. To the extent to which they achieve this integration, they are lively and intelligent individuals in vibrant health. They can seem somewhat undeveloped and childlike in their appearance, more like a boy or girl than a man or woman. When unbalanced, they may put on weight so that they appear to be uniformly heavy all over. Medically, this fat pattern is referred to as diffuse subcutaneous fat, which is commonly called baby fat. Their main food craving is for dairy products, such as a milk shake, yogurt, or a slice of cheese.

These individuals prefer situations that draw on their capacity for reasoning and judgment. Rather than being experienced as stressful, intellectual challenges—even unexpected mental challenges and demands—that require careful analysis and problem solving are energizing for them. Although these individuals tend to live in their heads and are confident in their mental abilities, they tend to doubt their ability to deal with situations that do not require mental prowess. And so they experience these situations as stressful and attempt to avoid them as much as possible. Accordingly, the prospect of being physically ill or injured and requiring medical care, of meeting with others socially for a meal, or of dealing with emotions and conflicts in interpersonal relationships, which cannot be reasoned away, can be quite stressful for them. As a result, they dislike seeking medical care; they avoid conflictual situations, and when they cannot, they easily give in. Furthermore, sexual concerns and difficulties can be major stressors for these individuals. It is not that they cannot enjoy sex with the right partner; it is rather that demands or perceived demands for sexual performance, or even talking about sexual concerns, tend to be anxiety-provoking for them.

Optimal Nutrition Strategy: The optimal nutritional strategy for P-Types to achieve balance includes plentiful amounts of beef, lamb, pork and organ meats like liver, eggs and poultry, and fresh vegetables; moderate amounts of fruits, legumes, whole grains, and yogurt; and rare use of sugar, caffeine, and dairy products other than yogurt. In short, the basic strategy is to eliminate craved foods (i.e., dairy products) and to emphasize beef and organ meats and vegetables.

Optimal Exercise Strategy: This type is characterized by an imbalance between mind and body. Accordingly, an optimal exercise strategy for these individuals is a program that focuses on mind–body integration and combines strength training and cardiovascular conditioning. This means that exercise done compulsively or to the point of exhaustion is counterproductive. On the other hand, 4 days a week of such cardiovascular conditioning routines as t'ai chi, karate, jazz dance, complex aerobic routines, or kick boxing require mental involvement and foster mind–body integration. Strength exercises, using weights or Nautilus three times a week, is recommended. The P-Type is over-represented among die-hard joggers and long-distance runners. Many report that they jog or run because of a spacey feeling called the runner's high. Needless to say, this form of exercise further unbalances their metabolism. Thus, exercises such as jogging and running are to be avoided. Similarly, repetitive exercises, such as calisthenics, that trigger obsessive rumination should also be avoided.

Optimal Stress-Reduction Strategy: Following the P-Type nutrition and exercise strategies should considerably improve the individual's capacity to stimulate body awareness and achieve a better mind–body integration. Because they have never really become friendly with their bodies, eating and meal times can be particularly stressful for these individuals. A key strategy is to specify ways to de-stress the process and to help them begin to understand the physical pleasure of eating. For example, these individuals are coached to create an atmosphere of relaxation that will be associated with mealtimes, in which they first think about what they might want to eat (besides their craved foods), then prepare the food or order it, and finally taste and enjoy it. Also, by applying a similar strategy to self-care, they can increase their comfort level with their body. Though at first this may be difficult, with practice it becomes much easier. Finally, because they tend to avoid emotional situations and conflicts, they need to learn to remain physically and emotionally in the situation. They learn that compromise is an alternative to avoidance and giving in, and that with time they can handle conflicts with minimal stress.

G-Type/Strategy 4

Unlike the other metabolic or energy types, the G-Type is recognized exclusively in women. Their energy pattern is noticeably good in the mornings, but may be better in the evenings. In terms of disposition, they tend to come across as warm, sensuous, and comfortable. They may be quick-tempered, but can be easily distracted from their anger by apologies or flattery. In terms of relationships, they seem to need close and warm relationships to feel good about themselves. They value nurturing relationship and are typically friendly team players with co-workers on the job or in community projects. Balanced G-Types are typically pleasant, energetic, and loving individuals. Physically, they tend to be smaller above the waist than below, and the lower body is likely to be more well developed and stronger than the upper body. When unbalanced, they tend to put on weight so that they appear disproportionately heavier below the waist, and tend to carry that weight on their outer thighs and rear. Their main food craving is for rich and spicy food and also salty foods, such as tacos, barbecued ribs, and cashews.

These individuals tend to prefer situations that require patience, persistence, and responsivity. They easily form intimate, emotional relationships with others and are energized by engaging in worthwhile activities, even when these involve tedium, boredom, or a lack of stimulation. Not surprisingly, they gravitate toward the helping professions, such as teaching, counseling, nursing, and other forms of pastoral ministry. However, they tend to experience interruptions, disorderliness, and change in routine as stressful. Furthermore, the expectation that they act competitively, particularly in situations involving peers and co-workers, can be very distressing. Similarly, situations that require them to respond or act assertively can be very stressful. Finally, they are likely to avoid situations that require risk-taking.

Optimal Nutrition Strategy: The optimal nutritional strategy for G-Types to achieve balance includes plentiful amounts of fruits, vegetables, whole grains, and light dairy foods such as yogurt, cottage cheese, and skim milk; moderate amounts of whole grains, poultry, fish, eggs, and light desserts; occasional use of red meat, cream, butter, rich desserts, and caffeine; and rare use of spices and spicy foods. In short, the strategy is to eliminate craved foods (i.e., spicy and salty foods) and emphasize fruits, fresh vegetables, whole grains, and light dairy.

Optimal Exercise Strategy: This type requires better coordination between the upper and lower body, as well as eye–hand coordination. Accordingly, the optimal exercise strategy for these individuals is a program that focuses primarily on moderate amounts of cardiovascular conditioning and full-body strength, emphasizing the upper body; secondarily, it should also focus on eye–hand coordination and mind-body integration. The recommendation is for 4 days a week of cardiovascular conditioning routines, such as complex aerobic routines, jazz dance, or t'ai chi, to promote coordination and mind–body integration. In addition, walking is also recommended. Upper-body strength routines should be done three times a week, in addition to lower body strength routines twice a week. A personal trainer can tailor and monitor strength training that emphasizes upper-body muscle development. Because bicycling, roller skating or roller blading, and horseback riding primarily exercise the lower body, these should be avoided.

Optimal Stress-Reduction Strategy: Following the G-Type nutrition and exercise strategies should considerably improve the individual's capacity to handle risky, challenging, or unexpected demands. Feeling more in control of their lives and learning to become more assertive, as well as more comfortable in competitive situations, will significantly reduce stress in these individuals' daily lives. Making minor changes in their work or home environment, such as rearranging furniture or changing décor, allows them to feel more in charge of their lives. Presumably, with time and effort this can generalize to outside areas of their lives. It is also important for them to reduce the routine in their lives and to slowly but surely begin to take small risks. Finally, because of their high need to nurture and be nurtured, they find it very stressful when they do not receive the kind of caring they expect. They assume that others should read their minds and respond to their need for love and attention; not being loved back is very stressful for them. Consequently, they must learn to ask for what they need from others.

Maximizing Executive Performance Through Health Promotion

A Case Example

Jeffrey Lyden has been senior vice president of product development for 8 years, as well as the favored inside candidate for the company's top position when the current president retires in 1 year. Jeff is 51, has been married for 26 years, and has two college-age sons. For the past 3 years, he has collaborated with an executive consultant, meeting for a half day each month. Most of the concerns discussed with the consultant dealt with personnel issues, usually involving problems with prototype development and project management. In the past 2 years, his division had met or exceeded its productivity and profit projections, turnover was less than 3%, and his employees rated him highly as an effective and trustworthy manager. In terms of overall leadership effectiveness, he would be rated as functioning in the highly effective range. Were it not for some chronic health concerns that last year accounted for 11 sick days, declining energy levels, and occasional periods of moodiness and irritability, he might easily be considered a peak performer.

Three months ago, feeling confident that his division was on target, he thought that it was time to focus on his health concerns as they related to job performance. He revealed his misgivings and apprehension about his candidacy for president, given his health concerns. He imagined that the job of president would be more stressful and would require even more air travel than his current job, and he knew that younger, presumably more healthy-appearing, candidates were under consideration. He asked the consultant to be frank and forthcoming with feedback and advice. Should he save face, bow out of the competition, and continue to do his best in the current position?

Focusing on such health concerns was not new for the consultant. The consultant had made a personal commitment several years previously to achieving and maintaining optimal health. He had some formal training in health psychology, and his resource network included physicians, nutritionists, and sports medicine experts who were specialists in health promotion. Although he occasionally referred his executive clients to these specialists, he was reasonably comfortable working within a scope of practice that included health–work issues.

Over the 3 years they had worked together, the consultant had mentally noted several observations about Jeff's energy pattern, stress response pattern, body type, and weight gain pattern, in addition to his personality and relational patterns. With some focused questioning, the consultant learned that Jeff's diet consistently mostly of complex carbohydrates, no red meat, and only occasional fish and chicken. Jeff said that he was embarrassed to admit that his craved snack foods included chocolate-covered nuts, donuts, and chocolate chip cookies, but added that he also snacked on apples, grapes, and bananas. Except for an occasional glass of wine, he used no other alcohol or recreational drugs, and had never smoked. He took a number of vitamins, some minerals and herbs, but no prescription medicines. Jeff indicated that he had begun the Zone diet—a high-carbohydrate, low-fat nutrition plan—about 16 months previously at the suggestion of his wife, who had started it and steadily gotten down to her ideal weight for the first time since the birth of their first son. Whereas she had lost weight on this nutrition plan, it seemed ironic that Jeff, who previously was only 10 pounds above his ideal weight, had gained 15 additional pounds, despite his 4 hours of exercise a week! He had been jogging for the last 20 years, even though his knee joints had become increasingly painful and arthritic. The consultant noted that Jeff closely matched the T-Type profile. Specifically, his energy level was inconsistent throughout the day; he craved sweet and starchy food; he was creative, impatient, irritable, and easily angered; he appeared to have a T-Type body shape, which included carrying most of his weight around his waist, the so-called love handles; he had a variety of friends and colleagues and was most attracted to individuals who were original thinkers and stimulating conversationalists; and he seemed energized and exhilarated when initiating new projects, but most stressed when finishing projects and engaging in work that was repetitive, detailed, and tedious.

Mr. Lyden was referred for a complete executive medical evaluation. It had been more than 3 years since his last comprehensive medical evaluation. This included extensive lab testing and, given his family history of heart disease, a cardiac stress test. The report of that evaluation indicated that Jeff was approximately 22 pounds above optimal weight for someone his age and level of conditioning. His cardiac stress test was in the normal range and exhibited a level of exercise conditioning usually seen in amateur athletes. He was noted to have chronic sinusitis and mild to moderate levels of osteoarthritis in both knees and the right hip. Two treatment recommendations were provided. To reduce sinus symptoms, it was recommended that he reduce sugar and eliminate dairy products from his diet. In addition, a trial of glucosamine sulfate, an extraordinarily effective natural remedy, was suggested for 12 weeks and a referral to a joint specialist if the trial was not successful. The diagnosis of insulin-dependence, which the examining physician said was the first stage of adult-onset or Type II diabetes, was also given, along with the recommendation for an initial trial of either weight loss or medication. Overall, his health was assessed as being average to above average for his age and gender.

The consultant described the T-Type patterns that Jeff exhibited, and they talked about ways to optimize his diet so that he would reduce his food cravings and lose weight. It appeared that the high-carbohydrate diet that he had been on was a poor match for him. The nutritional strategy that better matched the T-Type was a higher-protein diet that emphasized eggs, poultry, and fish, with some complex carbohydrates, but that limited nonstarchy vegetables. It appeared that Jeff's exercise plan needed some fine tuning. A more optimal exercise strategy would emphasize strength training, with some aerobic conditioning. Jeff expressed interest in working with a personal trainer who could design and monitor a strength-training program for him. Given Jeff's joint pain and damage, the trainer urged him to replace jogging with lap swimming. Another key part of the recommended changes involved stress reduction and management. Jeff was overly stressed by job functions that required extensive involvement in detail-oriented and project completion. Because it was possible to shift much of this activity to two associates who enjoyed these job functions, this delegation was made, which increased Jeff's job fit considerably. It was mutually agreed that Jeff would try these recommendations for 4 months and evaluate the outcome.

After 4 months, Jeff indicated that he was feeling considerably better. He felt less pressured and irritable since he had delegated all of his daily responsibilities to oversee project management. Now he was simply monitoring progress on a weekly basis. Though this was not one of his stated job functions, Jeff had believed that he needed to roll up his sleeves and show his employees his personal commitment to these projects. It had become even clearer that he was a "big picture" person, rather than a "detail" person. Using his creativity to conceptualize and plan new projects was not only immensely gratifying for him, but also more energizing and less stressful. Furthermore, the new diet plan seemed to be working. He was now within 5 pounds of his ideal weight, and his sinus and joint symptoms were considerably lessened. His physician indicated that his lab tests revealed no indication of diabetes or insulin resistance.

At 6 months Jeff continued to do well. For the first time since college, he was at his ideal weight. He enjoyed lap swimming and strength-training workouts with his trainer. He was able to exercise without joint pain, and cutting dairy products from his diet had almost eliminated his sinus congestion. He had taken only 1 sick day in 10 months, and jet lag seemed to bother him less. Finally, he felt more confidant as he embarked on interviews for the job of president.

This case illustrates the application of a number of executive-development strategies. Clearly, the consultant functioned as a diagnostician—particularly in identifying Jeff's type and basic patterns—as well as a sounding board and an expert adviser. This represents executive consultation. He instructed and coached Jeff on beginning and continuing the health promotion program. This is, of course, an executive coaching function. But he also worked with Jeff to challenge and work through the core belief of "doing it yourself if you want it done right." This involved some aspects of executive counseling.

CONCLUDING NOTE

Executive health is increasingly being recognized as an essential factor in understanding and maximizing executive performance. For centuries, executives and the researchers who studied leadership have worn tailored suits and business garb. The fact that the average executive male in the United States is a size 40 regular does not mean that he will buy and wear a 40 regular suit if he is another size. Presumably, he buys clothing that fits him, based on the belief that tailored clothing creates a better appearance. Executives differ not only in clothes size, but in a vast number of other physical dimensions. I hope that this chapter and case example have succeeded in making the point that consulting with executives on health issues has to move beyond "one-size-fits-all" prescriptions for exercise, nutrition, and stress management to advice and coaching that are tailored to the executive's unique physiological and psychological make-up. Effective consultants recognize, if only intuitively, that significant individual differences, as well as cultural and gender differences, exist in executives, and that consultants must tailor their advice and other interventions to accommodate these differences.

REFERENCES

Abravanel, E. (1999). *Dr. Abravanel's body type diet and lifetime nutrition plan.* New York: Bantam (1983; revised edition).

Gilbert, R. (2000). Executive commentary. *Academy of Management Executives, 14*(2), 44–46.

Karasek, R., & Theorell, T. (1990). *Healthy work: Stress, productivity and the reconstruction of working life.* New York: Basic Books.

Neck, C., & Cooper, K. (2000). The fit executive: Exercise and diet guidelines for enhancing performance. *Academy of Management Executive, 14*(2), 72–83.

Nelson, D., & Burke, R. (2000). Women executives: Health, stress, and success. *Academy of Management Executives, 14*(2), 107–121.

Quick, J., Gavin, J., Cooper, C., & Quick, J. (2000). Executive health: Building strengths, managing risks. *Academy of Management Executives, 14*(2), 34–44.

Quick, J., Nelson, D., & Quick, J. (1990). *Stress and challenge at the top: The paradox of the successful executive.* New York: Wiley.

Seligman, M. (1999). Positive social science. *Journal of Positive Behavior Interventions, 1,* 181.

Seligman, M., & Czsikszentmihaly, M. (2000). Positive psychology: An introduction. *American Psychologist, 55,* 5.

Appendix A
Leadership Skills and Competencies

Leadership Skills

Technical/Analytic Skills

Mastering Job-Specific Skills: Job-specific skills are the basic competencies related to a job position and are typically specified in a job description or job analysis. These specific skills can be learned in several ways: through a management training program, apprenticeship, and so on. Because they are job-specific, they will differ from position to position. For example, some requisite skills of a vice president of human resources (HR) for a service corporation might include:

1. Managing HR program directors
2. Overseeing policies and procedures on benefits
3. Overseeing policies and execution of employee selection, training, and termination
4. Overseeing compliance of regulatory policies regarding HR

Problem Solving and Decision Making: Both decision making and problem solving are action processes that overlap—in other words, decision making is a step and a skill in the problem-solving process. Nine skill requisites are involved in the problem-solving process:

1. Identifying symptoms
2. Collecting information
3. Comparing desired results with actual results

4. Stating the problem and its effects
5. Listing, analyzing, and eliminating possible causes
6. Choosing the most probable cause(s)
7. Identifying and examining possible courses of action
8. Deciding and implementing the best course of action
9. Evaluating

Time and Priorities Management: Managing priorities is irrefutably linked with being a successful leader. Effective management of priorities is related to time management. Five skill requisites are involved in time management:

1. Analyzing current use of time
2. Eliminating nonessential and inappropriate tasks
3. Delegating tasks
4. Improving performance of essential tasks
5. Maintaining control of time

Project Management: Unlike day-to-day responsibilities, projects are one-time undertakings that are divided into specific sections that can be sequenced and independently evaluated. Effective project management is a sure-fire test of both project team and leader performance. A number of requisite skills are involved in effective project management:

1. Choosing a project manager with requisite leadership ability
2. Establishing project objectives and requirements
3. Selecting the project team
4. Managing the project
5. Monitoring the project
6. Coordinating follow-up activities

Performance Monitoring: Monitoring is the continuous process of checking progress on performance and goal outcomes. It involves both formal and informal checks, and when the leader renders feedback based on performance monitoring, the process becomes proactive. Effective performance monitoring involves the following requisite skills:

1. Establishing a monitoring plan
2. Communicating the plan
3. Evaluating performance with periodic or continuous monitoring
4. Providing feedback and guiding performance

Training and Development: Training provides individuals with the necessary knowledge and skills to perform a job, whereas development prepares individuals for increasingly responsible or complex jobs or careers. Four skill requisites are associated with training and development:

1. Building skills to improve performance
2. Advocating for continuous, ongoing learning
3. Aligning training with the organization's mission
4. Measuring the outcomes of training and development

Relational Skills

Communication: Communication is considered the most important of the leadership skills. It is the "bridge" for transferring knowledge and guidance, as well as for receiving information from inside and outside the organization. Effective communication involves the following requisite skills:

1. Improving face-to-face communication
2. Writing clearly
3. Being conscious of nonverbal communication
4. Improving team and organizational communication
5. Being sensitive to informal communications networks, such as the "grapevine"

Team Development: A team is a group of individuals that collaboratively accomplishes specified goals; effective leaders promote optimal teamwork. Effective team development involves the following requisite skills:

1. Selecting appropriate team members
2. Discussing team processes and teaching a team attitude
3. Reviewing team goals and developing a mission statement and implementation plan
4. Determining team roles and responsibilities and obtaining commitment
5. Building team trust, belonging, and team spirit
6. Training and coaching individual and team performance
7. Monitoring the flow of information and resources
8. Rewarding the team appropriately

Diversity: Diversity in a work team may involve gender, age, race, ethnicity, religion, and lifestyle factors. Effective leaders have the capacity of facilitating subordinates to work together as a team—despite their diversity—to perform optimally. Skill requisites for accomplishing this include:

1. Viewing diversity as a resource, rather than as a problem
2. Learning what will maximize diversity in the team and organization
3. Communicating with, involving, and getting commitment from others
4. Aligning the team and organization with diversity

Motivation: Motivating subordinates to function effectively involves at least five skill-requisites:

1. Knowing what motivates others
2. Being sensitive to others' needs
3. Rewarding properly, immediately, and equitably
4. Rewarding desired behavior and sanctioning undesirable behavior
5. Eliminating demotivators—that is, sources of job dissatisfaction

Conflict Resolution: Leaders who are effective in resolving conflict demonstrate the following skill requisites:

1. Separating misunderstandings from conflicts
2. Creating a positive environment for resolution of conflict
3. Focusing on individuals' interests, not on their positions
4. Communicating clearly
5. Negotiating win-win solutions

Coaching: Coaching is a process of guiding and encouraging subordinates to achieve optimal performance. It is considered the pinnacle of the relational skills, requiring a high degree of competence in the other relational skills. Assuming that the subordinate and the leader/coach have previously developed and agreed upon job standards and goals, coaching can proceed. Five skill requisites are involved in coaching:

1. Comparing current performance with job standards and goals
2. Offering feedback
3. Asking for comments and analyzing performance
4. Collaborating on a solution
5. Honoring the subordinate being coached

Strategic Skills

Visioning and Strategy Formulation: Vision is the capacity to perceive possibilities and create an ideal depiction of where an organization will be or needs to be at a future time. It involves setting a clear, focused, desirable direction that points toward and energizes an organization toward a specific destination. Five skill requisites are involved in visioning:

1. Cultivating a visionary attitude
2. Understanding the organization's trajectory from the past to the present
3. Developing a vision for the organization that extends that trajectory in terms of external threats and opportunities
4. Communicating the vision and obtaining commitments
5. Supporting the vision

Strategic Implementation and Management: Strategy is an integrated, long-term way of perceiving, thinking, deciding, and acting that produces viable plans for achieving an organization's vision. Four skill requisites are involved in strategic management:

1. Understanding the organization's environment and assets in relationship to the vision
2. Involving subordinates and others in strategic planning
3. Developing requisite strategies to accomplish the vision
4. Aligning day-to-day missions with vision and strategy

Guiding Change: Guiding change involves preparing for, initiating, and implementing the change process. Five skill requisites are involved in guiding change:

1. Understanding change from the perspective of the organization, its environment, its members, and its leaders
2. Maintaining a positive attitude toward change
3. Promoting continuous learning and fostering an attitude of innovation
4. Eliminating barriers to change
5. Monitoring change efforts

Financial and Information Technology Skills

Mastering the Budgeting Process: Planning and implementing a unit budget requires a number of requisite skills, which include

1. Utilizing budget guidelines
2. Anticipating expenditures and revenues for a reporting period
3. Compiling an operating budget

Understanding Balance Sheets and Financial Reports: Financial performance analysis and decision making that involves financial considerations require sufficient understanding of financial statements. Specific requisite skills include

1. Conducting basic financial and operating statement
2. Analyzing cash flow statements utilizing ratios that measure profitability, liquidity, market value, and asset and debt management

Monitoring Financial and Human Resources: Akin to monitoring and analyzing employee performance, monitoring financial resources and human resources in a given organizational unit is essential to effective leadership. Basis requisite skills include

1. Setting up a simple approach to monitoring work flow, staff output, budget allocations, accounts received, and so on
2. Monitoring these various indices weekly in a short time frame—that is, in less than 30–60 minutes

Using Data to Guide Management Decisions: Managerial decision making can be greatly enhanced when data are appropriately utilized. The capacity to effectively utilize data in such decision making requires that the manager

1. Seek converging data sources to accurately assess the situation or concern
2. Specify alternative solutions and likely outcomes
3. Translate this data to information in deciding upon the best alternative solution

Personal and Self-Development Skills

Stress and Lifestyle Management: The capacity to control and cope with stress requires a number of requisite skills. These include

1. Analyzing job strain—that is, the extent to which psychological demand and decisional control of one's job impact health and well-being
2. Assessing one's personal coping resources
3. Assessing organizational resources, including support of peers and superiors that buffers or neutralizes work stressors
4. Enhancing both organizational and personal resources

5. Maintaining a healthful lifestyle by increasing positive health behaviors and reducing health risks

Balancing Family, Work, and Personal Life: Individuals who can effectively balance job, family, and personal dimensions tend to be healthier and more productive than those who do not. Requisite skills in balancing involve

1. Setting boundaries and limits about work demands seeping into family and personal life
2. Coming to terms with relational issues, intrapsychic or psychological conflicts, work addiction, and other factors that tend to unbalance the three dimensions

Developing/Utilizing a Personal Mission Statement and a Career Plan: The trajectories of personal development and career development tend to remain in parallel and in sync with job/organizational goals for highly effective individuals. Establishing a personal mission statement can facilitate both personal and career development. Requisite skills include

1. Assessing and analyzing the correspondence between one's personal goals and values with the corporate goals and values of one's job
2. Delineating a long-range statement of personal and career growth, with 1-, 5-, 10-, and 20-year goals and benchmarks
3. Comparing that statement with the corporate mission statement
4. Taking appropriate action to increase "fit" between personal, career, and corporate missions, which may include job change, mentoring, additional education, and so on

Leadership Competencies: Behavioral Indicators

1. Acts with Integrity and a Sense of Balance

Highly Effective

- Genuinely lives with integrity and courage—that is, consistently listens, responds, and serves others authentically
- Consistently keeps ego in check; humble about accomplishments; recognizes the efforts of employees and colleagues and the impact of family
- Leads by example and consistently models fairness, courage, and honesty

- Effectively maintains a balance among corporate, personal, and family values, needs, and demands

Moderately Effective

- Is considered honest; has reasonably good listening and responding skills
- Is viewed as a team player; is somewhat inconsistent in acknowledging the contributions of others
- Usually models fairness and honesty
- Reasonably balances corporate, personal, and family needs, values, and demands

Minimally Effective

- Anticipates what others want to hear and emphasizes managing a good impression over responding and acting with honesty and forthrightness
- Places self-interest over the organizational need and publicly recognizes the contributions of others only when it is expedient
- Displays and models self-seeking behavior, defensiveness, favoritism, or self-protectiveness
- Is excessively preoccupied with work, family, or personal needs at the expense of the other two

2. Develops a Winning Strategy

Highly Effective

- Proactively scans the environment and develops long-term approaches that redefine problems or market opportunities in anticipation of changing business conditions or environmental trends
- Envisions the future when developing strategy; anticipates potential obstacles, competitive responses, and alternate scenarios; develops contingency plans
- Fosters internal and external commitment for strategy by involving broad constituencies and multiple perspectives
- Implements strategy through the organization by completely integrating organizational and individual goal planning, assessment, and rewards into strategy

Moderately Effective

- Recognizes changing environmental conditions that will impact the organization and its stakeholders; applies established approaches to address this impact and aligns organizational resources to deliver results

- Anticipates long-term consequences while developing plans and strategies that address current issues
- Considers impact on other units and constituencies when developing strategies
- Consistently communicates strategy and creates broad understanding of direction within appropriate constituencies

Minimally Effective

- Communicates unclear or conflicting information regarding strategy formulation and implementation
- Hesitates or fails to incorporate changing business conditions into strategies and plans
- Fails to consider unwarranted assumptions, projections, and the broader impact of issues and opportunities
- Fails to include others in strategy development or is too dependent on a single person's input

3. Mobilizes Employee Commitment

Highly Effective

- Identifies and develops organization strengths to match opportunities
- Anticipates employee and leadership competencies needed within the organization and actively develops others' competencies to meet those needs
- Effectively demonstrates how the organization's services or products meet customers' needs
- Is significantly involved in coaching, developing, and supporting staff and effectively models this to others
- Exudes enthusiasm and proactively garners employees' commitment to the organization by creating and maintaining a culture of trust and cooperation

Moderately Effective

- Continually upgrades core competencies through selection, training, coaching, or rotational assignments
- Shares corporate goals, expectations, time lines, and status in order to increase employee understanding of the organization's purpose and direction; builds appropriate cross-functional teams to address challenges
- Manages expectations and appropriately delegates decision-making authority
- Considers the impact of structure and culture on corporate success

Minimally Effective

- Neglects key stakeholders in achieving buy-in for goals, strategies, and direction
- Displays favoritism or ignores employee issues and concerns
- Fails to plan for long-term needs of employees
- Refuses to acknowledge negative information or conveys it without discussing potential solutions

4. Possesses the Requisite Job Capabilities and Understands Corporate Dynamics

Highly Effective

- Draws broadly on resources, knowledge, and expertise to thoroughly and systematically analyze a strategic initiative
- Works to achieve an equitable outcome in a negotiation, cognizant of relevant facts and data, as well as of the needs, wants, objectives, and constraints of the involved parties
- Demonstrates the capacity to make and accept difficult decisions
- Proactively develops contingency plans in anticipation of changing market, regulations, or resources

Moderately Effective

- Gathers essential data and consults with appropriate stakeholders before making a strategic or important tactical decision
- Routinely tracks business plans and objectives of internal and external stakeholders
- Creates opportunities for staff to share ideas and information with similar functions across divisions
- Seeks out internal resources, expertise, and knowledge across divisions when trying to resolve business problems

Minimally Effective

- Fails to share goals, results, or activities with others or to receive information from others
- Ignores suggestions for improvement or fails to learn from situations and replicates ineffective or unproven processes
- Regularly makes decisions based on initial reactions; fails to question, clarify, or confirm information
- Becomes overly invested in a course of action or refuses to initiate alternate courses of action that could produce better outcomes

5. Engenders Corporate Capability

Highly Effective

- Seeks out opportunities for partnership in setting goals and proactively integrates these goals with appropriate functions within and across divisions
- Consistently sets the bar higher and searches for new tactics to improve results
- Challenges current perceptions that limit effectiveness and results
- Effectively maintains and manages organizational boundaries to deliver results

Moderately Effective

- Persists in pursuit of goals despite obstacles
- Actively implements new ways to improve old processes and increase productivity
- Pursues the "spirit," rather than the "letter," of a strategic initiative
- Establishes performance measures at beginning of project; utilizes these measures to monitor and communicate project accomplishments

Minimally Effective

- Dictates goals without gaining buy-in of those responsible for delivering results
- Limits efforts to the success of the executive's own unit while ignoring the potential for benefit to the rest of the organization
- Develops plans that lack sufficient monitoring and feedback systems
- Establishes overly optimistic or unrealistic time frames
- Sets goals that are too conservative

6. Communicates Effectively and Encourages Knowledge Sharing

Highly Effective

- Encourages and rewards diversity of opinion in discussing issues
- Redesigns organizational structure and operational systems to support effective corporate communication
- Seeks, quantifies, and responds to employee input in large and small issues
- Creates and routinely utilizes two-way communication networks to facilitate corporate-wide exchange of best practices

Moderately Effective

- Creates multiple processes for two-way communication and information sharing
- Regularly shares relevant information with entire organization
- Utilizes technology to facilitate the exchange of best practices and rapid access to knowledge and expertise
- Seeks and effectively responds to personal feedback

Minimally Effective

- Insists on functioning as the sole information processor and decision maker
- Reacts ineffectively to negative information
- Limits the dissemination of important information
- Refuses to focus attention beyond the organization's current boundaries

7. Exhibits a High Level of Energy and Health Status

Highly Effective

- Exudes a high level of energy and stamina, which ensures the capacity to tolerate, when necessary, long work hours, extensive travel, and other arduous job demands and deadlines, while also leading an active social life
- Undergoes exposure to ongoing stressors without compromising health and well-being; has unlimited ability to socialize in situations where a wide variety of food and drink is a focal point of business entertaining and negotiation
- Recovers rapidly from minor illnesses—a cold or flu in 1–2 days—as well as injuries, physical exertion, and emotional stress, without undue disruption of normal schedule; is unlikely to develop chronic health conditions that reduce productivity and work involvement
- Withstands arduous job demands and deadlines while remaining in excellent health

Moderately Effective

- Exhibits moderate levels of physical energy and stamina, which limits the type and extent of involvement in physical, social, and leisure activities
- Exposure to ongoing stressors occasionally compromises the executive's health and well-being, which sometimes limits the ability to socialize in situations where a wide variety of food and drink is a focal point of business entertaining and negotiation

- Recovers at a medium pace from minor illnesses, injuries, physical exertion, or emotional stress
- Is occasionally affected by jet lag, insomnia, chronic health problems, and so on, which impact productivity and absenteeism to some degree

Minimally Effective

- Exhibits low levels of physical energy and stamina, which limits the type and extent of involvement in physical, social, and leisure activities
- Exposure to ongoing stressors takes its toll on the individual's health and well-being, which significantly limits the ability to socialize in situations where a wide variety of food and drink is a focal point of business entertaining and negotiation
- Recovers slowly from minor illnesses, injuries, physical exertion, or emotional stress; uses excessive health benefits and sick days, which can significantly disrupt productivity
- Is prone to chronic health problems, jet lag, insomnia, and so on, which significantly impacts productivity and time away from the job as a result

Appendix B
Personality Styles in Executives by Level of Functioning

The Self-Confident Personality

Healthy: These are energetic and self-assured individuals who believe in themselves and their own value, without expecting special treatment or privilege. They tend to be attractive and charming individuals who become outstanding in a profession or in an avocation. Because they embody widely admired qualities, others want to model their achievements. Highly competent, adaptable, and focused, they are very likely to achieve challenging goals. They can expertly present and advocate for an idea or a proposal in ways that are both acceptable and compelling, and they easily enlist the support and commitment of others to worthy projects that serve the common good. At their best, they are genuine and authentic individuals who fully accept themselves. Their worth as people is not based on success, fame, or the appearance of either. Accordingly, they can live modestly, and relate to others with heartfelt simplicity and grace.

Average: Although emotionally vulnerable to negative assessments and feelings of others, they can surmount these with style and grace. They are shrewd in dealing with others, utilizing the strengths and advantages of others to achieve their own goals. Usually, they are quite effective in selling themselves, their ideas, and their projects. They believe in themselves, their abilities, and their uniqueness, yet favor special treatment and privilege. Also, they tend to be able competitors who love getting to the top and enjoy staying there. These individuals can visualize themselves as the best or most accomplished in their field. They readily accept accomplishments, praise, and admiration, gracefully and with self-possession. They possess a keen awareness of their thoughts and feelings and have some awareness of others' feelings. Finally, they expect people to treat them well at all times.

Disorder: Individuals at this level of functioning tend to react to criticism with feelings of rage, stress, or humiliation. They are interpersonally exploitative and take advantage of others to achieve their own ends. They possess a grandiose sense of self-importance and believe that their problems are unique and understood only by other special people. Preoccupied by fantasies of unlimited success, power, brilliance, beauty, or ideal love, they have a sense of entitlement and unreasonable expectations of especially favorable treatment. Not surprisingly, they require almost constant attention and admiration. They lack empathy, have an inability to recognize and experience how others feel, and are preoccupied with feelings of envy.

The Adventurous Personality

Healthy: These individuals are confident, assertive, and effective in getting what they need and want. Disposed to taking the initiative and making things happen, they value independence and foster it in others. By nature they are strong-willed, impassioned natural leaders whom others respect and turn to for direction. They earn respect by acting honorably, by using power constructively, by championing and protecting others, and by promoting worthwhile causes. They seek justice and fair play and have a positive vision for their world. At their best, they become compassionate, merciful, and forbearing individuals who have achieved a great degree of self-control and who protect and support the rights of others with their strength and the courage of their convictions.

Average: Executives who function at this level prefer to follow their own drummer and typically live by their own internal code of values. Although they are seldom influenced by others or by society's norms, they can respect others' values. As adolescents, they were usually high-spirited hell raisers and mischief makers. Most of the time they are generous with money, believing that as it is spent, more will turn up somewhere and somehow. Though they are often driven by wanderlust, they are able to make plans and sustain commitment, albeit for limited time spans. They have a gift for communicating and easily befriend others, although they may not offer much depth to these relationships. Typically courageous, physically bold and tough, they will stand up to those who take advantage of them. They seldom worry about others, but rather expect others to be responsible for themselves. They often have strong libidos and although they may desire others, they can remain monogamous for long periods of time. They usually focus on living in the present and seldom experience guilt feelings.

Disorder: At this level of functioning, individuals are unable to sustain consistent work by their talents, skills, ingenuity, and wits. They fail to conform to social norms with regard to lawful behavior, performing antisocial acts toward others or flouting society's norms, which could be either grounds for arrest, or merely rule breaking. They are irritable and aggressive, as indicated by their physical fights or assaults. They may repeatedly fail to honor financial obligations, may fail to plan ahead, or may be impulsive. They seem to have little regard for the truth and may lie and "con" others for personal profit or pleasure. Furthermore, they can be reckless regarding their own and others' personal safety. Thus, they may drive while intoxicated or engage in high-risk driving behavior, such as speeding in school zones. As a parent or guardian, they lack the ability to function responsibly. Showing remorse and sustaining long-term monogamous relationships are difficult for them.

As noted earlier in this chapter, although the *DSM-IV* clinical counterpart to this personality style is the antisocial personality disorder, few executives would fully meet criteria for this diagnosis. Nevertheless, some executives will manifest a few of these behavioral indicators. This less extreme form is known as antisocial trait disturbance.

The Dramatic Personality

Healthy: These individuals are deeply empathetic and compassionate. They put themselves in the place of others and are caring and concerned about others' needs. They see the potential and goodness in those around them and readily respond with appreciation and encouragement. Because serving others is their basic priority, they are extraordinarily generous, giving, and helpful. Even if it requires personal sacrifice, these individuals go out of their way to provide others with what they really need. In the course of meeting others' needs, they are able to maintain healthy boundaries, while attending to their own needs as well. Because they have found the love they seek within themselves, they can be altruistic and unconditionally giving, without any expectation of reciprocity. At their best, they are deeply humble, gracious, and patient individuals who have mastered the art of nurturing both self and others.

Average: Individuals at this level of functioning typically enjoy compliments and praise. They are charming, engaging, and appropriately seductive in appearance and behavior. Usually, they are most attentive to their appearance and grooming; they enjoy colorful clothes, style, and fashion. Though lively, fun loving, sensation-oriented, and often impulsive, they can delay gratification. They enjoy being the center of attention, and they can rise to the occasion when all eyes are on them. Others enjoy being around them because they are interesting, emotionally demonstrative, and physically affectionate. They react emotionally, but appropriately, most of the time. Furthermore, they display a style of speech that is appropriately global and specific at the same time.

Disorder: These individuals seem to continually seek or demand reassurance, approval, or praise from others. Physical attractiveness is often very important to them, and they may spend an inordinate amount of time and money on their appearance. At times, they may be inappropriately sexually seductive in appearance and behavior. They express emotion with inappropriate exaggeration and are often self-centered and have little tolerance for delaying gratification. Most notable is their level of discomfort in situations where they cannot be the center of attention. They display rapidly shifting and shallow expressions of emotion. They utilize a style of speech that is excessively impressionistic and lacking in detail.

The Leisurely Personality

Healthy: They are emotionally stable and have a refreshingly positive outlook on life. Though coming across as easygoing, patient, and gentle, they remain firm in their convictions and are not easily fooled or misled. Their steadiness, common sense, and quiet demeanor have a calming and healing influence on others. Though usually laid back, they can act decisively and courageously when the situation demands. They exhibit an unhurried attitude and pace and will conscientiously set and make realistic deadlines. Because they easily can appreciate others' points of view, they make effective negotiators and counselors. At their best, they are autonomous and fulfilled individuals who exude genuine contentment, optimism, and equanimity. Because they maintain a high degree of centeredness and composure, they achieve an unparalleled level of balance in their lives.

Average: They can be somewhat pessimistic about the present and the future and, when tired or stressed, will typically complain about the demands in their lives. They can usually fulfill their given responsibilities, but they seldom function at or above their level of ability. Although they are not likely to be exploited, they will effectively resist unreasonable demands. Relaxed about time, they typically display a Type B personality. They can cooperate with others and are usually comfortable with groups and family members. They are not overawed or impressed by authority.

Disorder: They resist fulfilling their given responsibilities through procrastinating, "forgetting," sulking, or being argumentative. An underlying pessimism pervades their thoughts, attitudes, feelings, and actions. They protest, without justification, that unreasonable demands are being placed on them. They deliberately work slowly or do a bad job on tasks that they don't really want to do. They obstruct the efforts of others and fail to do their share; they are uncooperative. They resent other people's useful suggestions about how they could be more productive or effective.

The Conscientious Personality

Healthy: These individuals are highly principled, conscientious, and constantly strive to be impartial, fair, and objective. Truth and justice are primary values for them and they are models of the highest levels of personal and professional integrity. They are willing to make personal sacrifices and delay gratification for the greater good; they utilize their time, energy, and passion to fulfill their calling in life. Because of their moral sensitivity and articulateness, they make excellent teachers and role models. Furthermore, because they can maintain a sense of centeredness and composure even under pressure, they are likely to achieve an unparalleled level of excellence and balance in their lives. At their best, they become extraordinarily wise and humane, with a superb sense of vision and discernment. As a result, they tend to make realistic choices and provide wise counsel to others. Because of their acceptance of shortcomings in themselves and others, they are an inspiration to many. They are life-affirming, hopeful, and kind, while balancing personal integrity with generosity. They experience a deep sense of serenity and peace that comes from accepting their lives and life circumstances.

Average: Individuals at this level of functioning desire to complete tasks and projects without flaws or errors. They take pride in doing all jobs or tasks well, including the smallest details. They want things to be done "just right" and in a specific manner, yet they have some tolerance for how things are done. They are dedicated to work and are capable of intense, single-minded effort. They carefully consider alternatives and the consequences of these in making decisions; they have strong moral principles and strongly desire to do the right thing. They are no-nonsense individuals who do their work without much emotional expenditure. Generally speaking, they are careful, thrifty, and cautious, but are able to share their abundance. Furthermore, they tend to save and collect objects and are reluctant to discard objects that have, that formerly had, or that someday might have value for them.

Disorder: Individuals at this level are characterized by perfectionism that interferes with task completion. They tend to be preoccupied with details, rules, lists, order, organization, or schedules, to the extent that the major point of the activity is lost. They maintain an unreasonable insistence that others submit exactly to their way of doing things, or they have an unreasonable reluctance to allow others to do things because of the conviction that others will not do these correctly. They exhibit excessive devotion to work, and to the exclusion of leisure activities and friendships. Most of the time, they are indecisive, meaning that decision making is avoided, postponed, or procrastinated. Overconscientiousness, scrupulosity, and inflexibility about matters of morality, ethics, or values are common. Restricted expression of affection is characteristic, as is lack of generosity in giving time, money, or gifts when no personal gain is likely to result. Furthermore, they may be unable to discard worn-out or worthless items even when these have no sentimental value.

The Vigilant Personality

Healthy: They are self-assured and confident in their ability to make decisions and take care of themselves. They tend to be intuitive, sensitive, and perceptive individuals. Superior listeners, observers, and interviewers, they are keenly aware of subtlety, tone, and multiple levels of meaning. They excel at sizing up situations and people and at discerning motives and intentions. Accordingly, they are highly proficient scientific investigators, security analysts, detectives, document examiners, and trial attorneys. They are assertive and can defend themselves without losing control and becoming aggressive. At their best, they are loyal and faithful colleagues and friends who take criticism rather seriously, without becoming intimidated.

Average: They are individuals who are keenly aware of environmental and interpersonal cues and ascribe to the belief that "it is better to be safe than sorry." Because they are thin-skinned, they can be rather sensitive to criticism, even positive criticism. Questioning persons and circumstances is a part of their vigilant outlook, as is careful foresight and discernment. They are keenly observant of others and are particularly sensitive to how others react to them. Not surprisingly, they are careful in their dealings with other people and maintain a certain level of detachment, while sizing up the potential threat that others may pose.

Disorder: These individuals are reluctant to confide in others because of unwarranted fear that the information will be used against them. They regularly read hidden meanings or threatening intentions into benign remarks—for example, they might suspect that a neighbor put out trash early to annoy them. They bear grudges and are unforgiving of insults or slights. They may routinely question, without justification, the fidelity of a spouse or sexual partner, friends, and associates. They also expect, without sufficient basis, to be exploited or harmed by others. Finally, they are easily slighted and quick to take offense and react with anger or to counterattack.

Index